THE BEDFORD SERIES IN HISTORY AND CULTURE

Schools and Students in Industrial Society

Japan and the West
1870–1940

Peter N. Stearns
Carnegie Mellon University

BEDFORD BOOKS　　Boston　✖　New York

For my well-schooled children

For Bedford Books

President and Publisher: Charles H. Christensen
General Manager and Associate Publisher: Joan E. Feinberg
History Editor: Katherine E. Kurzman
Developmental Editor: Charisse Kiino
Managing Editor: Elizabeth M. Schaaf
Production Editor: Tony Perriello
Production Assistant: Deborah Baker
Copyeditor: Barbara G. Flanagan
Text Design: Claire Seng-Neimoeller
Indexer: Steve Csipke
Cover Design: Richard Emery Design, Inc.
Composition: ComCom

Library of Congress Catalog Card Number: 96–86781

Manufactured in the United States of America.

2 1 0 9 8 7
f e d c b a

For information, write: Bedford Books, 75 Arlington Street, Boston, MA 02116

ISBN: 0–312–13913–6 (paperback)
ISBN: 0–312–16381–9 (hardcover)

Acknowledgments

Cremin, L.A., excerpt from *The Republic and the School: Horace Mann on the Education of Free Men* (New York: Teachers College Press, © 1957 by Teachers College, Columbia University. All rights reserved.) Reprinted by permission of the publisher.

Fukuzawa, Yukichi, excerpt from the *Autobiography of Yukichi Fukuzawa.* Copyright © 1966 by Columbia University Press. Reprinted with permission of the publisher.

Ishimoto, Baroness Shidzue, excerpt from *Facing Two Ways: The Story of My Life.* Copyright 1935 © 1963 by Shidzue Ishimoto. Reprinted by permission of Henry Holt and Co. Inc.

Keene, Donald, excerpt from *Sources of Japanese Tradition.* Copyright © 1958 by Columbia University Press. Reprinted with permission of the publisher.

Tanizaki, Jun'ichiro, excerpt from *Childhood Years: A Memoir by Jun'ichiro Tanizaki.* Kodansha International, Ltd.

Photographs:

Japanese girls doing calligraphy, the hoisting of the flag, and the Japanese boy at the machine, courtesy of Yoshida, K. & T. Kaigo, *Japanese Education,* Board of Tourist Industry, Japanese Government Railways, Feb. 16, 1938.

Higher storm, courtesy of Donald Roden.

As the teacher dissects, Library of Congress, Frances Benjamin Johnston (photographer).

Chem lab, courtesy of the Boston Public Library, Prints Department, Boston Public Schools: Roxbury High School, by A.H. Folsom, 1892.

French students and separate entrances, Prost, Antoine, *H.G.E. IV,* Paris Nouvelle Librarie de France, 1981.

Schools and students in industrial society

Stearns, Peter N.

370.952 S799s

Foreword

The Bedford Series in History and Culture is designed so that readers can study the past as historians do.

The historian's first task is finding the evidence. Documents, letters, memoirs, interviews, pictures, movies, novels, or poems can provide facts and clues. Then the historian questions and compares the sources. There is more to do than in a courtroom, for hearsay evidence is welcome, and the historian is usually looking for answers beyond act and motive. Different views of an event may be as important as a single verdict. How a story is told may yield as much information as what it says.

Along the way the historian seeks help from other historians and perhaps from specialists in other disciplines. Finally, it is time to write, to decide on an interpretation and how to arrange the evidence for readers.

Each book in this series contains an important historical document or group of documents, each document a witness from the past and open to interpretation in different ways. The documents are combined with some element of historical narrative—an introduction or a biographical essay, for example—that provides students with an analysis of the primary source material and important background information about the world in which it was produced.

Each book in the series focuses on a specific topic within a specific historical period. Each provides a basis for lively thought and discussion about several aspects of the topic and the historian's role. Each is short enough (and inexpensive enough) to be a reasonable one-week assignment in a college course. Whether as classroom or personal reading, each book in the series provides firsthand experience of the challenge—and fun—of discovering, re-creating, and interpreting the past.

Natalie Zemon Davis
Ernest R. May

Preface

Education is hardly an innovation of modern society, but the idea that most children should spend considerable time in schools and that societies owe the citizenry a formal educational system is relatively new. Accounting for these dramatic changes is an obvious challenge to historical analysis worldwide. Why have so many societies moved in this direction? What new goals is formal education presumed to serve?

At the same time, educational systems are sensitive barometers of the values and assumptions of their specific societies. Some countries find it obvious that schools should also be sports centers, but others do not. Some societies are quite comfortable distinguishing elite students by tests and other performance results, while others are more ambivalent, looking to education to confirm the capacities of the masses.

This book is stimulated by these two features of modern education. The ubiquity of school systems makes the rise of education a vital aspect of social, political, and cultural history. But the need to compare systems, to show how and why they differ, is equally intriguing.

Three modern industrial, democratic societies—the United States, France, and Japan—open both avenues of exploration. Their common educational patterns help explain why formal education has become so widespread and important. Their differences focus on the comparative effort. All three societies generated important debates about educational history that spice this study. All three produced abundant documents about educational goals and experiences, allowing comparison to proceed through the interpretation of primary sources as well as through the analysis in the text.

Once the three modern educational histories are sketched and compared, each reader may seek to answer two obvious questions: If you could choose where to be born and start school, in which of these countries would you prefer to be educated? And on what grounds would you make your choice?

ACKNOWLEDGMENTS

A number of scholars provided valuable suggestions for this study. My thanks to Helen Hopper, Donald Sutton, Daniel Resnick, Steven Schlossman, and Scarlett Townsend. The book greatly benefited from critical readings by Kevin Reilly, Charles R. Day, Linda L. Clark, Sheldon Garon, William R. Keylor, and Merry White. I am grateful to Charles Christensen, Joan Feinberg, Katherine Kurzman, Charisse Kiino, and Tony Perriello, and the rest of Bedford Books for supporting the project. Thanks, finally, to Derek Davison, Perrin Rowland, Karen Callas, and Alicia Brown for assistance with the manuscript.

Peter N. Stearns

Contents

vii

1

Introduction:
The Rise of Modern Education

The spread of formal education is one of the most striking features of modern world history. Two centuries ago most children, after a few years of infancy, defined their lives in terms of work, assisting parents or other adults in farming or craft manufacture while learning, sometimes informally, skills that would serve them in the same jobs later. Since 1800—and more recently still in many cases—the primary tasks of childhood have shifted to school-based learning, with its requirements of literacy, numerical skills, and new forms of discipline. In three disparate societies—France, the United States, and Japan—government-run education developed at the earliest date and by some measurements most successfully. Those societies shared an emphasis on education as part of a general effort to advance the economy and develop modern political loyalties. But they also exhibited very different implementations, for the rise of education built on and sometimes extended specific national traditions, strengths, and weaknesses.

Children in any society need to be educated, of course. Teaching children appropriate emotional cues, gender roles, and manners has always been a vital part of family life, and it remains so in the present day, though nonfamily influences, like the modern media, play a role as well. Religions have always sought to train children in certain beliefs and practices, and in many religions ceremonies testify to a child's mastery of religious materials as an entry to adulthood. And of course children have always been trained for work. In urban crafts in many different societies, apprenticeship systems provided guidance toward the acquisition of skills in areas like carpentry, tailoring, and goldsmithing. Children on the farms—and farmers constituted the majority of the population in all civilizations until quite recently—learned somewhat less formally, usually from their

1

fathers and mothers, the methods needed to grow crops and tend live-stock. In all civilizations also, a minority of young people encountered out-right schooling, learning how to read, becoming acquainted with past lit-erature and philosophy, and perhaps even studying medicine or law (including religious law). Before modern times, indeed until the late eighteenth century, education for members of the upper class and top offi-cials was most fully developed in China, for the training of gentlemen and bureaucrats in literary classics and Confucian philosophy. Schools in other societies—like the Koranic schools in Islamic areas or the uni-versities created in the European Middle Ages—also played significant roles in educating a minority of the population.

The rise of modern education in key countries such as France, the United States, and Japan redefined these traditional processes in a num-ber of ways. Most obviously, large numbers of children were brought into schools. The family role in education declined. The difference between elite children and the children of the masses persisted in some cases, but that distinction became more complicated as large numbers of children learned to read and attended formal classes. Education still trained for work, but the skills involved were more general, in some ways more abstract, and the period of schooling was increasingly separated from actual work. One result of this change to modern education was that chil-dren now became expenses for families and society rather than eco-nomic assets. In traditional farming communities, children began to con-tribute to their own upkeep, through useful work, by around age five, and by age ten they often were doing enough to cover the costs of feeding and clothing them. With modern education up to the present, children not only do not work, at least until their early teens, but they actually cost additional money in terms of books, supplies, appropriate clothing, and teacher salaries.

Studying the development of modern education involves some intrigu-ing analytical issues. Why was such a change in the treatment of children necessary? What has prompted so many societies to go to the expense of setting up huge school systems and of creating a massive group of pro-fessional teachers? It is vital to note that all societies, when they began to develop modern schools, were relatively poor. Early schools often reflected limited resources—but why did they seem worth extra fund-ing at all? Modern education first arose in Western societies, in places like the United States, France, and other European nations. Here is where the questions of causes are most intriguing, particularly because Western Europe had not been a world educational leader before the eighteenth century. The success of Western countries, from the eighteenth century onward, in creating dynamic industrial economies and powerful military forces led other societies to the realization that they had to alter their ways of doing things to catch up—and new education was vital to the process, even in training different kinds of military leaders. Even where schools were already important, as in China or Japan, they needed to be redefined. New-style education, which could in part be copied from the Western example, seemed a key ingredient in a broader process of change. The spread of modern education to places like Japan, in other words, is not as hard to explain as the rise of the phenomenon in the West in the first place. Some societies found it easier to produce modern educational systems than others, which means that some special factors were involved. Unusual causes must be sought particularly for cases of rapid educational expansion such as in Japan.

Creating a modern education system involved tensions with traditional cultural values and sources of authority. What should the role of religion be in a school system designed largely to train loyal citizens and effective modern workers? How should cherished educational values of the elite, such as a veneration for classical literature, be combined with new emphases on subjects like science or engineering? How should the values and habits of particular families—for example, the dialects of a region or the language of an immigrant group—mesh with the homogenizing impulses of national school systems? Issues of this sort provided genuine drama in the creation of modern schooling, and some of them have not disappeared, since the phenomenon itself is so recent.

Partly because of tradition but partly because of tensions within modern economies, school systems also created conflicts between elite and mass goals. Modern education systems were designed to produce a well-trained elite, capable of providing top management for business, effective professionals in fields like medicine and teaching, and leading government bureaucrats. At the same time, the system was called upon to provide some training, at least literacy and numeracy, for everyone. How did the framers of a system decide what the differences were between elite and mass schooling, and which should receive more attention? Dealing with these questions involved deciding how and at what stage children were selected for elite training and what the masses were told about their chances for advancement. The need for special elite education is not a modern phenomenon; all civilizations provided some education for their elite. But the need to distinguish an elite in a context where everyone receives some formal schooling raised new and complex issues that societies resolved in various ways depending on their own values. The relationship between education and social mobility was and continues to be a vital but complex topic in all modern societies.

Similar dilemmas apply to gender. In most traditional societies, any formal education applied primarily to young men. Women were far less likely to be schooled outside the home. Modern education, in contrast, has applied to both genders (and here too, the causes are important). Should it nevertheless promote major differences between males and females, or should it largely seek to provide similar values and skills? The questions modern education raised were fairly standard across most societies, but they were answered very differently.

How, finally, is modern education best viewed—from the top down, or the bottom up, or somewhere in between? All modern education systems have resulted from explicit policies established by governments, sometimes along with religious groups and other official agencies. It is possible, as a result, to frame the history of education from the top—in terms of key laws and decisions. Beneath this official level are the practitioners of modern education —the hundreds of thousands of teachers. Teachers may share official educational goals, but they usually have some goals and needs of their own. It is possible, then, to deal with modern education from this middle perspective. Finally, modern education consists of the actual students and to some extent their families. What students experience may be rather different from what governments intend and teachers profess. This bottom layer—the students themselves—though the hardest to document, may be the most interesting perspective from which to view modern education.

The multiple layering of modern education invites attention to a number of specific topics. Attendance is one. Governments may require attendance of certain age groups, but this does not mean that children and their families uniformly obey; the real history of school attendance often differs from official policy. Multiple layering shows in more subtle ways as well. Modern schools often present themselves primarily in terms of subjects taught and tested. The development of school curricula thus can be studied—the rise of science subjects, for example, or the development of nationalistic presentations of history. But schools also teach in less explicit ways that policymakers may be scarcely aware of but that students experience keenly. Schools, for example, teach children habits of time and socialization, exposing them to ways of dealing with strangers; different kinds of students, however, may learn rather differently. Schools also try to teach values and morals, presenting ideals for family life and standards of personal success and group relations.

Key issues in assessing the rise of modern education—from the causes of the whole phenomenon to the differences between formal policy and actual student experience—apply literally across the world. Globally, modern educational history is nowhere more than two centuries old. Most major societies began to set up modern education systems in the nineteenth century (a few, in the West, began even in the eighteenth century), and literally every society has expanded the systems rapidly during the twentieth century.

Studying the entire process of modern educational history would be a mammoth task. This book looks instead at three significant national cases—France, the United States, and Japan. They are atypical of world experience in that all three involve educational systems that began early in the modern era and managed to spread to virtually the entire society by the early twentieth century. They are atypical also in that they involve societies that industrialized successfully. This success partly reflected early educational achievement, in providing a literate labor force and a supply of trained professionals. But industrial success also encouraged further expansion of the educational system, for example in proliferating expensive research universities and other costly facilities. At the present time, international literacy rates average under 50 percent, and only 1 percent of the total world population are college graduates; but in the United States, Japan, and France, the rates are over 90 percent and over 16 percent, respectively. These societies were and are unusual, though they are not the only ones with high education rates. Their distinctiveness means that their histories may be studied to shed light on what other societies will grapple with as they build their own modern systems. The implications of focusing on these three countries are considerable for a larger understanding of world history in the past two centuries and for anticipating the role of education in the future.

Yet Japan, France, and the United States are also very different educationally, which is where the work of comparison comes in. Choosing three educationally advanced societies for special attention does make the process of analysis somewhat more manageable. Comparing education in an industrializing society with efforts to set up schools in a largely peasant society risks being a case of apples and oranges: it is hard to get beyond very gross distinctions. Japan, France, and the United States provide a more coherent framework. The three countries have operated amid some key economic and social similarities over the past century and a half. But they also differ, and the differences are both important and intriguing in showing the various answers possible to the issues of modern education. The differences must be explained, through partially separate causation, and their results assessed, in terms of broad social results and individual experiences. As you read about three somewhat different systems, all modern, all at least partially successful, you can do a personal tally of strengths and weaknesses: Which system would suit you best, and why? The goal is a probing comparison, focused on similarities as well as differences, that might then be applied to other educational explosions in one of the fundamental areas of change in modern world history.

Comparing France, the United States, and Japan involves two kinds of alignments. Most obviously, the first two nations are part of a Western tradition, broadly speaking; Japan is not. This helps explain why France and the United States began the process of constructing modern educational systems earlier than Japan, as they reacted to changes in culture, such as the rise of new science, and to expanding commercial and industrial opportunities that occurred earlier in the West. Japan was a slight latecomer, though an extraordinarily successful one. While all three countries infused modern education with nationalism, the Western countries tempered nationalism with a belief in individualism, and Japan emphasized patriotic loyalty through emperor worship, group identification, and a long-standing belief in Japanese cultural superiority. The trio of cases in this book, then, invites exploration of the differences between Western values and Japanese values in the construction and operation of vigorous, institutionally rather similar education systems.

The second alignment is one of historical tradition. Japan and France were both older societies, with well-established premodern aristocracies. The United States was much newer, without fixed traditions and with a much more diverse population. Key educational issues in the United States were different from those in the older nations. The balance between democratic and elitist educational goals varied as all three mod-

Debating the Present

Pride in one's own educational system (which does not preclude recognizing some problems) is a key aspect of cultural identity in advanced industrial societies in the late twentieth century. Pride can also entail a denigration of other people's systems. Many advanced industrial countries note, with a mixture of compassion and condescension, the lower literacy levels and incomplete school systems of less-developed areas like India or many African nations. But they save some of their most telling shots for each other, as education becomes a measurement of national self-worth.

In 1986 the Japanese prime minister, Yasuhiro Nakasona, created a political storm when he compared Japanese and American intelligence levels: "On the average, the United States is lower because of a considerable number of blacks, Puerto Ricans, and Mexicans." In 1992 the speaker of the Japanese Lower House, Hoshio Sakurauchi, extended the attack, arguing that poor education explained why the United States lagged behind Japan in economic growth: "U.S. managers cannot issue written orders because about 30 percent of American workers cannot read." His remarks embarrassed the Japanese people, but only because they seemed tactless; it was "common knowledge" in Japan that American schools were doing a bad job.

While many Americans agreed that their nation faced problems in education, they also liked to claim some patriotic advantages over Japan. In 1995 the New York Times *published an extensive analysis of Japan's schooling under the headline "Orderly and Crime Free, but Not Much Fun." "Schools are like cookie cutters in Japan," the article explained, "assembly lines that press students into the same shape." While the article granted that the results included impressive discipline and achievement, it argued not only that young people were more joyless in Japan than in the United States, but also that the Japanese approach would soon begin to harm the nation's standing because it placed so much emphasis on rote learning and memorization, so little on creativity and imagination. The* Times *rather gleefully quoted a former prime minister as saying, "I seriously believe that if we do not change our educational system, it will be the ruin of our country." Another critic likened Japanese students to "trained seals" who would "not be able to master the information age in the coming decades."*

Education bashing had not yet become an Olympic sport, but it was clearly a popular currency in the competitive Japanese-American relationship. A key point in more extensive analysis must focus on determining how these mutual criticisms stand up.

ern educational systems were launched, but the United States diverged more from France in some ways than France diverged from Japan, and it has remained different even in the late twentieth century.

Sharp contrasts in some aspects of modern education reflect the complex contexts in which school systems developed. Deeply held values, changes in youth culture, and official policies shaped the systems, and thus the tenor of education varied even among systems that function in successful industrial economies and political democracies. Contrasts among France, Japan, and the United States are all the more striking given substantial mutual influence. Both American and French educational policies were shaped by the values of the eighteenth-century Enlightenment and the revolutionary era that swept both countries before 1800. Americans directly copied some elements of the French system (for example, aspects of medical education) while French educators inevitably had to react to growing American cultural prestige after World War II. (Other European countries, particularly Germany, also provided influential educational models for both the United States and France.) Japanese modern education not only was based in part on the Western model at the end of the nineteenth century but was explicitly reformed by American occupation forces after World War II. Yet, even with these mutual influences, the systems continue to differ, and advocates of each system continue to question claims made about rival systems.

The comparative framework is not simply an academic exercise. Differences in current educational results and perceptions flow directly from larger historical contrasts. Distinctions of the kind described in this book among societies with well-developed, structurally similar educational apparatus provide one of the most intriguing features of modern world history: that societies can grow alike in many ways, even through explicit imitation, while remaining vividly distinct, even loudly different.

Exploring the modern educational trajectories of France, the United States, and Japan involves a focus on three main stages. First we look at the educational backgrounds of the three nations that allowed them comparatively rapid educational development but also set the basis for some ongoing divergences. Then we look at the actual process of setting up the modern educational apparatus in the nineteenth and early twentieth centuries and at how it was experienced by policymakers, teachers, students, and families. Finally, we look at how the modern educational apparatus has reacted to change and challenge in the twentieth century, for modern educational history did not end with the creation of the institutions of mass schooling and elite universities. Qualities that created educational vigor at one point may prove less appropriate at a later stage of a nation's history—this is what some Japanese think has happened to the United States, as they see a clear process of deterioration in recent decades, and what some Americans think will soon happen to Japan. Education continues to change, and so do key comparisons; it is time to turn to the beginning of this modern process.

2

Before Modern Education: Schooling up to 1800

Most people in most preindustrial societies did not attend formal schools at any point in their lives. There were several overlapping reasons for this. Schools cost money—for teachers' salaries, for building maintenance, and for materials—and preindustrial societies were relatively poor, without the tax or tuition base for massive educational investments. Governments did not think of mass education as one of their responsibilities. Individual families needed child labor. Peasants and farmers used children to assist in field work and around the house, while craft workers assumed that children would begin to clean and perform the simpler supporting tasks at a young age. Most children began to work at around age five, and by eight or ten they could be productive enough to cover the costs of their support. Because most work occurred in the family setting, this child labor was absolutely essential; families that were childless because of infertility needed to hire children from larger families to help out. One of the reasons couples continued to have children into their forties, indeed until the wife's menopause, was to try to ensure a supply of assistants into old age. In this situation, sending children off to school, even for brief periods, was too expensive in terms of resources sacrificed. The biggest reasons, then, for the rarity of schooling in world history before the nineteenth century were the costs to societies and to families.

It was also true, however, that the lessons available in formal schools did not constitute the most relevant kind of learning for the masses of people who were farmers or craft manufacturers. What children needed to master, above all, were the skills they would use in their work through adulthood. These skills were most readily learned through formal or informal apprenticeships, rather than through school-based lessons. Even some professionals, such as doctors, picked up a good bit of their training through apprenticing with established practitioners, rather than going to classes; and certainly this was true for peasants, farm wives, carpenters, or shoemakers. To be sure, many societies also wanted children to gain knowledge of religion, which meant receiving some instruction from priests or shamans. Even this, however, did not necessarily require a classroom setting; knowledge could be transmitted in a few sessions along with some home instruction and children's participation in relevant rituals. Education in the sense of schooling thus did not clearly mesh with the training children required to become effective adults. This gap between the society's goals for children and the training that schools might offer them lingered even after modern education began to gain ground, leaving many families—including many children—unsure that classroom experience had much relevance.

A final deterrent to widespread schooling resulted from the profound social divisions of most preindustrial societies. Groups at the top of society that could afford formal education for children—providing them instruction in reading and mathematics and perhaps a deeper treatment of legal or religious texts—knew that they had an advantage over the masses of people who remained illiterate. Even these elite, however, did not see the need for elaborate education for all their children; often, extensive opportunities were reserved for younger sons destined for priesthood or university. But the elite had a clear self-interest in not encouraging more extensive schooling of the lower classes that would challenge their own hold over certain skills and knowledge. To be sure, just as not everyone in the upper classes acquired formal schooling, there were usually opportunities for some individuals lower on the social pyramid to gain academic skills either because they rose in trade or because they were exceptionally bright. But education and social hierarchy were usually tightly linked. The same held true for education and gender. Groups that had access to some education always favored boys over girls. The most common functions of women—in the familial, domestic realm—were less related to formal education than were those of men, and implicitly men also realized that depriving women of educational skills like literacy could help keep women in their "place." Again, there were exceptions: most preindustrial societies had some educated women. But their numbers always lagged, as education and inequality went hand in hand. The traditional relationship between social and gender hierarchy and education meant that, even when new school opportunities began to develop, many people in authority worried that members of the lower classes or women might become dangerously restive if they had access to learning that "confused" them about their proper roles or gave them grandiose ideas. The limits on formal education before modern times applied quite generally around the world. Certain societies, however, offered more extensive schooling than others, even before the pressures of political and industrial change entered the picture. France (along with most of Western Europe), the British colonies in North America, and Japan all had greatly expanded schools and literacy during the eighteenth century. In France and colonial America, these changes followed from some important developments in religious and intellectual life, along with growing commercial prosperity that made formal education affordable at least for people with some property. Familiar landmarks of early modern history such as the rise of the printing press, the Protestant Reformation, and the eighteenth-century Enlightenment fed educational expansion. Japan's leading position in formal education had a different basis, particularly in the Confucian tradition; an isolated nation, Japan did not participate in Europe's scientific revolution or the Protestant Reformation. Yet the Japanese population was the most literate in the world outside of Western societies.

The premodern rise of education in the three societies did not eliminate the classic limitations on schooling. Costs, goals for children, and social inequality continued to serve as constraints, depriving many people of formal educational opportunities and limiting access for many others. But nonetheless Japan, France, and the American colonies unintentionally prepared for the modern era by providing an unusually strong educational apparatus. Later educational achievements built on these gains, and so, by 1900, the United States, Western Europe, and Japan were even further ahead of most of the rest of the world in schooling and school results such as literacy. We can understand the rise of modern systems only by first understanding premodern trends and also the differences between them and later educational regimes.

CAUSES OF CHANGE IN WESTERN SOCIETY

Europe before 1500 was a largely oral society, with fewer schools than in most Islamic or Confucian regions. In one French village of 250 people, only 4 could definitely read in the 1480s. Most merchants relied on memory aided by carved notches in tally sticks to record numbers.

As written documents became more common, people wondered whether they were as reliable as a person's spoken word. Formal education was largely a matter for the priests, and even some of them could not read but simply memorized Latin phrases for use in church services. By 1800, Western Europe had become an unusually literate society, compared with other regions of the world. A growing minority of people could read. While religious leaders and the upper class dominated schooling, some education became available to ordinary merchants, urban artisans, and even a few wealthy peasants. What forces pushed for change?

The Renaissance, beginning in the fifteenth century, had an important impact on education. More and more intellectuals and urban leaders argued that it was vital not only to learn to read, but to have a command of the classics in Latin and Greek while also gaining the ability to write polished prose at least in one's own language. Ancient history began to receive attention, along with carefully defined manners. The Renaissance indeed helped define a classical, humanistic upper-class education, remnants of which still exist today. This movement did little for mass education—indeed, the crudeness of the peasantry came in for unfavorable comment—but it certainly widened the urban base. It was the Renaissance, also, that provided the context for the rapid development of the printing press after its invention in 1455. Early printing was devoted mainly to religious works, and it included a lot of woodcuts and other illustrations; it did not, in other words, automatically encourage new levels of education or literacy. But the fact was that books and pamphlets became much more widely available than ever before, in a process that unquestionably facilitated considerable literacy gains during the sixteenth century. The new technology of printing plus new intellectual currents that associated classical learning with upper-class status helped set a new, brisk educational pace.

During the Protestant Reformation in the early sixteenth century, Martin Luther and other Protestant leaders worked hard to make the Bible accessible to ordinary people, beginning by translating it from Latin into the vernacular, be it German, French, or English. Priests were no longer seen as intermediaries between the people and the word of God, though Protestants did hedge against too many diverse interpretations of religion by insisting on long church services that guided people's thoughts and on pastoral supervision of children's religious training. Nevertheless, the emphasis of Protestantism on reading the Bible gave a huge spur to training in literacy. Both schools and family religious education proliferated; one of the moral tasks of a good Protestant father was to read the Bible and prepare his children to understand it, which could include teaching them to read. While Catholics were less affected by these developments, the outpouring of religious pamphlets, for and against the Reformation, encouraged Catholic literacy as well. The Council of Trent, convened in 1545 to revivify the Catholic Church against the Protestant threat, specifically called for parish priests to set up local schools to educate ordinary people in the faith; not all priests did so, and the decree was not clearly intended for universal application in any event, but it did gradually create new opportunities for schooling. Key agents of Catholic defense in the Counter Reformation, such as the new Jesuit order, emphasized education as a means of keeping the flock loyal to the church yet trained enough to be active in its behalf. Jesuit schools, though primarily open to the upper classes, spread throughout Catholic Europe. Religion, then, guided much of the new impetus to education throughout Western society.

Less formally, new merchant activity and gains in science also prompted growing attention to schooling, as well as providing funds that could pay for teachers and tutors. These final factors began to emerge most clearly by the seventeenth century, even as religious education continued to predominate. A fairly steady stream of craft books, for example, began to emerge in Western Europe and, later, the American colonies, introducing readers to methods in such trades as weaving, cabinetmaking, and locksmithing and sometimes, indeed, purporting to convey trade secrets not usually available to people outside the craft guild. By 1800, some Americans claimed that they had picked up even complex skills like engraving by reading how-to articles on the subject. Another category of practical reading advice involved medicine and health, with books in French, German, and English on caring for various diseases at home, identifying medicinal remedies, and so on. During the seventeenth-century scientific revolution and thereafter, treatises also appeared to explain major discoveries to a lay public. French aristocrats, both male and female, delighted in learning about astronomy or physiology in this popularized form. Clearly, as books and reading gained ground, additional reasons for the acquisition of reading material quickly emerged, as part of the West's commercial and scientific expansion. The desirability of acquiring some formal education proceeded accordingly;

it even became possible to replace apprenticeship by careful reading in some instances.

These trends were capped, from the 1680s onward, by new theories of learning and by new locations in which reading could be performed. John Locke, in England, argued that children were born with "blank slates" for minds. Arguing against traditional Christian beliefs that children were tainted by original sin, Locke asserted that education and experience made people what they were. The young had immense learning capacity, and it was up to adults to organize appropriate sources of education for them. These optimistic views spread widely after 1700 in France and the American colonies as well as in England. They promoted new parental interest in fostering children's development and helped create an intense faith in the power of education to triumph over superstition. The Enlightenment, centered in eighteenth-century France but with ramifications throughout the West, emphasized the importance of learning as an engine of personal and social progress. With so much new knowledge being generated, particularly in the sciences, people had every reason to expose themselves to education, however informal. New encyclopedias, such as the *Encyclopaedia Britannica* in England, were created to provide information to adult readers; these books both reflected and encouraged extensive education. It was now possible for the first time in Western history for writers and encyclopedia promoters to support themselves by providing information and reading matter to a literate public. Other centers of literate discussion arose, such as the coffeehouses that began to dot European cities and in which the increasing array of political pamphlets and weekly newspapers served as sources of facts and controversies.

Europe's education was thus affected by most of the major currents of the centuries just prior to 1800. Religion probably had the greatest impact in encouraging formal education, but science, Renaissance culture, and commercial interests all left a mark, as did new technologies such as printing. Not surprisingly, at least rudimentary literacy gained ground rapidly. Among English merchants in the Norwich area, for example, 61 percent were illiterate in the 1580s, but only 34 percent were in 1720; among independent farmers, the figures were 55 percent down to 26 percent respectively. Only adult male laborers lagged, with 87 percent still illiterate in the early 1720s. Illiteracy in some parts of Sweden decreased from 79 percent in the early seventeenth century to only 10 percent a century later. Shifts of this sort meant that formal schooling was advancing, but they also served as preconditions for even more education—for with reading, additional training in many subjects became possible, including religion as well as various secular areas. Personal habits changed under the impetus of growing facility in writing: diary keeping began to emerge in Protestant areas by the seventeenth century, a sign that ordinary people had a new skill in writing but also an indication of how these skills empowered a new sense of self and personal expression.

EDUCATIONAL GAINS IN FRANCE AND NORTH AMERICA

How did these general factors shape the actual educational experience in a major Western country such as France? The French participated actively in the Renaissance, in science, in printing, and in the enthusiasms of the Enlightenment. Most did not turn Protestant, and though French Catholicism generated some enthusiasm for direct reading, the Protestant-Catholic distinction held French literacy back somewhat compared with England and Sweden before 1800. Changes in France also confirmed some of the ongoing limitations in educational development: few other than the elite social classes were affected at all, and even educational advocates had a difficult time believing that educational opportunity should be extended to the lower classes. The result, by 1800, was a decidedly mixed picture: literacy had gained substantially, and chances for professional education for privileged classes were at an all-time high; but massive inequality prevailed as well, with large numbers of the population depending on traditional oral transmission and individual apprenticeship for information and training.

Following the Council of Trent and the spirit of the Catholic Counter Reformation, the French church began to set up village schools during the seventeenth century. Called "little schools" (*petites écoles*), these were staffed by religious orders such as the Brothers of the Christian Schools, many of which were explicitly established for this purpose. The schools taught reading, but their main emphasis was moral and religious education, accompanied by strict discipline. Hard work and virtuous behavior received extensive attention, as did drill and memorization exercises. The schools were not designed for everyone, nor were they equally available throughout the nation. More boys attended than girls. Wealthy peasants were more likely to be able to forgo some labor, to allow their sons some schooling, than were peasants with little land or agricultural laborers with no land. Some boys were able to attend only irregularly, and perhaps only for a year or two around the age of religious confirmation. Students of this sort might learn little more than a memorized catechism, taught orally. Other students did gain literacy, but only on the shakiest basis; thrust back into peasant life and labor, with no real chance to read or reason to do so, their skills might quickly atrophy.

Nevertheless, this growing elementary education did produce a new "reading public" among the urban artisanry and wealthier peasantry. A new industry of popular books arose during the seventeenth and eighteenth centuries, called the "blue library." Easy-to-read pamphlets dealt particularly with religious life but also with family matters, advice about health problems and the proper handling of death, and a variety of other topics.

Literacy rates reflected the uses of the schools, as parts of France gained reading skills almost as rapidly as key regions in England and Scandinavia. In the late seventeenth century, 44 percent of all men in northern and northeastern France—the most prosperous and commercially active parts of the country—were able to read; a century later, on the eve of the great revolution of 1789, the figure had risen to 71 percent. Southern France was a different story: greater poverty combined with widespread use of dialects and languages other than standard French (particularly Provençal) limited opportunities. Here, 14 percent of all males were literate in the late seventeenth century, and only 27 percent by the later eighteenth. Women's gains were notable, but again different from the patterns of men. For the whole nation, 14 percent of all women seem to have had some level of literacy in the late seventeenth century, while the figure rose to 27 percent a hundred years later. In a few special cases, however, women were more likely to be literate than men: among some urban artisans, it made sense to have a wife who could read and do arithmetic, to keep accounts in the family store, while men did the work of production, where school skills counted for less.

Overall, educational gains in the century and a half before 1800 divided the French masses, in city and countryside alike. A growing group gained some experience of school, and a segment of this group maintained the ability to read as well as other traces of school discipline and religious indoctrination. A large number of people, however, had little or no contact with school culture; this group was disproportionately composed of women and the poor, many of them southerners.

Above these masses, the French middle and upper classes—lawyers, merchants, aristocrats—had their own educational system. Basic reading and arithmetic skills were acquired in childhood, sometimes through parental instruction or use of a tutor. The crucial school experience came in early adolescence, when boys, particularly, would be sent off to a *collège*, or secondary school, run by a religious order such as the Jesuits. (Some families, including wealthy peasants, even sent their sons to board during the school term.) By the late eighteenth century, as many as fifty thousand students a year were attending *collèges*. Discipline in these schools was fierce, directed among other things against any sexual misbehavior. Corporal punishment was frequent. Lessons aimed at teaching Latin and perhaps a smattering of Greek, as badges of educated status but also as opportunities to extend moral training. Students were set to work translating Latin passages that stressed religious orthodoxy or family hierarchy. A typical passage, for example, highlighted the importance of obedience to one's father: "Do you not fear that your father will become angry with you? I hope that he will use all the means that his love and his severity may inspire in him to correct you." Students gained some acquaintance with literature in this process, but the emphasis was on discipline and virtue, not a quest for beauty or even a humanistic appreciation of classical style. The basic values and manner of this education differed little from those of the *petites écoles,* though the system was socially separate and the emphasis on Latin gave students skills that ordinary schooling did not provide, thus creating another education gap that mirrored the larger social order.

France also had several universities, for training in law, medicine, and theology. Prestigious during the late Middle Ages, universities had dropped in significance, though school-trained doctors, taught mainly by memorizing classical texts like that of Galen, tried to assert their prestige over other practitioners.

No coherent educational system existed in premodern France, but some consistency of purpose was clear. Education was increasingly valuable, but inequitably available. Its sponsors, concentrated in the church, saw its goals in terms of religious obedience and social and family stability; clearly, many school graduates, as they read the new popular religious pamphlets, seemed to agree. At the same time, however, education already had some unintended results. Various observers commented on a type of peasant, literate and aggressive, who was pressing forward with new ideas about farming for the market, often disrupting traditional village arrangements with attempts at land acquisition and attacks on communal practices. A key reason for northern France's educational lead was the uses to which peasants and artisans could put literacy and numeracy skills, to assist them in record keeping, commercial transactions, and the making and reading of wills. Religious books remained more popular than commercial manuals, but the literate artisan could and did learn about manufacturing methods by exercising his reading skill. Another source of innovation involved the provision of education, not just its uses. The French government was largely content to leave schooling to the church, but by the eighteenth century the monarchy faced growing pressure to limit religious influence. One response, in 1761, was the expulsion of the Jesuit order from France, which created a need to find alternatives for the operation of the secondary schools.

Government sponsorship was even more directly involved in the most radical educational innovation of the later eighteenth century, the formation of the first great technical training schools in France. French industry and commerce were beginning to advance rapidly enough that professional engineers were essential, and the French government began to take on the responsibility for their education. In 1747 the state set up the School of Bridges and Roads (École des Ponts et Chaussées) to train civil engineers; this was followed, in 1783, by the École des Mines for mining engineers. The French Revolution added even more important schools: the École Polytechnique, which became the premier engineering school in the nation, and the Conservatoire des Arts et Métiers. All these schools tried to recruit students according to aptitude; they drew in middle-class boys primarily, but they could reach farther down in society. The Conservatoire emerged from an earlier attempt by the king to set up a collection of machines that ordinary workers and artisans could look at to further their own mechanical aptitude; the revolutionary leaders who founded the school saw it as a means of encouraging new inventive powers among this group of urban craftsmen, creating a second tier of technical personnel below the engineers emerging from the polytechnical school.

Beyond specific measures, educational growth in France encouraged further thinking about schools and their purposes. Various Enlightenment thinkers discussed innovations in the teaching of reading. The great philosopher Jean-Jacques Rousseau, in his widely sold book *Émile*, launched a movement to relax school discipline in favor of giving children greater latitude for their innate creativity. The French Revolution of 1789 provided yet another source of change. The radical Convention, in 1792, proposed a national school system, from the primary grades to the university, that would allow access to education for everyone and would replace the church with the state as the source of educational funding and policy. The scheme built on Enlightenment excitement about human capacity for education and the personal and social benefits a secular school system could provide. Political and economic disarray prevented the realization of this great scheme, but a portion of the revolutionary approach was taken up by Napoleon soon after 1800.

Yet the potential for further change, on the eve of the nineteenth century, must not be exaggerated. The majority of the French population remained unschooled. Reformers' ideas about educational change, though promising, often continued to reflect traditional limitations. Many Enlightenment intellectuals found it particularly difficult to envisage education for all, because of their disdain for the capacities of the lower levels of French society. Dictionary entries dealing with the word *people* emphasized the modest talents of the lower classes: "The people does not know what it wants most of the time"—which could mean that education would be positively dangerous, in promoting half-baked ideas and unrealistic expectations. A French official in 1764 warned against giving ordinary people anything more than religious instruction: "In order to render society happy it is necessary that a great number of its members be ignorant as well as poor . . . each hour that poor children spend on books is that much time lost to society." The knowledge needed by a few experts, including literacy itself, "is highly pernicious for poor folk."

France ended the eighteenth century, clearly, with more educational questions than answers, despite important changes over the previous 150 years. If the church's leadership in education was to be challenged, how and according to what purposes could schooling be organized? Was it worthwhile even thinking about schools for at least the poorest third of the population or for most women? What was the relationship between the growing excitement about modern, specialized training for a few new professional categories and the content as well as the inclusiveness of education in general?

Educational patterns in the English colonies of North America—the area that would become the United States—differed from those in France in many respects. In some ways, the pre-1800 trends toward expanding education emerged more clearly in this partially European outpost. Some

Figure 1. A traditional primary school in France around 1900. The school mixed ages but not sexes, as boys and girls entered separately and took classes apart. Uniforms marked another concern for appropriate decorum and discipline.

basic educational issues were different as a result, not only in 1800 but well beyond. Nevertheless, questions about inclusiveness, about curriculum, and about discipline were on balance quite similar, as the colonies combined measurable gains in educational experience with some vigorous constraints on what it might accomplish and on who might participate.

A fair number of the colonists who came over from England in the seventeenth century were already literate—indeed, evidence from New England to Virginia suggests that migrants had higher literacy rates than the English average, which means that schooling somehow helped encourage emigration to the New World. Certainly many colonists tried to teach their children to read and write, though the difficulties and scattered settlement of the early seventeenth century limited major gains. Much teaching occurred in the home. A 1647 Massachusetts law required that every town support a public school, and while compliance was incomplete, a modest network did emerge. Several religious groups, such as the Quakers, operated schools, and widows or unmarried women conducted "dame schools," giving classes in their homes. In cities like Philadelphia, master craftsmen established evening schools for their apprentices.

By the eighteenth century these varied activities produced a definite increase in literacy rates, particularly among white males. New England, where religious impulses particularly spurred education, pushed toward the highest levels of literacy in the world. By the late eighteenth century, more than 90 percent of all white males in this region were literate enough to sign their names, thanks largely to their childhood attendance at reading-and-writing schools. The desire to make sure that children could read the Bible, reinforced by frequent family sessions where fathers read as part of their responsibility for the moral upbringing of their children, presumably accounts for this development, for New England was not the center of American commercial activity at this point. Elsewhere, literacy levels did not gain ground so strikingly, hovering at about 60 percent among men—which means that North America, like France, exhibited pronounced regional differences in educational achievement and interest on the eve of the modern age.

American schooling, whether expanding or status quo, was routinely accompanied by strict discipline. As in France, the religious purposes of most primary education made it easy for teachers and parents to associate severity with lessons in reading. Corporal punishment was common. Reading primers repeated Bible stories, drawing appropriately somber moral messages, and urged docile behavior. One alphabet book thus illustrated some of the final letters as follows: "T: Time cuts down all, Both great and small"; "W: Whales in the Sea, God's Voice obey"; "X: Xerxes the great did die, And so must you & I"; "Y: Youth forward slips, Death soonest nips." And accompanying these moral imperatives were injunctions to obedience:

Now the child being entered in his Letters and Spelling, let him learn these and such like Sentences by Heart, whereby he will be both intrusted in his Duty, and encouraged in his Learning. . . . I will fear God and honour the KING. I will honour my Father & Mother. I will obey my Superiours. I will Submit to my Elders. . . . I will as much as in me lies keep all God's Holy Commandments.

Substantial American interest in literacy and school-based docility had its limits. As in France, the poorest segments of the male population were largely ignored. As commercial activity increased, particularly in the middle colonies, the resulting literacy hierarchy helped relegate some groups to lower-level work as laborers or small farmers throughout their lives. The colonies also, however, presented a distinct racial twist in their educational patterns. Most colonists saw no reason to offer schooling to American Indians or African American slaves. Most Indians, in fact, had no interest in the white educational system, maintaining their own traditional patterns of training their children. Some white missionary and philanthropic effort, however, generated schools, and resultant literacy, among some Indians; one college, Dartmouth, was founded (in 1769) to advance Indian education and the Christianizing effort. Slaves posed a clearer problem. While some individual masters and mistresses taught their slaves, the general view held that slave education was simply a waste of time, or even a positive danger, for a group compelled to labor. Strong social efforts and, ultimately, outright laws worked against educating slaves, lest literacy and even Christianity itself encourage African Americans to question their social station. By the late eighteenth century some African Americans, like some Indians, were literate, but they were concentrated in the cities and the northern colonies and among the minority of freedmen.

Education was also less available to women than to men, even among established white settlers. Women did participate in some literacy, as a slipover from religious training; this was a vital source of the "dame" teachers the colonists patronized. Female literacy rates were higher than in England, though interestingly there was an actual decline in female levels in New England in the late seventeenth century because of the costs of training in a still-struggling colonial region and the ensuing shortage of schools. In the eighteenth century, however, white women in the northern colonies pulled ahead of women elsewhere in the world, with literacy rates of 50 percent or more. Particularly in the cities, but also on farms producing for the market, women were finding reading and arithmetic skills increasingly useful for economic reasons, as the basis for keeping accounts and reading correspondence and contracts. Though historians have not pressed the comparison, it seems that in education, as in some other aspects of life, conditions in the American colonies provided wider opportunities for women than existed in Western Europe, if only because the economic tasks were more varied.

Overall, educational conditions in the American colonies resembled those in France in key respects. Interest in education grew, particularly for religious and disciplinary reasons but with burgeoning commercial motivation as well. Most schools were church-sponsored or religiously inspired, though some government backing (local, in the American case) might be involved. Schooling was often sporadic, for many children could not be freed up on a regular basis; the resulting literacy might be quite limited, and some adults even forgot how to sign their names. Other restrictions operated, for neither society saw education as a universal goal: not only were the poor largely excluded, but also some regions lagged behind others. The American colonies featured less outright fear of educating the lower classes than did France, but they harbored racial restrictions that were irrelevant in the French setting. Women were differentiated from men, for educational purposes, though more rigorously in France than in the colonies.

The American colonies offered far less advanced training than did France. No widespread system of secondary schools existed, and nothing like the new French technical schools was sketched before 1800. There were a few universities, which actually took in fairly young teenagers, largely from the ranks of merchants and professionals, given the absence of secondary schools. Six colleges were operating in the colonies by 1763, almost all of them founded by religious groups and designed primarily to train Protestant ministers. Secular subjects gained some place in the college curriculum, so that astronomy and physics were taught along with theology, Latin, and Greek. In 1755, Benjamin Franklin and other laymen founded the Academy and College of Pennsylvania (later renamed the University of Pennsylvania) under entirely secular auspices; there was no theological faculty. Despite this initiative and a similar one in New York (King's College, later renamed Columbia), American higher education was distinctly limited, even if its existence allowed some opening to newer scientific interests. Aside from ministers, most professionals in the colonies, such as doctors and lawyers, were trained through apprenticeship rather than extensive schooling. At the level of advanced and technical education a gap existed between America and countries like France and Germany that would only gradually be filled.

Educational gains during the seventeenth and eighteenth centuries in both France and North America fell short of what people today would call a modern school system, but they provided a clear basis for further developments. Questions about inclusion and focus surfaced in both systems. There was active debate about the advantages or dangers of extending schooling to largely excluded groups. New issues were also emerging, not always explicitly, about the balance between religious focus and newer pursuits in science and technical subjects. The French grappled with the role of the church while establishing novel engineering programs; American leaders, in a more restricted higher educational setting, experimented with secular universities. At the theoretical level, intellectuals in both societies were also raising some new objections about conventional school discipline, arguing that harsh punishments contradicted the essential goodness and learning capacity of the child. Neither France nor the new United States had established definite paths to an educational future. Both, however, had some clear momentum. Both societies, also, while sharing many educational characteristics, had established somewhat different emphases, and these, too, would carry into the future.

JAPAN, ASIA'S NEW INNOVATOR

Like the West, but entirely independently, Japan in the early modern centuries forged a distinctive educational system, inadvertently setting the basis for modern developments. In the process the Japanese faced some of the issues being raised in the West—for example, about the educational place of women. But because of their separation from Western trends—indeed, their substantial isolation from almost all international contact, save in their active use of Chinese learning—the Japanese definition of schooling and of educational issues inevitably had a flavor of its own, and some features and debates were unique.

As in Europe, Japanese educational gains began to pick up speed in

Figure 2. A "storm"—wild revelry—in an elite Japanese secondary school in 1934. How did this kind of activity serve the broader purposes of Japanese education in this period?

the seventeenth century. Even before this point, Japanese culture provided some emphasis on schooling. Buddhism, imported from Korea, encouraged some education so that the religious faithful could read Buddhist writings and prayers and perhaps compose prayers of their own. Confucianism, imported from China, urged the importance of education for the political elite, to give them a sense of the traditional literature, philosophy, and history. While Confucian values encountered some obstacles in feudal Japan, the Japanese upper nobility did in certain periods enjoy reading plays, writing poetry, and in general displaying some of the benefits of literacy and education. The world's first novel, *The Tale of Genji*, was composed in this spirit by the court lady Murasaki Shikibu, around 1000 C.E. Even some ordinary people, however, gained literacy, thanks particularly to Buddhist temple schools.

What pushed premodern Japanese education to higher levels—well beyond the levels obtained, for example, in Confucian China—were the political and economic changes of the seventeenth century. The formation of a stronger central government, the Tokugawa shogunate, and the decline of feudal warfare created important new motivations for Japan's feudal lords and military samurai to improve their education in the interests of serving in the government's bureaucracy. The same shift led the government increasingly to encourage Confucian doctrine, with its emphasis on philosophical and literary training. A growing number of Confucian intellectuals emerged, and these leaders encouraged the educational process still further. Both the government and individual feudal lords invited their vassals—the samurai—to study. A manual for noble households included the insistence that "the study of literature . . . must be cultivated diligently," along with military skills. The government established a number of new schools for the samurai from 1630 onward, and leading feudal lords followed suit. Other samurai were simply tutored at home by a growing array of scholars, some of whom were based in the intellectual center, Kyoto. The new schools emphasized Confucianism and Chinese culture. Students learned to read and write Chinese, practiced calligraphy, studied the classics, and read Chinese and Japanese history, poetry, and other works, depending on their teacher's preferences. Classes ranged from large lectures to tutorial sessions. By the time students finished their studies, in a few months or years, they were usually literate, acquainted with key philosophical and literary materials, and also vigorously attached to the particular views of their main instructor, in a period when different brands of Confucian thought (along with elements of Buddhism and of Japan's traditional Shinto religion) vied for attention in Japanese intellectual life.

During the eighteenth century this elite educational system expanded, while educational access for other groups began to gain ground as well. By this point, Japan's growing internal trade, including market agriculture, was beginning to provide additional motivations for acquiring literacy and arithmetic skills, and successful families—including some propertied farmers—valued literary means of expression. (Elaborate diary keeping gained ground at this point in Japan, though there were earlier precedents.) Ideology entered in as well. Some feudal lords—the daimyo—wanted to encourage Confucianism, with its secular, political focus, against Buddhism, among subordinates such as village leaders, and set up local schools to this end. The government also promoted Confucian teaching, founding some schools that mixed samurai and commoners and emphasized basic Confucian texts. Some broadening of curriculum occurred also, at least for scholars. A decree of 1720 relaxed a previous ban on all Christian learning, allowing that while outright Christian teachings were still prohibited, other Western works (in practice, those dealing with science and medicine) could be translated and taught. (Contact with Western learning at this point occurred through exchange with Dutch merchants in Nagasaki, the only Western group allowed into even a single Japanese port.)

Most education during the eighteenth century was provided by private schools, called *shijuku*, that depended on fees paid by samurai or ambitious commoners (such as merchant families). Rural education, however, centered mainly in local schools or emanated from various branches of Buddhism, and so had greater religious overtones. The private schools for the upper classes ranged from large centers, with elaborate administration, to small tutorial arrangements, sometimes in the homes of scholars. In the most prestigious centers, samurai boys were taught, Confucian-fashion, the importance of their leadership role in a well-ordered society. Other schools, however, favored merchant families, in part because they could pay higher fees than the poorer samurai. One school, for example, eliminated seating privileges for samurai by 1760, arguing that "interchange among students will take place without regard to high or low status and entirely as colleagues of like mind." In this school as in others, students learned how to read and write and use the abacus for counting (a vital skill for merchants) while imbibing Confucian lessons on loyalty and filial piety; more advanced classes taught Confucian philosophy and literature. Schools spread rapidly, some with low tuition, so that almost all merchant and samurai families acquired education by the later eighteenth century. These trends accelerated during the first half of the nineteenth century. Japan's preindustrial age lasted longer than that in France and the United States—significant political and economic change came only after 1853—but important educational gains continued, if largely in the traditional mode. Many schools set up by feudal lords continued to admit samurai only, aiming to produce a cultured and moral ruling elite. Confucian schools spread widely, along with a smaller number devoted to "Japanese" studies (including Shintoism). The sheer quantity of schools going beyond rudimentary education more than tripled in the early decades of the century. A typical school contained some samurai and Buddhist priests, with a majority of doctors, merchants, farmers, artisans, and village heads. The most elaborate schools, recruiting people in their late teens, required two to six years to complete. Emphasis rested on Chinese language and classics, with drill sessions designed to produce a reverence for the social order plus solid preparation for practical careers.

The biggest debate in Japanese elite education during the early nineteenth century involved steady pressures for more practical training, even for the samurai—more knowledge of fiscal issues and law, for example—and a small but growing interest in "Dutch" studies, particularly medicine but also military topics, through which students gained contact with Western learning. Only a small minority of schools provided any Western science, as late as 1872, but leaders of the "Dutch" current, even earlier, vigorously denounced the sterility of Confucian training.

The greatest educational expansion in Japan occurred beneath the level of the discussions of curriculum and the attacks on and defenses of Confucianism. The number of local schools increased by more than 600 percent between 1803 and 1843, and they became steadily more secular, with the role of Buddhist and Shinto priests declining. Teachers in the schools gained considerable prestige because they were seen to provide an esteemed public service. Lessons focused on basic literacy and practical subjects, with texts dealing (confusingly) with old historical topics or a mixture of Confucian and Buddhist ethics. Once students mastered reading, they were exposed to texts in commerce or farming, with a few written explicitly for female students.

By the middle of the nineteenth century, about 760,000 young people were in school (more than double the figure of 1829). The vast majority of these were in village schools, but about a fifth were in the more elite lords' schools or in the *shijuku*. About a fifth of all students were female, mainly in the cities. This level of schooling was producing substantial literacy. Again around midcentury, about 45 percent of all males and about 11 percent of all females in Japan could read and write at least on a rudimentary basis—figures well above those of any other society outside the West. Education was firmly established as a vital part of Japanese life, long before the need to react to Western example began to reshape the nation's experience.

CONCLUSION: A COMPARATIVE DEBATE

Similarities among French, American, and Japanese schools on the eve of major political and industrial change were striking. No nation had a full educational "system"; everywhere, schools were often local and haphazard, and while governments were involved they had yet to take primary leadership. Men gained far more education than women, though women acquired a foothold. Social hierarchy was pronounced. Japan and France had at least three major tiers: a set of schools for the elite (but including a few students from lower classes), elementary schools for a wide range of commoners, and no schools at all for the poorest groups. The United States, without a well-defined elite system, focused more on a division between those with some schooling and those with none (some, like the slaves, were positively discouraged from any attempt). Education had a variety of practical uses but was also designed to instill respect for the established order, through religious or Confucian emphases and rigid discipline. Finally, however, education was a changing commodity—all three societies were experiencing marked expansion and vigorous debates about educational purpose by the late eighteenth and early nineteenth centuries.

Similarities should not, however, be exaggerated. The difference between the traditional dominance of the Catholic Church in French schooling, the somewhat more diffuse Protestant direction in American schools, and the largely secular Confucian influence in Japan was considerable, raising distinctive issues in each case for the future. By French or Japanese standards, the United States had yet to define a special educational level for its elite. While educational discrimination against women was universal, the gender gap was least pronounced in the United States, most severe in Japan. All three countries were discussing the relationship between practical subjects and more traditional religious and philosophical emphases, but clearly the French were taking the most explicit steps toward new technical curricula. Patterns varied: on some issues France and Japan were more alike, on others Japan divided from the West, and in a few cases France followed the most distinctive approach. The differences mattered in three societies that, on the whole, were unusually well positioned to utilize an active, evolving educational structure to help adjust to new needs and opportunities in the nineteenth century. How education changed, in this adjustment, inevitably reflected some of the national characteristics already present. The substantial educational achievement ensured, in fact, that none of the three societies would wish to change its approach entirely.

3

Education for Industry and the State: Reforming the System in France 1800–1900

Both France and the United States began to modify their schooling patterns early in the nineteenth century, launching a process of educational change that would go on for at least a hundred years. This chapter deals with the patterns of change in France, from early attempts to adjust well-established patterns of schooling to the fuller emergence of a modern system. The focus is on shifts that were cumulatively decisive, but also surprisingly gradual, a mixture present in other Western countries like the United States. France created a new secondary school system beginning in 1808, but only in 1905 fully resolved a massive battle between church and state over which institution should dominate education. Change did not end even in 1905, but it is possible at that point to see a well-defined structure and, indeed, something of a national approach to education and its role in society.

Before dealing with change, however, it is important to ask why change was necessary in places like France and the United States, where education was already rather well developed and seemed to be meeting various social and personal needs. By the 1820s, both nations had launched a process of industrialization, involving new technology, installation of factories, and growth in manufacturing. Historians have debated how much education industrialization demands. It is not clear, for example, that literacy improved the productivity of early factory workers—and, in fact, many workers were illiterate either because they came from the poorer ranks of the farming population or because the disruptions of early industry reduced the time available for schooling in many cities. Industrialization did create new needs for trained technical personnel, like engineers and certain kinds of lawyers. Even here, most inventors and machine mounters were self-taught, rather than formally educated in secondary schools, until the later nineteenth century. The relationship between growing industry and schooling is complex, though some link certainly exists.

Some new motivations for education resulted from more specific aspects of industrialization. Very early factories frequently used many child laborers, but as machines became more complex the need for these workers diminished. At the same time, industrial work pulled parents out of the home (unless, as often occurred, mothers withdrew from the formal labor force). The result was new needs for child care, and schools might serve this purpose (though no educational leader explicitly admitted this fact).

Alongside the demands of an industrializing economy, political changes pushed for education. As more people moved into cities and as pressure for democracy increased, in response, for example, to the American and French revolutions, many political leaders believed that increased education was a vital preparation for an informed (and possibly loyal) citizenry. Growing attention to nationhood prompted the belief that education should help people identify with the national entity. Obviously, the political and the economic purposes of modern education did not entirely mesh. Lessons that emphasized political obedience might differ from those that stressed the need to change established economic habits or simply provide a technical mindset.

Finally, political and economic changes were complemented by new beliefs about education coming from various sectors of the population in Western society. Many middle-class liberals began to argue that education was essential for children to have proper social opportunities, and they certainly wanted to make sure that their own children had educational access. The idea that societies owed schools to the citizenry as part of the standard functions of government gained ground. Many lower-class people began to think that education was vital for them or their children to take advantage of new knowledge and gain access to better jobs, especially since many established positions were threatened by machine competition. Early labor movements frequently featured demands for popular schools. Again, these impulses did not fully mesh with the other spurs to educational change. Questions arose, for example, about whether education should emphasize social stability and political order or should encourage people to strive for new achievements; whether it should train people in the skills needed for factory work or should promote more ambitious social and technical goals.

The three forces of industrial development, political change, and new cultural aspirations and beliefs did combine to promote more educational opportunities and revised curricula. They did not, however, generate precise definitions for the educational agenda. France, as its system developed over several decades, provided one distinctive approach.

STAGES OF CHANGE

France took a major step in educational reform early in the nineteenth century by focusing on elite training. The motivation was political: the government of Emperor Napoleon, on the heels of the great revolution, wanted to firm up central government controls and reduce the role of the church, while also for the first time providing a coherent system of training for the bureaucrats needed by a growing state. There was no interest at this point (despite earlier proclamations at the height of the revolution) in doing more for mass education. Napoleon saw no need for a more educated populace, which might in fact raise new demands. He was content with an incomplete educational network staffed by priests and nuns, which would emphasize religion and obedience while relieving the government of any additional expense.

But training government officials, drawn largely from the ranks of business and professional families, was another matter. Napoleon devoted considerable attention to education, as part of his attempt to reconcile groups bitterly divided by the revolution and to establish an effective, forward-looking authoritarian state. A law of 1802 began the process of centralizing the educational system in principle, and by 1808 a single institution, called the University, had acquired a monopoly over all public instruction, including individual colleges and universities. Private institutions could continue, but under the University's supervision; they were also required to pay fees to the state. Continuing initiatives launched during the revolution, Napoleon focused a second main innovation on the secondary level. Alongside the traditional *collèges*, a new set of secondary schools, called *lycées*, was established. These schools were highly disciplined, featuring drills and military-style uniforms. They emphasized a severe classical curriculum, including Greek and Latin. Science was downplayed, but national literature, logic, and mathematics received considerable emphasis. Admission went mainly to children from upper-middle-class and even aristocratic families, but other students, identified for their talent by government officials, might win scholarships. The purpose of this system was to recruit and train a solid corps of bureaucrats, accustomed to hard work and convinced of their cultural superiority. Forty-six such schools existed by 1812, somewhat short of the number Napoleon had envisaged. Finally, Napoleon actively encouraged technical education. He provided improved funding and facilities to the École Polytechnique, into which the older engineering schools had been regrouped. Napoleon also funded another professional school, the École Normale Supérieure, which had been set up to train nonreligious teachers but became a leading source for France's intellectual elite.

Napoleon's educational goals were several, and partly contradictory. He wanted the state to control a centralized system, and this feature proved so convenient to subsequent French governments (of various ideological stripes) that it has continued with minor modifications ever since. In principle, the University had to approve all teachers at all levels. Even in primary schools, localities could only nominate an instructor; the central agency had to agree. But the emperor also wanted to appeal to different ideological camps, so he left many Catholic schools alone, and thus his centralization effort was hampered in practice by the lack of available tax revenues. He hoped to please liberals by the new secular schools and the opportunities for the upper middle class. He wooed Catholics by giving free rein to religiously run primary schools and he provided little supervision for the seminaries that trained priests. Inspection of private and religious schools was in fact minimal, for the state could not afford many agents. The head of the University—called the Grand Master—was a Catholic conservative named Fontanes whose major appointments, even for the *lycées*, were influenced by the advice of bishops. Catholic orders continued to provide the bulk of France's teachers. Socially, Napoleon obviously believed in hierarchy. He wanted to attract the loyalty of the upper classes, and of course he largely ignored mass schooling. But he qualified upper-class dominance in two ways. First, entrance to the prestigious *lycées* was demanding, based on tests. Few students could succeed without prior tutorial (rather than attendance at village primary schools), but merely being upper class did not assure entry.

Second, limited access to really talented people from other social levels provided a glimmer of genuine mobility through education; some political leaders of subsequent generations, like the liberal Adolphe Thiers, rose through their educational attainments. Napoleon also sought impact on curriculum, by encouraging science and technical subjects, but the emphasis on more traditional training, not only religious but also classical, modified results in this category.

Napoleon's changes pleased no group entirely. Liberals resented Catholic influence, but Catholics feared the implications of fundamental state control and centralization. Actual student patterns changed far less than did organization and principle. Local church schools began to expand again, though many areas had no facilities. Far more middle-class students went to *collèges*, usually religiously run, than to *lycées*, though the public secondary schools did begin to cut into private school numbers. In 1810 the public *lycées* and *collèges* had 38,000 students, while in 1813 they had moved up to 44,000, mostly at the expense of private attendance. The various universities by this point took a minority of these graduates, mainly for higher professional training. A total of 8,859 young men studied law (45 percent); medicine (24 percent); humanities subjects (20 percent), mainly to become secondary school teachers; theology (6 percent); and science (5 percent). The figures for science, though low by later standards, actually surpassed those of other European countries at the time, giving France a solid scientific basis for years to come. And while Napoleon left many questions unanswered—including, ultimately, the role of the church and religion—his measures had two durable outcomes: first, the extreme centralization of French education in principle, if not always in fact; and second, the emphasis on rigorous (though still mainly humanistic) training for an elite, separate from the educational conditions of the majority. Along with the earlier initiatives in technical training, which coexisted with the elite *lycées*, these features continued to mark the French approach to modern schooling.

During the fifteen years after Napoleon's fall in 1815, the imperial system was largely confirmed while increasingly bitter debate focused on the role of the church within it. Church-state issues were not the only features of French educational history during this period and beyond, and probably not the most important ones, but they were unquestionably the loudest. Neither Catholics nor liberals wanted to compromise on educa-

Debating the Past
Napoleon's Achievements

Historians have not been kind to Napoleon's educational measures. American historians, relying on what they value in their own pattern, commonly take potshots at the "rigidity" and "centralization" of Napoleon's approach. One historian, Joseph Moody, blasting the "needless rigidity of curricula," sees the emphasis on state control and discipline as "an indictment of [Napoleon's] own drill-sergeant's idea of education." Many French historians, writing as liberals or radicals, emphasize more the emperor's failure to limit Catholic impact. And almost everyone notes the neglect of mass education and the various compromises Napoleon had to make.

Several points might be suggested in assessing these chilly arguments. First, what criteria should be used in evaluating educational change? Napoleon's goals clearly differed from American educational values, with his centralization impulse. How can historians decide, save by their own value system, whether centralization is good or bad? Is it ever possible for a historian committed to his or her own nation's pattern to note that a foreign system differs significantly but works well? The same dilemma, about the role of value judgments, obviously applies to discussions about Catholic influence. Certainly if one measure of success is sheer durability, some of Napoleon's achievements may seem rather impressive. What measurements of good or bad seem useful in judging education history? How much, furthermore, can one expect a leader—for whom education was important but not nearly as interesting as foreign conquest—to push beyond the common conditions of his time? To be sure, Napoleon ignored the democratic suggestions of the revolution, but he also grappled with budget limitations and internal dissent. Could he reasonably be expected to have been bolder, say, in implementing his clear commitment to modern science? Because education is costly and because it tends to be conservative, with each generation recalling its own educational experience in judging innovation, actual change in this area often comes slowly, however radical the official pronouncements. How do Napoleon's initiatives fare when judged with this in mind?

tional control. The Restoration monarchy that ruled between 1815 and 1830 could not bring itself to dismantle centralization, but it did increasingly turn the system over to conservative Catholic educators. By 1821 Catholics controlled the state secondary schools, the *collèges,* while a vigorous priest, Frayssinous, became Grand Master of the University and later minister of public instruction and ecclesiastical affairs (the merger of state departments of education and religion was revealing in itself). Liberal teachers were fired in favor of priests, even at the university level. The government increased funding for seminaries, though many priests continued to be poorly trained, particularly in terms of coping with new scientific and political ideas. Catholic gains inevitably roused liberal opposition, and French education risked becoming a battleground, with directions shifting according to the faction in power.

Alongside this public furor, technical training in France advanced further. The 1820s saw the spread of new factories, and many businessmen and artisans sought formal instruction that would improve the skills of the upper tier of the labor force (the business interest) or provide new opportunities for people whose traditional craft training was now outdated (the worker interest). City governments and chambers of commerce set up adult classes in accounting, industrial chemistry, and the like. A few big companies established schools for their child workers, from humanitarian concern and also to upgrade their future labor supply. Here were clear signs that industry did require educational innovation—though not necessarily mass education. In 1829 a group of businessmen and scientists founded a new engineering school, the École Centrale des Arts et Manufactures, to provide sons of middle-class families with practical training; from its graduates would come many of France's leading railroad engineers a decade later. French medical schools began to tighten their training, with more clinical and pathological work. On a variety of fronts, then, education continued the emphasis on scientific and technical training, both for a part of the nation's elite and also for a middle level of practitioners.

The next big step in France's pattern of educational change came after the moderate liberal revolution of 1830, with the Guizot law of 1833, which directly encouraged new initiatives in the area of mass schooling. François Guizot was not only a liberal but a Protestant and thus had a double stake in educational advance. He saw education as a means of allowing people to gain their place in society by merit, an idea that appealed to the "ambitious foresight" of French families but was also a key issue for the state now that religion no longer exclusively dominated people's loyalties. As Guizot put it, "The great problem of modern society is the government of men's minds." Debate about the very desirability of mass education continued among the French upper classes. Some continued to see schooling as dangerous, giving people ideas and expectations beyond their station. Guizot disagreed, but he shared the belief that schools must emphasize social order. His solution, practical also in the climate of French political debate between liberals and conservative Catholics, involved facilitating state-run schools that embraced continued religious involvement.

The Guizot law of 1833 effectively served as the charter of modern French primary education. At the time, as many as 38,000 localities in France still had no school of any kind. The new law required every commune to establish a public primary school and provided for expanded teacher training facilities. The law did not guarantee education for everyone, and church influence continued in many localities. Guizot realized that many areas could not afford teachers without help from religious orders, and he also believed that religion was an essential educational component for the lower classes. As he put it, "Popular education must be given and received in the midst of a truly religious atmosphere permeated from all sides by religious attitudes and habits." Otherwise, people would soon abandon morality and restraint. At the same time, however, Guizot advanced the state's role. Each local school board was to have a majority of laymen. Furthermore, the teachers emerging from the new training programs were secular in orientation and sometimes actively opposed to religion. Guizot's law did not provide a uniform primary school system across France, and in some regions the church continued to monopolize education at this level. It did expand schools while giving the teaching profession higher status and better working conditions. By 1848 the number of teacher training schools had risen from forty-seven to seventy-six, and enrollment in public primary schools had almost doubled.

The expansion of schooling under the Guizot law was not accompanied by major rethinking either of school discipline or of curriculum, though there was some theoretical discussion and a few brief experiments in, among other things, methods to help teachers handle larger classes. Though policymakers did attempt to limit corporal punishment, the practice continued as rules became even stricter than before and an atmosphere of rigid discipline prevailed. Few schools offered more than basic reading, writing, and arithmetic, but officials encouraged attention to history and geography after the basics were mastered. Though some new books were available for young students, traditionalism and lack of resources prompted many schools to fall back on religious catechisms. In other words, the system altered more rapidly than its content.

Even with such limitations, however, the social and personal role of education began to change as well. Under the auspices of the Guizot law, in fact, France entered a period of fascinating debate over the purposes of primary schooling. The debate involved middle-class people talking about what schools might do to and for the lower classes; even more important, it involved lower-class people themselves figuring out whether primary education now made sense for their children. As schooling expanded during the decades after 1833, and before outright compulsory education was mandated in 1882, growth resulted from hundreds of thousands of personal decisions about the role of education in modern life — decisions about whether to go to the expense, trouble, and uncertainty of sending a child to school, about what kind of school, and about how long to continue schooling. These decisions riveted on primary schooling. The Guizot law maintained a substantial separation between elementary education and the most prestigious secondary and higher education facilities open mainly to the upper classes, who also used their own primary feeder schools or private tutoring.

Middle-class people, increasingly devoted to education for their own children, actively discussed lower-class schooling during the 1830s and 1840s. The principal focus was the growing number of children in the cities, some of them working in the new factories. Was a life devoted to work, beginning as early as age five, appropriate in modern conditions, without some opportunity to acquire basic education? Some middle-class people continued to answer yes. They feared the effects of schools on popular loyalty, or they shied away from additional public expense (arguing often that decisions about children should be left to the fathers of families, without intervention from the state), or they sincerely believed that their own livelihood depended on cheap child labor uninterrupted by even a few hours of school each week. But a growing number, headed by some passionate reformers, saw things differently. They felt that children deserved the chance to gain basic skills that would allow some of them, at least, to rise in life; education might encourage mobility and so make society more just. Better-trained workers would help French industry itself, providing a higher-caliber labor force. Reading ability would help workers understand instructions and written work rules. Schools could also instill the habits of discipline, accustoming children, for example, to work according to clock time; these implicit lessons, in new behaviors demanded by industrial life, would generate more disciplined labor later. Understanding how society works might actually reduce random protest, and education certainly might save children from the brutal exploitation of some working-class parents. Arguments varied, but they increasingly led to the conclusion that children should have access to schools. This belief prompted a minority of employers to set up classes for their own workers' families. A few big operations, like the Le Creusot metallurgical firm, launched huge educational operations, providing primary training for all children of employees, from which particularly able students could be selected for technical courses and subsequent jobs as skilled workers, foremen, or even middle managers. This was a tight paternalistic system designed to tie workers to the company while meeting its labor needs. More generally, middle-class sentiment helped generate a law in 1841 that in principle limited child labor in the factories and required schooling for children under twelve who were employed. The law was not strictly enforced, but along with more general humanitarian pressure it did encourage more urban school attendance.

Middle-class reformers, sincerely interested in children's welfare, tended to distrust workers and peasants, whose horizons seemed limited and who might care more about short-term earnings from child labor than from longer-term opportunities. But middle-class outlook had only limited impact. The crucial changes in primary school resulted from new calculations by lower-class parents themselves. Education was not of course new to French rural life—it had already made inroads before 1800. It was between 1830 and 1880, however, that schooling definitively gained the majority of French peasants, along with growing numbers of urban workers, including, increasingly, females as well as males.

Why should peasants want an education for their children by this point, even when it became slightly easier through the formation of more widespread local schools? The barriers were still considerable. Children's work was valuable. Many attended school, at most, for a few months in the winter and forgot most of what they had learned before they returned after the months of farm labor. Schools might be at some distance from a particular village, which meant precious travel time and some expense. Schoolrooms were often desolate, kept in bad repair because the localities begrudged the money. Teachers, even with Guizot's training, were not always competent; sometimes children could spend two years in the classroom without learning to read at all, because the teacher merely had them memorize sentences after he read them himself, beating them if they did not make the right sounds. Even good teachers often ran afoul of the local priests, many of whom were hostile to anything but memorization of the catechism; many villages were divided over what the school should do beyond religious training. Language was another issue: the teachers worked in French, but many peasants used a local dialect while counting in traditional units rather than in the official metric system.

But change did begin to break down the barriers, sometimes after a decade or more. Better roads were built, making travel to school easier. Teachers improved, gradually, becoming more adept in effective teaching methods. Headed often by village artisans, rural families began to see advantages in formal schooling. Counting (including use of the metric system) began to matter more as the village sold its produce more widely and engaged in more elaborate commercial transactions. With many families adding some shopkeeping or craft production to their farming, to make ends meet in an increasingly market-driven economy, girls needed some basic skills as well as boys. As more male peasants were drafted into the army, reading became more useful—otherwise they could not write home or read letters from their families. Greater rural prosperity made the taxes and fees for schools easier to manage. Active electioneering, particularly in hotly contested political battles during the 1870s, made more peasants eager to read political pamphlets. It began to seem shameful not to know how to read—by which time the battle for schooling had been won, for all but the poorest minority. A steady increase in French literacy, even in the previously laggard southern region, by the 1870s meant that upwards of 70 percent of all males nationally, and almost half of all females, could read and write at least to sign their names.

During these transition decades, when French primary education gained ground but before a full national system was in place, a real corps

Figure 3. Schooling in the old style: French artisans complete an apprenticeship with their craft guild toward the middle of the nineteenth century. The skill was carpentry, and the students have completed a "masterpiece" to demonstrate their competence—the equivalent of a final examination.

of teachers also emerged, trained in the state-run normal (that is, teacher training) schools. When they were tactful and alert, teachers could gain significant status in their communities, particularly when they were of peasant origins themselves. State support was also vital in the increasing status of teachers: a reform-minded education minister in the 1860s, Victor Duruy, advocated improved salaries and pensions, making teachers a full part of the lower middle class, and these measures were gradually realized. But community standing counted, even aside from this. Teachers could help draft letters and contracts for villagers who were not literate. They stood as symbols of rural mobility through education, for obviously schools had helped them move up the social ladder. Most of these teachers were secular in their loyalties. They might have some attachment to Catholicism still, but they knew that the state was their employer and they often experienced the hostility of local priests. By the 1870s they usually believed in the republic, rather than a monarchy, as the appropriate system of government for France. And they were nationalistic, using texts devoted to the glories of the nation as staples in their teaching of reading, literature, and history. They embraced primers like the

Debating the Past
School Clientele

Historians continue to debate the interesting issue of why people's enthusiasm for education began to increase, particularly before direct state compulsion and when schools charged fees — as in France before the 1880s. Several historians have gone to great pains to show that primary schooling did not necessarily lead to improved economic success in later life. Some of the highest-paid factory workers were illiterate. One historian, Harvey Graff, has highlighted what he calls the "literacy myth" — the widespread idea that literacy was essential for individual progress. Also, key skills could be picked up without going to school. Literacy itself had long been gaining ground in Europe through training in the home, while apprenticeships could generate the ability to count and calculate. Other historians, however, emphasize the power of a growing faith in education, granting that some particular groups (including minority language groups in France) often still held out. They stress the growing moral superiority with which schooling endowed its graduates, apart from specific benefits. Even here, however, there are questions about expectations. Did people look to schools to provide very particular, job-relevant training, so that farmers could be better able to cope with the market economy for example? Or did they have more ambitious dreams for their children, like the working-class mother in Paris who defined her vision: "How many wonderful dreams I had for my dear child. I wanted him to go to school, to be well brought up, how happy I would have been if one day chance had smiled on me and my son would have become a doctor." To be sure, the reference to chance shows that this woman did not assume that education alone would do the trick. But how many people, sending children to school for the first time, shared her dreams? And what would happen when the more modest results of schooling became apparent?

one, in the 1870s, that ended with a boy saying "I love France, I love France . . . I wish the whole world answered me and that every nation on earth said, 'I love France.' "

COMPLETING THE BASIC SYSTEM, 1880–1900

By 1880, the spread of primary education and the new band of professional teachers did not create a full national system of schools. First, battles over the role of the church had not ended. When the vaguely liberal monarchy that had sponsored the Guizot law collapsed in revolution in 1848, it was soon succeeded by a more conservative empire that sought to conciliate Catholic opinion by an 1851 law that gave the church more educational control. Liberals once again worked against this trend, and a showdown loomed by the 1880s after the empire had been overthrown (in 1871) and a moderately liberal republic installed. Even aside from these political disputes, the French system remained incomplete, in that some boys and even more girls were still not drawn in. It remained incomplete also in the division between mass education and education for the middle and upper classes, who gained separate primary training and then monopolized the secondary schools. To be sure, a few bright peasants went beyond elementary education, most commonly in teacher training but occasionally in a technical or classical school that led to even higher status. But for the most part the mass elementary and elite secondary systems were not linked. Furthermore, most peasant and worker families, even after being convinced of the utility of some primary schooling for their children, had no explicit ambitions beyond this. Education was intended to provide skills helpful in modern agricultural or factory work, not to take children to a more elevated station. Modern education remained compatible with profound social inequality and basic divisions in aspiration.

Some of these issues were tackled from the 1880s onward, under sponsorship of the new republican regime. It was during the two decades to the turn of the century that France's modern educational system was essentially completed, though further adjustments would be made in the twentieth century. Between 1878 and 1881, liberal republican leaders, in a movement spearheaded by Jules Ferry, rapidly expanded the primary school system, and the teacher training normal schools, in preparation for universal education and freedom from dependence on church personnel. A series of laws between 1879 and 1886, commonly called the Ferry laws, made primary education free and tax-supported (thus cutting into church competition); a measure in 1882 required schooling for all girls and boys between ages six and thirteen. A further provision decreed that "civic and moral" teaching must replace religious instruction in the schools. Ferry argued that it was time to "liberate the souls of French youth" from Catholic influence; the expanding numbers of state-trained teachers were regarded as "lay missionaries" in spreading new beliefs in science and nationalism. A law in 1886 provided for the replacement of all Catholic personnel, mostly within five years. The Ferry program also limited the rights of Catholic universities, creating a largely state-run higher education system and new secular secondary schools. This measure was particularly important for girls, whose secondary training previously had been concentrated in Catholic hands. The rights of members of religious orders to teach in any school, even a private one, were limited, and the Jesuits were again expelled.

These measures inevitably aroused controversy. Catholics, from the pope to ardent lay advocates, protested, largely in vain. The government did allow some Catholic schools to continue, as voluntary options, but the bulk of education became resolutely secular. New geographies of France omitted emphasis on the great cathedrals; histories downplayed Catholic heroes like Joan of Arc. The French system, with no formal religious teaching, stood out for its secularism among European programs at this time. And most Frenchmen seemed, if not to approve, at least not to object; Catholic political candidates made little headway. Amid these changes, the more fundamental shift—the provision of education for all children—passed almost without comment. By this point everyone agreed that all children should gain basic skills in school. Quickly, French literacy rates showed the impact, as they moved from 60 percent of the entire population, male and female, in 1870 to 95 percent by 1900. Parallel legislation preventing the use of child labor supported universal education by limiting the alternative uses of children and making parents and employers alike see that schooling now provided the only reasonable setting for children, at least before the teen years.

The expansion of the French teaching corps continued many of the trends established earlier. French teachers felt a sense of mission in bringing enlightenment and rationalism to the masses, along with a commitment to the secular republic. Paid rather poorly, many of them also unionized by 1900 and became attached to radical or socialist political parties. Before 1914 they also remained nationalistic, though this stance softened later. The new laws did spur the dramatic growth of a new group of women teachers, in essence replacing the nuns who had previously run most schools for girls but also expanding into boys' classrooms. By 1906, when almost no nuns were teaching, there were 57,000 state-trained female teachers in France (up from 14,000 just thirty years before), falling only a few hundred under the figure for men. This feminization of French teaching was a logical result of the increased numbers of female students. It also created a corps of teachers willing to work for less pay than men (about 20 percent less, at the highest level, though with scant differentiation in the lower levels). By the 1880s, the development of a female teacher corps roused considerable male resentment, with terms like "humiliating" tossed up. On the whole, however, French teachers drew together in common fear of Catholic counterattack, particularly as religious disputes resurfaced in France during the 1890s. The gender change was assimilated, and many women joined the teachers' unions.

The mass education system completed by the Ferry laws brought other changes or reemphases in its wake. The first involved the implications of France's commitment to centralization, which now covered virtually the entire school system. Ministers of education were known to boast that, because of curriculum plans drawn up in Paris, they knew what was going on in every classroom in the nation at any point in the school day. This was a gross exaggeration, but it was true that central controls, combined with the republican, anti-Catholic zeal of the Ferry plans, produced a strong standardization. This had important implications for some outlying regions. Educational officials vigorously pushed teaching in standard French, hoping to eliminate minority dialects and languages such as Provençal and Breton. Cultural resistance resulted, but without question the conversion to a national language proceeded rapidly.

The new mass system also sought novel means of implementing some highly traditional social and educational goals. Despite the attacks on religion, the desire remained to use schools to promote morality. And policymakers did not want to see schools become seedbeds for social discontent and skepticism. Moderate republicans implicitly agreed with conservatives on this point. Thus, emphasis on fervent nationalism, already present in the French system, escalated. From early reading manuals onward, primary school students were taught a highly laudatory view of French history and of the distinctive beauties of the French language and literature that was meant to attach them to their country. As Ernest Lavisse, a French historian-educator, put it in 1912, "If a student does not grow into a citizen imbued with his duties and a soldier who loves his rifle, the teacher will have wasted his time."

Messages about personal goals were frankly mixed. On the one hand, education was touted for its role in helping students improve their lot in life, and in fact some individuals did rise into the more elite schools and, subsequently, in social standing. On the other hand, there was no desire to encourage unrealistic expectations. Reading lessons instilled the importance of sticking to one's station in life, working hard, taking pleasure in simply providing for one's family. Other lessons urged thrift, obedience to authority, orderliness, and patience in the face of adversity, a remarkably traditional set of values even with the religion removed. Combined with nationalism — in lessons that, for example, hailed the conscientious French peasant and his agricultural production as the backbone of national strength — this approach sent powerful signals of social stability.

These messages, or at least the intent behind them (because the messages by no means always succeeded) particularly undergirded the approach to girls' education. Universal schooling and an unprecedented parity with men in literacy were important shifts in French gender relations, but they did not eliminate the desire to ensure that schools maintained separate roles for males and females. To be sure, girls and boys both studied reading, writing, arithmetic, history, science, geography, and moral education. Boys had more athletic training; girls had sewing classes. Girls were also told about the virtues that were expected of them in their main role as wives and mothers: "modesty in dress, attitude, and language," along with "perseverance, the spirit of conciliation, love of peace, and mutual respect." They should expect to provide support for their husband's work in the world, arrange a calm and orderly home life, and serve France by bearing and raising children. Special texts for girls in reading, home economics, and moral education drove these lessons home, while the examination for the certificate of primary studies for girls at age twelve or thirteen involved drills in the same vein. Essay questions were on topics such as "Why I love my mother" and "What are the qualities of a good housewife?" The certificates were preconditions for lower-level government jobs, for example in the post office, and were the first step for those aspiring to be teachers; girls did increasingly well on them, almost matching boys' scores by 1907.

Moral and nationalistic lessons, while forming a major part of the primary school curriculum, did not necessarily take hold. There is evidence that many girls found the domestic message silly, and lower-class boys and girls often became politically radical in later life, not confining themselves to national loyalty. Common methods of teaching, involving repetitious drills and memorization, did not necessarily inspire confidence. Nevertheless, the goals of the exercises were clear. Primary schools were designed to give the French masses some essential basic skills, including some training practical in later work; they should also underpin social and familial stability, while basically maintaining the existing class structure.

The new primary school system remained separate from the state-run network of secondary and higher schools, which had been created earlier and for a different clientele. Of course there were links. Ferry's reforms drove religious teachers out of most higher schools, save for a few private academies and universities that still managed to attract students. Secularism, faith in reason and science, and nationalism dominated curricula at this level as they did in the primary schools. It was also possible for a minority of talented children, former peasants as well as former urban workers, to move from the primary schools into a secondary normal school for teacher training or occasionally into a *lycée* or a prestigious technical school. Education did serve mobility. But for most people, schooling stopped with the primary school; as late as 1934, only 40 percent of all students even bothered or managed to get the graduation certificate. A key question in French education then, as it had emerged by the late nineteenth century, was the relationship among different academic and social levels.

Secondary schools changed in the last decades of the century in other ways besides secularization. New kinds of schools developed between the primary system and the elite level. This expansion from the 1860s onward was essential partly to replace the declining network of Catholic *collèges* but also to feed the middle-class thirst for educational qualifications that would take their children beyond the level of the masses. Master artisans, shopkeepers, and clerks as well as middle-level businessmen and professionals realized that certain kinds of training were increasingly necessary for middle-class status. It was not enough to have basic skills; some further knowledge of literature, perhaps a foreign language, and more advanced mathematics provided both practical tools and an assurance of respectability in the modern world. In addition, even more than the working class and peasantry, middle-class families needed outlets for their offspring between early childhood and near-adulthood; it was impossible to provide respectable, constructive work even to teenagers in most middle-class settings. Sons could not usefully enter their fathers' businesses before their mid-teens, key professions from teaching to medicine offered nothing to people lacking some advanced training, and there was not much to keep growing girls busy around the house. In this respect education seemed crucial, so long as it took students beyond the primary levels. The middle classes were even willing to continue to pay fees for this extra training, and fees thus remained part of state-sponsored secondary schooling into the twentieth century (though with some scholarship opportunities).

During the 1860s and 1870s, a new category of secondary programs gained popularity, under the heading of "special education." Different from the more prestigious but also more academic *lycée* curriculum, these state-sponsored programs were introduced as separate, lower-track operations in existing schools. They offered practical instruction, combining some general education in literature, language, science, and history with commercial courses and even some manual training. The programs caught on with the lower end of the middle classes. In the 1880s, however, they became more academic, though they were still kept separate from the *lycée* curriculum. Called the "modern" stream, as opposed to the classical orientation of the *lycées*, these programs now emphasized more theoretical science and French literature. There was fierce debate as to whether real culture could be obtained without Latin, but on the whole the middle classes welcomed a more prestigious, if less immediately practical, option than the special education stream had offered. Most of the

Figure 4. A Catholic college around 1920. Uniforms and careful posing mark the impression the school wished to make, though each student expressed clearly individual characteristics.

expanding secondary schools for girls followed the modern approach, with three- to four-year programs in literature, history, and the basic sciences.

Finally, in 1902, the main branches of the secondary system were coordinated, and the "modern" curricula were placed on a par with the classical *lycées*. A full seven-year program was laid out, beginning at age eleven; the program was divided into two cycles. During the first cycle, which lasted four years, students opted for either a classical or a modern program. The second cycle, three more years for students who had continued this far, involved greater specialization in classical languages, Latin and modern languages, Latin and science, or modern languages and science. In the second year of the second cycle, students from all programs took the first part of the *baccalauréat* examination and then spent a final year working on philosophy and mathematics for the second part of the examination.

The *baccalauréat* exam, or "bac," had long been part of the certification for *lycée* students. Generalized now to the whole secondary system, it remained a formidable challenge. More than half of all students, undergoing the exam initially at age sixteen or seventeen, failed one of the two parts on first taking and then had to repeat a year of their school program to prepare anew. Success on these examinations, in turn, was a prerequisite for entry into universities and other higher schools, though the École Polytechnique accepted only a handful of the highest scorers and required additional testing as well. Many secondary school students did not choose to go further at this point—the percentage of the eligible population pursuing higher technical, medical, legal, administrative, or other training remained small. Nevertheless, the growing prestige and coherence of French higher education, building hierarchically on the secondary school experience and rigorous testing, provided an increasingly integrated apparatus for the training and recruitment of the French elite. Not surprisingly, success in government, the professions, and even the upper reaches of business correlated closely with school results in France by 1900—it was rare to achieve upper-class status without school experience to match. By 1900, private and public centers such as the École Polytechnique, the École Normale Supérieure, and a new School of Political Sciences (École des Sciences Politiques) were justly known as France's "great schools" *(grandes écoles),* producers of the leaders of the next generation.

The evolution of French education during the nineteenth century and the assumptions of key policymakers at most stages of the process had thus created two largely separate school systems. The primary schools existed for the masses. Reforms including the Ferry laws added an upper primary level for students who wanted further training for two or three years after age thirteen, which could help prepare them for certain jobs, including primary school teaching. Intermediate technical training, such as at the École des Arts et Manufactures, was also available to qualified graduates of the upper primary schools. But the real secondary system was distinct. Many *lycées* ran their own primary programs, beginning to teach Latin, for example, to nine-year-olds who were preparing for entry. A handful of students managed to shift from the standard primary schools into the secondary school program, usually around age eleven; they had to be identified as particularly talented and of course needed financial assistance. The number of children of working-class or peasant background able to make this huge jump remained very small. Even most scholarship holders came from lower-middle-class backgrounds.

The secondary and higher education system served the middle class well and produced significant mobility. Lower-middle-class children, from families of clerks and shopkeepers, were well represented in the great schools and were on their way to substantial social advance. Children of teachers and lower bureaucrats, however, did noticeably better than those of shopkeepers and clerks in gaining entry to secondary and higher education; mobility remained complex. Tough examinations— and the years spent preparing for the "bac" were agonizing indeed— gave students an understandable belief that they deserved their success. Secondary schools and the higher technical schools, in particular, imposed rigorous work regimes, and many people learned habits of working long days and avoiding frivolous distractions that would define their whole adult lives. Students who could not stand the pressure and the constant assignments left the programs; small wonder that one historian has termed some of these schools the "factories of the bourgeoisie." To be sure, wild celebrations and occasional street riots followed the days of the *baccalauréat* examinations, as students let off steam. But this was a severe educational regime—far more severe than traditional upper-class schools had been before—if in many ways an undemocratic one at base.

A combination of social tradition and policy innovation had thus produced, by 1900, both universal education and near-universal literacy in France and an elitist educational track in which enrollment was effectively limited though open to hard work and merit for a minority of the population. While some features of early modern schooling could still be discerned, the French educational landscape had altered dramatically in the space of a century. In the process, key questions about the role of religion had been answered, somewhat brutally, and a mixture of classical and technical training defined beyond the basic skill levels. Tensions within the system were obvious; the relationship between elite levels and opportunities for the masses would have to be revisited. Extreme centralization, plus a tendency to neglect certain educational areas such as the newer social sciences (economics, for example, was

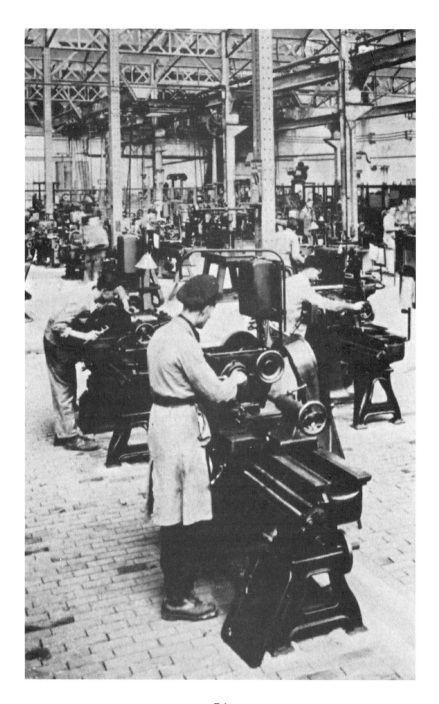

available only in some of the law schools) in favor of more specialized classical or technical emphases, made the system vulnerable to becoming rigid as well. French higher education was also known for its devotion to theory and abstraction, rather than more practical specializations in the technical fields. But this was a system that worked well in many respects for one of the world's leaders in political democracy and a growing industrial power.

Using the Sources: Issues in French Secondary Schooling

What was secondary schooling for? Tradition and ongoing practice suggested it was to help identify and school an elite, but how? As secondary training expanded, without losing elite status, new issues arose about what kinds of preparation it should entail. Should it focus on mental discipline? On certain kinds of sophistication, for example in speech or in mastery of a classical language? How practical should it be? Various French approaches provided different answers for these questions, in part (but not entirely) related to the different kinds of secondary schools that developed through the century. The following passages give some flavor of complex, sometimes implicit discussions of what purposes the schools served, in the context of a modernizing society. In the first selection, an eminent historian looks back, fondly, on his training. What was its purpose? Does he value the same emphases that his teachers did? In the second passage, an eminent Catholic educator talks about the utility of Latin. Finally, the leading educational reformer of the 1860s, Victor Duruy, takes quite a different slant, arguing for a much more varied menu for secondary training. How would Lavisse and Dupanloup answer Duruy's appeal? Would they accept the need for variety (and would they view the results of this variety as of equal value)? How does this implicit debate relate not only to changes in the French economy and social structure but to the ongoing issue of relating specialization and open opportunity in any modern educational system?

Figure 5 (*opposite*).   The rise of French industrial engineering at the beginning of the twentieth century.

ERNEST LAVISSE

Reflections on Education in the Lycée
1902

I feel I was raised in a noble, foreign, and distant setting. I've lived in Athens in the time of Pericles, Rome in the Augustan age, Versailles under Louis XIV. The ideas and passions which shape men's lives were presented to my mind in the most delightful forms. The permanent fund of human wisdom was communicated to me through slow penetration. . . .

Rhetoric was the true goal of study back then, and the best students spent two years at it. Everything focused on speech. We composed two speeches per week, one in French and one in Latin. Our professors rated them according to merit, read aloud the best one entirely and the best passages from the ones that came next. . . . Thus our French pleasure in doing well and being told we did well was manifested. . . . M. Lemaire dictated "materials" to us which we were supposed to put into three, four, or five paragraphs, and woe to the student who tried to add a paragraph. "I forbid you from touching my material. Is that understood?" And we were not supposed to introduce any ideas; the exercise of the speech was an exercise in order and regulation, that was its true value.

Ernest Lavisse, "Souvenirs d'une éducation manquée," *Revue de Paris,* November 15, 1902.

MGR. DUPANLOUP

Defense of Latin in Higher Education
1873

Children never think, feel, imagine, or write as well in French as in Latin, and what is more, as in Latin verse. In French, they are almost always common, vulgar . . . because they know only the French of their recreations. . . .

What is the goal of higher literary education? It is to attain, not plain and

Mgr. Dupanloup, *Seconde lettre . . . sur la circulaire de M. le ministre de l'instruction publique relative à l'enseignement secondaire* (Paris: Ch. Douniol, 1873), 43–51.

vulgar language, but real language, full and strong, language expressive of thought, of the spirit of the great thinkers.

For this, we must break with primitive language, and give it by art, by true culture and real education, a kind of new form, nobler and more elevated.

VICTOR DURUY

The Need for a Special Education Track

1901

[In a small *lycée*] I found a young man twice as tall as his classmates, with broad shoulders. While he repeated a few words of Greek and Latin, which he spoke rather worse than well, I examined him and finally asked: "What does your father do?" "He's a farmer." "What do you want to do?" "I want to be a farmer too." I stopped dealing with his lame Latin. . . . Obviously, his father had made some money selling meat and butter, and said to himself: "Since I'm making some money, I want my boy to know more than I did." . . . So the University took this son of a farmer, this aspiring farmer, and taught him about agriculture by having him read Latin. . . . What I've seen in two years of inspecting *lycées* and *collèges* convinces me that, if it's useful to use classical studies to form literati, lawyers, and doctors, it's no less useful to give future employees of commerce, industry, and agriculture the special knowledge that their profession demands.

Victor Duruy, *Notes et souvenirs*, vol. 1 (Paris: Hachette, 1901), 167–68.

4

Emerging Patterns in the United States
1800–1900

Starting from different bases—with only a rudimentary gesture toward higher education, but a more elaborate elementary system, at least in the northern states—the United States differed from France in its answers to the basic questions of modern education during the nineteenth century. Though the causes of educational reform overlapped with those in Western Europe, American emphases, by 1900, were noticeably distinct. The questions, however, were shared: how to provide professional skills while also addressing middle-class people's interests in securing opportunities for their children; how to expand basic training; and how to include groups previously slighted without losing all differentiation. As in France, the issue of religion loomed large. With no single established church, the United States avoided the pitched battles between Catholicism and secular liberalism that defined so much of France's educational history. Nevertheless, American schools had strong religious content, drawn from the Protestant majority; this posed problems for the integration of larger numbers of Catholics and Jews. The religious element lingered longer in higher education than it did in France, clashing with growing interest in science and the social sciences.

One institutional factor marked American developments. While France was an extreme case of centralization in education (despite mixed initiatives in practice), the United States constituted the opposite extreme. Educational policy rested with localities, modified somewhat by state legislation; the federal role was modest, and there was neither national guidance nor consistent national results. The organizational contrast with France obviously complicates generalizations, for any American pattern must be qualified by hosts of exceptions and local variations. How much difference localism made in actual school experience is another matter, though the prolonged North-South gap in the United States surpassed any of the regional divisions in France during the century as a whole.

DEMOCRATIC IDEAS AND MIDDLE-CLASS INTERESTS

Two changes ushered in a new educational age during the first decades of the nineteenth century in the United States. Earlier than in France, a number of northern states began to move toward requiring education. This was motivated in part by strong educational interest but also in part by a desire to force schooling on some groups, such as urban immigrants—to a greater extent than in France, where the decades of transition after the Guizot law saw many grassroots conversions to the equation of childhood with schools. During the same decades, middle-class groups began to deal with their special educational aspirations by patronizing a wide variety of new secondary schools, setting up another cluster of needs that would later be more consistently addressed.

Many revolutionary leaders believed that expanded education was vital for the new United States; democracy could be preserved only with an educated electorate. A host of leaders argued that education should focus on republican virtue, as the foundation of the new American nation—a theme that would reecho later. Jefferson, for example, advocated to the state of Virginia a universal primary education system, with higher schools for the gifted. But no state actually took up this challenge directly for some time, if only because of cost concerns. In 1789 Massachusetts revived the colonial law requiring a school in each town, but it was not well enforced.

In practice, the first main educational change in the new nation came from the proliferation of private academies, involving primary and also some secondary education, for the middle and upper classes. Tuition charges, though often modest, effectively kept these new schools exclusive. The expansion occurred because of growing middle-class belief in the need for education—similar to beliefs by the same class in France, including the fact that children in this group could perform little useful work. The middle-class idea of separating itself from the less-educated masses was an unexpected but not entirely surprising reaction to the establishment of the new nation and the growth of popular democracy during the Jacksonian era. Throughout American history, democratic and elitist impulses have warred, and this was one example. Scores of schools opened between 1780 and the 1830s. In the South and the Middle Atlantic states, most of them were run by Protestant religious groups. In New England, the schools were secular, though with great emphasis on nondenominational religious and moral training. By 1815 there were thirty academies in Massachusetts, including Andover and Exeter, and thirty-seven in New York. And expansion continued: it has been estimated that by 1850 there were more than six thousand academies nationwide, with 12,000 teachers serving more than 250,000 students. This was a very checkered development. Some schools were shoestring operations, pulling in students (including sons of farmers) for a few months a year. Student ages ranged from eight to twenty-eight. Curricula were unsystematic, usually emphasizing basic skills plus moralistic reading matter (including, strikingly, a variety of primers inviting students to dwell on the ubiquity of death and the resulting need for constant virtue in this fleeting life). While fees were not high, they ranged well beyond what the average family could afford. Most of the leading centers were frankly elitist in outlook, combining schooling in basic skills with some Latin and other upper-class accoutrements. While the leading academies admitted only males, there was a growing movement for women's education as well, to improve the training of the nation's future mothers and their own ability to impart early education to their offspring. Female academies for the upper class sprang up in many cities, and the 1789 Massachusetts law in principle required educational access for women. Halting movements toward gender equity in education in the United States outpaced those in France. Finally, above the level of the academies, colleges and universities proliferated. There were twenty-two in 1800 (up from nine at the time of the Revolution). Some had state charters but all depended on tuition and were confined primarily to small numbers of upper-class males. Instruction was fairly unspecialized, with attention to the classics and ethical subjects; these were not institutions focused on professional training so much as social prestige and moral uplift.

The surge of interest in education in these early decades was not accompanied by any clear standards for teacher training. Because of great local variety and the lack of clear professional goals in schooling, American patterns differed from trends developing in France. Correspondingly, teachers had relatively low prestige. Many were primarily disciplinarians, and on this score, from primary schools through the academies and colleges, little had changed from colonial days. Beatings were common. A teacher on winter vacation from studies at Harvard described his treatment of a ten-year-old boy who told a lie: "I took my ruler, it was a large round ruler made of Cherry tree Wood, this I applied to his hand, quite moderately at first; . . . I repeated the operation of the ruler again to his hand till I made him confess the crime and say he was sorry." Conflicts with parents over severe punishments were endemic, particularly because teachers depended on local support; but belief that children were naturally unruly plus the teachers' lack of prestige encouraged severe punishments. In return, students in academies and colleges often carried out elaborate pranks, such as pouring cow urine on the pulpit in the college chapel, sometimes even attacking teachers directly or rioting outright. American students picked up adult political language in the period, talking of "sacred regard for their rights" and the "high and imposing duty of resistance." These student beliefs, along with uncertain school authority, help account for the surprising amount of disorder in this period and beyond, exceeding levels in the more disciplined French classrooms (though French boarding schools had serious outbreaks as well). There was a battleground quality to American schools on occasion.

More decisive developments occurred between the 1830s and the 1850s, when a more extensive primary school system was sketched beyond the colonial levels. Educational reformers also discussed modifications in traditional school discipline, launching an American interest in accommodating children at a time when France and other European nations maintained a more rigorous stance. Finally, at another level, American universities began, very tentatively, to grapple with the implications of modern science—though still at a considerable lag compared with their counterparts in higher education in Europe, where science teaching, though shaky, was gaining greater support.

Led by several New England states, the North began to move toward a system of tax-supported primary education, increasingly available to all. Reformers like Horace Mann headed this charge. Mann, head of the Massachusetts Board of Education (established in 1837), believed that widespread education was vital to provide individuals the skills and intellectual independence necessary to survive with dignity in an increasingly capitalist economy. He and other reformers in these midcentury decades also believed that an educated electorate was essential to the working of a free political system. By this point, most northern states had granted universal male suffrage, so democracy was a reality; the reformers were arguing that education must be adjusted to match. Massachusetts led not only in expanding free primary schools but also in lengthening the school year, broadening the curriculum, and improving teacher training and also pay (though with a wide gap still between men's and women's wages). Teachers' colleges spread, while school buildings began to replace classes in homes and makeshift structures. Finally, some states began to require education in principle. Massachusetts moved first: an 1852 law required twelve weeks' attendance per year for youngsters between ages eight and fourteen. By 1862, the state even passed a law providing for jailing of chronic truants. Other northern and midwestern states passed similar laws during the 1860s and 1870s. In fact, however, attendance remained incomplete (about 72 percent of all children in the North went to school by 1860), and those who did attend sometimes dropped out recurrently. But there was a definite move— early, by European standards—to make schooling an obligatory part of childhood. Literacy rates soared, reaching 94 percent of the population in the North by 1860, a world record at that point for men and even more so for women. Only the South stood apart from this trend. Laws continued to forbid the education of slaves, though about 10 percent of all slaves gained literacy anyway; and only a third of all southern whites went to school (though a larger percentage became literate).

The burst of primary education in the northern states followed from long-standing American belief in the importance of widespread literacy, plus the new sense of the educational needs of a democratic political system. Increasing trade and the beginnings of manufacturing provided funds to support more schools, though the notion of taxpayer obligation was a major extension of the role of state and local governments. The same economic changes created greater needs for literacy and numeracy. Use of young workers in the factories of the 1820s and 1830s, mainly drawn from the farms, prompted reformers to insist on schooling as a protection against exploitation (though actual child labor laws came only slowly in the American states). Education, in other words, increasingly seemed a prerequisite for key features of modern political and economic life. By the same token, provision of education demonstrated the moral responsibility of society; once schooled, people should be able to make their own decisions, regardless of the powerful economic forces surrounding them.

The spread of education and the enthusiasm of reformers like Horace Mann also involved some complex changes in the thinking about the nature of children and the moral environment of the schools. Traditional beliefs about sin and discipline were shifting in the American middle class by the 1840s. Greater emphasis was placed on the innocence of children and the need to protect their essential goodness and creativity. These new values, spread gradually in mainstream Protestant denominations, increasingly confronted some of the conventional disciplinary habits of many schools. Corporal punishment, particularly, came in for criticism. At the same time, however, educational leaders saw the need to provide children with an embracing moral context: young people might be good, but it was vital to keep them that way. Schools, in this view, had a pivotal role to play in surrounding children with guidance and restraint. Here was one of the motivations for lengthening the school year and also erecting relatively opulent school buildings, at least in the cities. Schools officials worried a lot about the proper location and construction of buildings and playgrounds. An 1847 report in Ohio reflected the general tone, calling for "commodious playgrounds, and attractive objects, inspiring correct taste, elevated feelings, and profitable associations, and conveniences, which would preserve youthful sensibility and morals from injury and pollution." Americans began to spend more on the physical infrastructure of education than did most other societies. Moralizing impulses also encouraged the use of female teachers, who were considered better with children than "coarse, hard, unfeeling men" (and also conveniently cheaper), and the practice of age-grading of classes, particularly in the cities, to keep younger children away from the contamination of older ones.

The emphasis on education as moralization, though under state rather than church control, raised a number of interesting issues. First, it tended to distract from a focus on the specifically intellectual functions of schools. To be sure, reading and writing were vital, and curricula allowed for a bit of attention to American history (reading celebratory biographies of George Washington, for example) and science. But attention to salutary moral lessons remained primary. Despite the new reform arguments, this approach had a traditional flavor. Though in different ways, Americans grappled with some of the same issues the French did, with their bitter debates over the role of religion; and both nations continued to see primary education in terms of guiding children to good behavior.

The second issue was even more complex. The moral environment educational leaders were talking about was very much a middle-class product. It involved emphasis on thrift, order, discipline, respect for authority, and punctuality (the need to instill a conscientious sense of time weighed heavily). To most middle-class parents, these values seemed obvious, beyond contest. But now, in states like New York and Massachusetts, this modern moral code was being imposed on many children who were not of the middle class. Growing numbers of Irish and German immigrants were flooding American cities, and educational authorities saw schools—often now obligatory—as a vital means of training children in proper habits their parents often seemed to lack. Horace Mann spoke of education's role in providing democracy and individual opportunity, but he also insisted on moral compulsion: "The unrestrained passions of men are not only homicidal but suicidal. . . . Train up a child in the way he should go, and when he is old he will not depart from it."

The moral impulses in American schooling, themselves in conflict over whether human nature was really good or in fact still evil, set a distinctive tone in the nation's education. French advocates of Catholic training wanted morality and discipline, but they conveyed a less vivid crusading spirit. French liberals came closer, in hoping to create a new republican ethic, but they did not really plan to instill universal middle-class values as opposed to political ideals plus obedience. Americans, in contrast, began to think of schools as critical institutions in making their children right. This impulse grew all the stronger in its interaction with immigrant and working-class groups, who (in middle-class eyes) needed to shape up. These groups, in turn, sought various protections against a school-based moralization that differed from their own values in some respects. They sought to influence local school boards and complained about attendance requirements (sometimes, additionally, because they still expected their children to work). They simply did not enforce attendance. They supported alternative systems, like the Catholic parochial schools that sprang up in contradistinction to the predominantly Protestant-influenced public schools. Still, there was lingering tension.

American educational history in the middle decades of the nineteenth century used to be seen in terms of unalloyed progress, one of the clear signs that American society was becoming better, more enlightened. Surely, the spread of free schools and the gains in literacy corresponded to desirable goals. The advance of primary education also illustrated vital democratic ideals. Unlike societies such as France, the United States did not set up clear distinctions between early education for the upper classes (through tutors or classes established by elite secondary schools) and that available to the masses. Some real social mixing could and did occur in the public primary schools, though the very rich might educate their children separately.

More recently, some historians have been taking a closer look at the underside of these undeniably extensive changes. They argue that schools, as defined in this period, must be seen as efforts at *social control*, designed to repress children and particularly to reshape the habits of immigrant and lower-class groups. They point out that in trying to require attendance while also emphasizing middle-class values, schools might drive a wedge between children and their parents, implicitly criticizing parents who did not live up to the virtues of thrift, sobriety, and a modern sense of time—a clock-based punctuality. They have shown that many families tried to resist the imposition of schools, precisely for these reasons. They argue that schools were not automatically progressive, but sometimes positively harmful to family cohesion and to the dignity and self-esteem of many children outside the middle class. Further, the clash could exacerbate larger social tensions. When school officials saw immigrant children preferring parochial schools or playing truant, they easily fell into sweeping condemnations of the families involved. Reformers like Horace Mann spoke of lower-class children as "little marauders," being introduced into "the Primary school of Vice," and they blasted parents who could let their children deteriorate so. Here, indeed, was a fascinating internal tension: reformers hoped that schools would preserve childish innocence or reform manners, but they often thought they identified children who were nearly hopeless. What, in a democratic society, should schools do with this group? American schools have struggled to answer this question for decades, and they struggle still.

The problem of interpreting American schooling in terms of value conflicts has an important comparative twist. The development of France's modern educational system also produced tensions between the

Debating the Past
Social Control

The social control argument has undeniably modified the conventional optimism about American educational history. Here's how historian Michael Katz puts the case:

The thrust of this study has been to try to dissolve the myths enveloping the origins of popular education in America. Very simply, the extension and reform of education in the mid-nineteenth century were not a potpourri of democracy, rationalism, and humanitarianism. They were the attempt of a coalition of the social leaders, status-anxious parents, and status-hungry educators to impose educational innovation, each for their own reasons, upon a reluctant community. But why pierce such a warm and pleasant myth? Because, first of all, by piercing the vapor of piety we have been able to see certain fundamental patterns and problems in the course of American urban educational reform. . . . We know better of what to beware. Because, second, to confront earlier urban reform is to dispel a kind of nostalgic romanticism. . . . Our reform movements must not be inspired by a vision of a once vital and meaningful schooling to whose nature if not specific features we must return. We must face the painful fact that this country has never, on any large scale, known vital urban schools, ones which embrace and are embraced by the mass of the community, which formulate their goals in terms of the joy of the individual instead of the fear of social dynamite or the imperatives of economic growth. We must realize that we have no models; truly to reform we must conceive and build new.

— *The Irony of Early School Reform* [Cambridge, 1968], 218

These views have not been uncontested, as many historians point to lower-class groups that did indeed welcome aspects of education, plus some school leaders who displayed flexibility in dealing with different groups within the schools. Nevertheless, a new complexity in judging the expansion of American education must be addressed. What might some alternatives have been that would have advanced student learning without some of the questionable side effects? How did class tensions over education fit into a society that prided itself on its healthy democracy?

values of middle-class policymakers and those of lower-class students and parents. The policymakers exerted extensive social control in undermining peasant dialects or (later) attacking Catholic beliefs or preaching new standards of hygiene. French leaders, too, could be obsessed with the issue of taming the working class. But the social control theme looms less large in French than in American educational history around mid-century, or at least it must be stated differently. Americans tended to want to remake the lower classes in the middle-class image, whereas French social control advocates looked more to modifying habits and instilling obedience. Several factors might have limited the tension in France. French educators were not as bent on middle-class moralism as were American leaders like Mann. Perhaps the greater sense of separation in France between the masses and the elite reduced the impulse to reshape mass behavior (though there certainly were serious attempts, in the name of orderliness or nationalism). The quarrels over the church's role perhaps diverted attention from other value clashes. It is also important to consider the different ways primary education spread: some states, like Massachusetts, passed compulsory education laws rather early, while France offered several decades of transition in which individual families could debate whether new school opportunities made sense for them. Finally, there is the obvious difference between a heavily immigrant United States and the more demographically stable France. The French worried about divisions in social class culture and about regional minorities, but they may have had more confidence in some widely shared values. Americans by the 1840s had more reason to think of education quite consciously as a tool for deliberate socialization of dubious newcomers. Both countries used modern education for social control, but the national patterns were different. This difference, in time, could contribute to different national political experiences, even differences in the authority parents could exercise over their school-based children.

At the other end of the educational spectrum in the United States, American universities in the midcentury decades began to make halting adjustments to the range of modern knowledge. Most schools continued to stress classical and moral subjects, with an eye to producing Christian gentlemen. But there was grudging recognition that modern science and engineering were generating findings that required advanced schooling. Some universities set up science departments. Yale established a separate science college, offering science training but keeping the school distinct from the more prestigious branch in which classical and moral philosophy still held sway. Beginning with the West Point military academy, some schools also began to train in engineering. These were straws in the wind, however. Most American professionals (apart from the clergy) gained knowledge through apprenticeship, not formal education. Doctors who wanted the most advanced training had to go abroad, mainly to Scotland or France. A major redefinition of American higher education still lay in the future. One other innovation did occur by midcentury. A few institutions began to admit women and African Americans. Oberlin College, founded in 1833, was the first institution to open its doors to women. Soon a few colleges were founded for women alone. With its emphasis on the important if separate roles of women, the United States continued to move somewhat faster than most Western societies in the area of gender.

The final vital development that took shape around 1850 focused on the secondary level, the bridge between mass primary schools and the still small ranks of the universities. Into the 1860s, most secondary education was still provided by the private academies. Nevertheless, several factors encouraged additional innovation, leading toward the distinctive American institution of the high school. More parents wanted some training for their children beyond the primary level, and the idea that local governments should extend their responsibilities and provide some opportunities gained ground. The introduction of age-grading encouraged separate institutions for teenagers. Middle-class Americans and self-styled experts on youth began to think in terms of a period called adolescence that could be particularly troubled, if only because of the strains of sexual maturation. They felt that young people going through this stage should be separated from the more innocent primary schoolers. At the same time, it was best to keep teenagers at home, rather than sending them to boarding schools, as one advocate of the local high school urged in 1858: "Early departure from the homestead is a moral crisis that many of our youth do not show themselves able to meet." Moral considerations, then, supplemented practical interest in some advanced training in the development of the high school.

Enthusiasm for expanding opportunities in secondary education was not unique to the United States around midcentury. But, unlike in France, the American movement did not involve a particular interest in defining secondary schools as places of intellectual rigor or as explicitly elite institutions. Only a minority of Americans could attend the new public high schools, to be sure (only 5 percent by the 1870s), because most teenagers had to work to help their families make ends meet. It was also true that most schools had an entrance test that not all applicants could pass, though the practice was vigorously debated and gradually declined. To this extent, high schools remained privileged institutions into the twentieth century, though a small minority of working-class children managed to attend. But there was a real commitment to merit and to at least a rhetoric of democracy; aside from the most prestigious private academies, there was nothing like the elite French *lycée* in the United States. Perhaps most important, high schools, though initially quite varied, emphasized practical training, not arcane classical learning, to prepare boys for business, girls for teaching or marriage. High schools stood, in principle, for considerable accessibility, an American response to the demands of democracy coupled, however, with practical limits on how much secondary education could be provided by tax-strained governments or afforded by most families.

Discussions of the desirability of public high schools increased steadily, and more and more commercial cities founded them. Attendance came mainly from the ranks of the middle and lower middle classes; graduates went on to become teachers, clerks, merchants, or college students. A French visitor in 1878 praised the schools as a continual source of replenishment for the middle class (though many middle-class children still did not attend). By this point a majority of middle-class children attended high school for at least a year or two in established cities, joined by a small minority from worker backgrounds. Increasingly, by the 1870s, these new schools prevailed over the competition of the academies, as all but the most prestigious private schools closed down.

A crucial feature of American high schools was their openness to girls. Indeed, because girls had fewer respectable work opportunities than did teenage boys, the majority of high school students were female by the late nineteenth century. There was some discussion about the appropriateness of so much education for females. The Cincinnati Board of Education in 1841 worried that education might prove unfeminine, taxing the weaker sex and possibly even disturbing the female reproductive capacity. But by 1851 girls were being admitted to high school and were performing better than boys in the Queen City. To be sure, many cities kept girls' and boys' schools separate. But the idea of providing education for girls made sense, given the growing need for teachers. It meshed with American beliefs in the importance of preparing mothers to provide enlightenment for children. And it provided a sense of status for the middle-class families who could afford to release girls from work demands. Along with piano lessons, high schools could give girls a sense of cultural familiarity, perhaps some sophistication with a foreign language, as well as some practical skills. Yet what was happening was, in a way, quietly revolutionary. Through the high schools, girls in many families were gaining educational parity with, and sometimes superiority over, boys. A trickle even made it to the university level, though here women remained a decided minority. Still, the permeability of American education beyond traditional gender barriers was a striking development.

COMPLETING THE BASIC SCHOOL SYSTEM, 1860–1890s

The United States entered the 1860s, the decade dominated by civil war, with much of its basic education system already sketched. Amid a mixture of local and state government activities, primary education in most regions was extensive and in a growing number of places mandatory. The need to offer basic schooling to all—or, as some would have it, the need to make sure schools helped socialize all children, to bring them into a common range of morals and beliefs—was widely felt. Atop this system, a distinctive kind of high school structure was beginning to emerge, though it drew a mainly middle-class minority. Extensive educational opportunity, though by no means equality of opportunity, was becoming established as a hallmark of the American approach. The juncture between education and more specific modern professional demands was less clearly set. While universities expanded, they largely aimed at producing generalists; only a handful of engineering institutions provided a clear alternative.

Two developments during and after the Civil War rounded out this picture in important ways. In 1862, the federal government passed the Morrill Act, turning over extensive holdings of public lands to individual states, which could sell them to finance education. This was the first decisive intrusion of the national government into American schooling. It led to a rapid growth of public universities—the "land grant" institutions. These institutions not only expanded the amount of higher education available; they also charged only modest tuitions, enabling some increase in the numbers of students attending university, including women, who began to trickle into the land grant colleges by the 1870s. In addition, the institutions were required to carry some practical courses. Research and instruction in agriculture were emphasized, but so was engineering. Some key state institutions helped lead to a significant redefinition of what the top centers of higher education were all about. Between the 1870s and the 1890s, a larger number of universities (like Johns Hopkins in Baltimore and the newly founded Massachusetts Institute of Technology) began taking serious research and professional training as the heart of their mission. In this, they not only expanded on the spirit of the land grant institutions but also copied the dynamic research universities of Germany. Johns Hopkins, for example, set up a new kind of medical school soon after its founding in 1876, emphasizing basic medical research as well as a more thoroughly scientific training. Even practitioners of older disciplines, such as history, began to recognize their fields as professional operations, forming research units and training graduate students.

The result was an amazing array of higher educational institutions: the religious college or the college emphasizing classical and moral training still thrived; ad hoc professional schools proliferated—the quality was so varied that a cleansing of medical schools, aimed at privileging scientific training, had to occur after 1900. Some leading institutions emphasized professional training alone, while others, including Harvard and Yale, added professional and research components while maintaining a more general undergraduate orientation. Along with variety, however, American universities were beginning to reach new levels in research and training. Growing prosperity allowed some institutions to hire leading European scholars to speed this process. The gap at the top of the educational pyramid between the United States and Europe narrowed rapidly.

The second key change, occurring after the Civil War, took place in the South, which for so long had been a laggard educational region. Reconstruction governments began to spread schools widely. At first, northern reformers and the strong educational interests of many freed slaves combined to produce a growing network of schools for African Americans. By 1870 there were four thousand schools, staffed by nine thousand teachers, half of them black, teaching about 12 percent of the

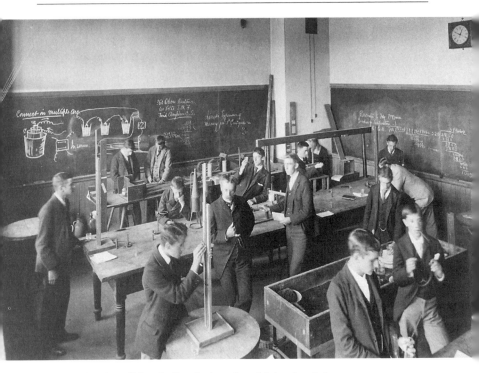

Figure 6. A traditional all-male American high school class.

school-age population of freed slaves. Then state governments moved into the picture, and by 1876 more than half of all white children and 40 percent of all blacks were attending at least primary school. A series of black academies also arose, offering more advanced education, and some of these gradually evolved into a network of black colleges. As Reconstruction ended, the burst of educational enthusiasm slowed somewhat. White southerners were particularly insistent that blacks and whites be educated separately, and state governments offered consistently poorer funds and facilities to the black schools. In this context, school attendance and literacy lagged among African Americans, though gradual gains continued and forces of change persisted. A number of black leaders, such as Booker T. Washington, insisted that education constituted the best route for racial progress, and the ranks of African American teachers and professionals trained at black colleges expanded steadily. On another front, increasing industrialization produced growing needs for basic skills. Many textile companies set up company schools in the South, for the usual mixed motives of providing a better-trained labor force but also tying worker families to the firm. Finally, soon after 1900, most southern states moved to require primary education in free, state-supported—but racially segregated—public schools. Massive regional differences in education remained in the United States—as they remain to this day—but the more glaring gaps narrowed.

The big news, by the 1890s, was the expansion of high school and university enrollments, the latter still comprising only a minority of the eligible population. In 1860, there had been only one hundred public high schools in the nation. By 1900 there were six thousand and by 1914, twelve thousand. Attendance began to become almost standard in the middle class, with a growing minority of working-class youth attending as well. University enrollments also grew, by 38 percent during the years 1890–1895 alone. Individual units expanded: Harvard had 358 students in 1850, more than four times that number by 1890. The state universities attracted growing enrollments, particularly in the Midwest and West, while a series of women's colleges, such as Vassar, Bryn Mawr, and Goucher, sprang up as well. Small clusters of women also began to gain entry to professional schools, including those in medicine and law, while the number of women training to be teachers, social workers, librarians, and nurses soared.

The expansion of high school enrollments reflected vital changes in the nature of the schools themselves. Increasing attention was given to practical courses, such as secretarial programs. A few high schools still stood out for classical training, but more curricula now emphasized modern languages and history rather than Latin and the classics. Entry tests began to recede: the long debate over how open high schools should be was increasingly resolved in favor of democracy. Some states, in fact, began to push compulsory attendance requirements to include at least two high school years. Women's attendance continued to surpass that of men. But young people from various social groups began to see high school as a prerequisite to suitable jobs, particularly in the service and clerical sectors, even when they had no thought of going on to college.

The role of university attendance was less clear. American institutions of higher education were quite varied in quality and curriculum. The growing state universities began to offer programs in agriculture, business, and engineering that could lead directly to careers. Some students also saw a bachelor's degree as preparation for law school or medical school. But many students attended universities that offered general courses in literature, history, psychology, and the sciences that were not highly specialized or professional. The definition of higher education in terms of moral training clearly receded. Many businesses now sought university graduates not because they had practical skills but because of their overall status and cosmopolitanism and the work discipline that success at this level entailed. University activities, including sports and fraternities, might have as much to do with producing these intangible qualities as academic life itself. In a society without an absolutely rigid upper class, the best universities seemed to generate a substitute kind of prestige and polish—what one observer called "good, heroic, wise, pure, honorable gentlemen." Highly specialized skills, of the sort generated by the French *grandes écoles,* seemed less relevant.

One other general change affected education at most levels. School discipline and rules continued to relax somewhat. Corporal punishment was now rare. As one result, outright student rebellion declined in American schools. Monitoring of students continued, however, sometimes in new ways. High school authorities were eager to repress troublemakers. Boys most commonly were identified as disorderly, but girls, when singled out for offenses against rules on sexual behavior, were treated more harshly. Both deviant groups might be treated as juvenile offenders and, if convicted, sent to reform schools. The spread of extracurricular activities plus school-related groups such as scouts helped adults supervise young people even after classes let out. At the high school level around 1900, authorities fought vigorous battles against fraternities and sororities, on grounds that independent groups of this sort "encourage wrong attitudes and a spirit of disregard for the established order." Growing interest in using the schools to regulate student hygiene introduced another morally relevant outlet. After 1900, and with increasing intensity after 1920, American schools began to teach children about cleanliness, require health examinations, and criticize families (particularly immigrant groups) whose standards of hygiene did not measure up. Commercial companies abetted this process, eager to prepare future consumers, by providing samples of soap and toothpaste. It was a commercial consortium, for example, that urged teachers to insist that children wash their hands after using the toilet and also have children "report on days they take baths at home" and on how often they changed their underwear. The overt purpose was physical health, but a strong undercurrent of morality—and moral disapproval of inadequacy—underlay these extensions of primary school oversight. Earlier ideas that education had primarily moral purposes now had a slightly old-fashioned ring, but the basic concept survived.

Ambiguities concerning moral control related to other important trends by the early 1900s. One was the growth of coeducation. Except for some private and parochial schools, primary education had long been coeducational in the United States. Now, around 1900, the growth of the high schools encouraged coeducation as well. Many girls' high schools in the larger cities were merged with other programs. Finally, while separate women's colleges flourished, coeducation also gained in the state universities and in some private postsecondary institutions. These changes provoked some anxiety. They helped fuel the ongoing attempts to regulate sexual behavior in and around the schools, including new rules about what cosmetics girls could wear. Some men worried about a loss of masculine qualities when boys shared schools with girls while also being taught by a largely female staff. With more shared classes, young men and women did change some key patterns of socializing, spending more time with each other, at least by later adolescence, and less time with same-sex groups. It was not surprising that dating, as an activity involving college and high school students, began to gain ground after 1920 as a major social focus.

At the same time, gender divisions still existed in the schools, and some of them increased in response to coeducation. In high school and college, girls took largely separate programs emphasizing secretarial training, home economics, and preparation for family roles. They enrolled rarely in manual arts programs, engineering, or the sciences. Extracurricular activities also divided the genders. Boys heavily dominated student governments and virtually monopolized school athletics. A few girls' sports not only were separate and lower-key but were carefully tailored to what most people still believed was the lesser physical strength of the gender; thus girls' basketball teams had special rules to limit running.

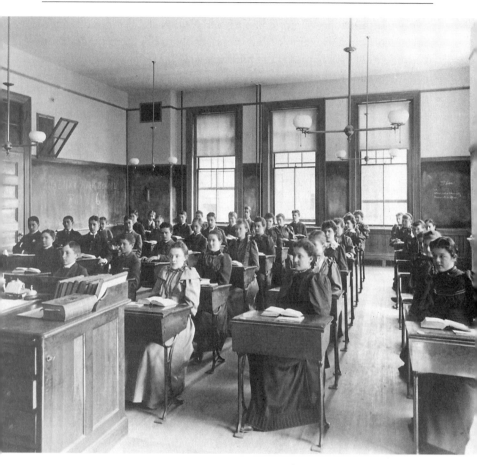

Figure 7.   A high school class in Roxbury, Massachusetts, in 1892. What differed in this kind of class setup from a more traditional school? What differed from patterns one would expect today?

Girls' clubs, in contrast, allowed separate expressions through dance or crafts that would help train future homemakers and instill ladylike qualities. The American response to gender and education reflected what leaders like the philosopher John Dewey regarded as a democratic commitment to sharing, but also a pronounced attempt to use school to reflect different qualities and prepare young men and women for different roles; the combination was complex.

School organization also changed around 1900. The United States remained committed to local control and great variety. Though a federal office of education was established, its role was limited, and even state governments exercised little direct educational control beyond attendance legislation and teacher certification. But American localism and variety had some drawbacks that began to be addressed. With growing interest in college, but with such a wide array of secondary schools, college officials found it increasingly difficult to identify measurements of ability. From the 1880s onward, various groups of colleges formed associations to inspect secondary schools and offer accreditation to those that passed muster—but most secondary schools did not participate. In 1899, several eastern colleges set up the College Entrance Examination Board to develop examinations for college admission. The principal examinations initially focused on subject matter—English, botany, and so on. But this approach was not entirely adequate: some schools prepared students for the examinations, which meant that good performance might mean little in terms of durable knowledge and understanding; and public high school graduates, with less rigorous academic training than that offered in the top private schools, were at a disadvantage. From 1915 onward, the board groped for more comprehensive tests that would show ability regardless of preparation; in 1925, bolstered by psychologists' claims that they could test for intelligence independent of content, the first Scholastic Aptitude Tests were administered. The College Board hardly systematized the links between secondary and higher education, and many schools did not participate at all; but the board did constitute a growing national influence on curriculum and admissions.

More locally, urban school districts around 1900 began to tighten controls over individual schools and teachers. This was the age of progressivism and business efficiency, when policymakers thought that formal organization could usefully be rationalized. Local school boards increasingly decided on curriculum, selection of books, criteria for hiring and firing teachers, and so on. An added result of this local consolidation was increasing ability for urban elites, politically powerful in the city as a whole, to maintain educational control over immigrant neighborhoods, which might have opted for different school decisions if left to their own devices. The result was the emergence of more formal school administration and the downgrading of teacher initiative and status. American teachers were struggling for their place in any event. They were increasingly educated in colleges or college-level normal schools (though rural schools were often still taught by high school graduates), but the standards of their training varied greatly. They could not claim the kind of uniform professional background that graduates of the state-run normal schools in France could boast, for example. Americans, while valuing education, may also have tended to look down on people who merely offered book learning. The growing place of women in the teaching ranks also reduced status; not only were women regarded as inferior, but most schools required women to leave teaching upon marriage (lest students be exposed to unwanted signs of female sexuality); thus, few female teachers gained advanced seniority. With urban school boards now also setting rules for the conduct of classes, teachers' positions became shakier still.

Along with the adjustments to coeducation and some new organizational controls, American schools during the late nineteenth century pioneered in a wide variety of extracurricular activities. The notion that schools could be centers of social and recreational patterns beyond the classroom seemed particularly appropriate in the United States. School athletics gained ground rapidly. Some sports, such as football, were first introduced at the college level. By the 1870s, most colleges were developing active intramural and team sports programs, and by the 1880s they were beginning to recruit talented athletes from the high schools. This helped generate student interest at the secondary level, and high school competition began to increase. Eager to make sure students did not gain undue control, school officials began to assert their authority, hiring coaches and incorporating athletics into the functions of the schools by the 1890s. Competition could be fierce. Detroit high school officials complained in the 1890s that some of their opponents were using professional boxers and wrestlers on their football teams, while Ann Arbor was cited for using "ringers" (semiprofessional players) in baseball. As authorities worked to regulate athletics, they mixed pious sentiments with open political and commercial interests. Successful sports teams increasingly solidified the position of high schools in communities and of colleges with alumni. Ticket sales could bring significant funding; it was around 1900 that universities like Michigan built stadiums capable of seating tens of thousands of paying fans. But the whole enterprise could be overlaid with an appealing and familiar moral ring: sports not only built men, they built character. As a high school principal in Michigan put it in 1895, "The greatest good that can come out of athletic games is their ethical relation. We are after honesty and good and in no way can we better inculcate truth than through these games." While athletics held pride of place in American education, other activities beyond the classroom included drama and music (the latter linked to sports through marching bands) and a variety of clubs and hobbies. This extracurricular thrust helped complete the formation of the unsystematic American system of education by the early twentieth century.

Using the Sources: Issues in African American Education around 1900

The emancipation of the slave population inevitably raised new questions about education, for slaves had long been largely excluded, a major contradiction to American assertions about educational opportunity. Initial expansion of school systems in the South provoked white resistance and a turn to segregation and unequal treatment along with a rather turgid development of southern education more generally. In the first passage, an Alabama school official explains segregation to a national audience of professional educators. What are his main arguments? What kind of education for African Americans do these views suggest, apart from the obvious claim that education must be separate? The second passage presents some of the views of Booker T. Washington, a strong advocate of education as the basis for the gradual development of African Americans' potential. Washington's foundation of the Tuskegee Institute and the school's emphasis on industrial education implemented his views that blacks must be able to improve their own conditions, amid admitted racial discrimination. What does his approach imply about the relationship of African Americans to educational equality? Does it suggest an attack on systems of segregation? Washington has become a figure of great controversy in American history, for his views clearly fall short of current ideals of racial justice; even at the time, many black cultural leaders, like W. E. B. Du Bois, criticized the limits of his approach. What is your interpretation? How does Washington fit into the complex history of actual (as opposed to rhetorical) educational access for excluded groups in the nineteenth century—how does his argument compare, for example, to pleas for the schooling of women or immigrants?

J. A. B. LOVETT

The Education of the Negro in the South: A White Statement

1890

The following propositions may be relied upon by all who are interested in this discussion as reflecting the views of the intelligent, law-abiding citizens, of Anglo-Saxon blood, in the South:

a. This class of Southern citizens would not, under any circumstances, favor the reenslavement of the colored people. Six millions of slaves at an average of six hundred dollars each, aggregates the enormous sum of three billions six hundred millions of dollars. This was all swept away by the emancipation proclamation, and should the Government propose to return this great loss of property to the Southern people in the persons of the negro population, as slaves, there would be a unanimous Southern voice against the resumption of such a burden.

b. They entertain the kindliest feelings toward the colored population: and, with their counsel and aid, they are ever ready to assist them in the acquisition of property, and to deal fairly with him [sic] along the line of his political, legal, and natural rights.

c. They have no fears of any serious or general trouble growing out of the fact of negro suffrage, if not interfered with by a low class of political agitators.

d. Were the question submitted to a vote, I feel quite sure that the representative Southern people would elect the negro to remain on his native heath, if he desired to do so.

With regard to the education of the negro, there is a variety of sentiment among our people. We have those among us who do not warmly favor the education of the masses of either race. This sentiment is shown in the fact that we suffer some opposition to popular education. A class similar to this may be found in all educating countries. We have also those who do not advocate negro education, because they have never become reconciled to negro citizenship. Their neutrality on the subject is about all the opposition that comes from this source; and, if their passiveness is an indication of doubt on the subject, it is plain that the negro gets the benefit of the doubt. But the most formidable opposition we have to negro education, is

J. A. B. Lovett, "The Education of the Negro in the South," National Educational Association, *Journal of Proceedings and Addresses* (Topeka: National Education Association, 1890), 502–5.

the positive declaration made by a large and respectable class of citizens that education is a decided detriment to the negro's best interest. It is claimed by these opponents that just as soon as the negro obtains a little learning, he is disposed to abandon manual labor, and seeks to engage in politics, preaching, or teaching. It is also claimed that the educated negro often becomes a firebrand among the more ignorant of his race, and uses his acquired talents in stirring up and perpetuating hatred and strife between the races.

Despite all these various phases of opposition to negro education in the South, their schools are generally well fitted with enthusiastic learners, and they are making as fair a headway as their limited facilities will admit. And this very fact shows that the majority of the Southern white people are strongly favorable to negro civilization; for it must be known to those who are familiar with the statistics of Southern education, that our legislators make, substantially, the same provision for the education of the colored children as they do for the whites. Nor do we ever hear of our representatives being arraigned by their constituents for supporting measures which give equal advantages to our colored youth. When this is fairly considered, in connection with the fact that the negro population contributes a very diminutive per centum of the State appropriations for public education, it will be seen that the white people of the South richly deserve the gratitude of the negro, as well as the commendation of all who are interested in his cause.

Having reviewed the opinions of the white people, North and South, on this question, it is proper that something should be said from the negro's point of view.

For the past several years my official relations in the field of education have been of such a character as to enable me to learn something of the purposes and ambitions of the representative negroes of the South. From various conversations with the most intelligent persons of this race, I have gleaned the following facts:

They believe that the intelligent white people of the South are their best friends. They know they are at liberty to leave the South, but they prefer to remain. They take but little stock in the exodus agitations. They think the time for such a movement is not yet. When the Good Father shall arrange his program of final destiny for the negro, possibly there shall be a great emigration of the race to the land of their fathers. At present the burning bush, the presence of a Moses, the inviting Canaan, are not in sight. However, when this day shall come, if ever it shall, there will be no wicked Southern Pharaoh that will detain the colored man from a brighter inheritance; and there will be no infuriated Southern host to be swallowed up in the angry seas, in the wake of his departure. But there will be should such an event ever occur, a mighty host of friends to the colored man in the South who would raise their prayers to Almighty God to protect and defend the negro, and make of his race a strong and mighty people.

The intelligent Southern negroes do not think that social equality with the whites is either practicable or desirable; not practicable, because it would be unnatural; not desirable, even on their part, because those who undertake to practice it with them inflict upon them a positive injury. In conversation with a highly-cultivated colored man, not long since, I asked him to give me his views on this subject. His answer was replete with wisdom, and full of good common-sense. He said: "The whites who put themselves on an equal social basis with us come to us in white skins, but their hearts are black—they always lower us in the moral scale."

The intelligent Southern negroes are also opposed to the co-education of the races. They generally have a natural parental feeling toward their children, and they would be unwilling to have their offspring to undergo the unavoidable embarrassments that would surely attend the presence of their children among those of the white race.

BOOKER T. WASHINGTON

On the Tuskegee Institute's Approach

1916

Industrial training will be more potent for good to the race when its relation to the other phases of essential education is more clearly understood. There is afloat no end of discussion as to what is the "proper kind of education for the Negro," and much of it is hurtful to the cause it is designed to promote. The danger, at present, that most seriously threatens the success of industrial training, is the ill-advised insistence in certain quarters that this form of education should be offered to the exclusion of all other branches of knowledge. If the idea becomes fixed in the minds of the people that industrial education means class education, that it should be offered to the Negro because he is a Negro, and that the Negro should be confined to this sort of education, then I fear serious injury will be done the cause of hand-training. It should be understood rather that at such institutions as Hampton Institute and Tuskegee Institute, industrial education is not emphasized because colored people are to receive it, but because the

Booker T. Washington, *Tuskegee and Its People,* edited by Emmett J. Scott (New York: Appleton, 1916), 8, 11–12.

ripest educational thought of the world approves it; because the undeveloped material resources of the South make it peculiarly important for both races; and because it should be given in a large measure to any race, regardless of color, which is in the same stage of development as the Negro.

On the other hand, no one understanding the real needs of the race would advocate that industrial education should be given to every Negro to the exclusion of the professions and other branches of learning. It is evident that a race so largely segregated as the Negro is, must have an increasing number of its own professional men and women. . . .

Tuskegee emphasizes industrial training for the Negro, not with the thought that the Negro should be confined to industrialism, the plow, or the hoe, but because the undeveloped material resources of the South offer at this time a field peculiarly advantageous to the worker skilled in agriculture and the industries, and here, are found the Negro's most inviting opportunities for taking on the rudimentary elements that ultimately make for a permanently progressive civilization.

The Tuskegee Idea is that correct education begins at the bottom, and expands naturally as the necessities of the people expand. As the race grows in knowledge, experience, culture, taste, and wealth, its wants are bound to become more and more diverse; and to satisfy these wants there will be gradually developed within our own ranks—as had already been true of the whites—a constantly increasing variety of professional and business men and women. Their places in the economic world will be assured and their prosperity guaranteed in proportion to the merit displayed by them in their several callings, for about them will have been established the solid bulwark of an industrial mass to which they may safely look for support. The esthetic demands will be met as the capacity of the race to procure them is enlarged through the processes of sane intellectual advancement. In this cumulative way there will be erected by the Negro, and for the Negro, a complete and indestructible civilization that will be respected by all whose respect is worth the having. There should be no limit placed upon the development of any individual because of color, and let it be understood that no one kind of training can safely be prescribed for any entire race. Care should be taken that racial education be not one-sided for lack of adaptation to personal fitness, nor unwieldy through sheer top-heaviness. Education, to fulfill its mission for any people anywhere, should be symmetrical and sensible.

5

Transatlantic Comparison:
Contrasts and Causes

During the nineteenth century, France and the United States grappled with essentially the same educational issues. The two nations followed roughly the same chronology in shaping a modern primary and secondary school system, even though specific moves occurred at different intervals and in a different order. Both nations introduced an increasingly secular school system, with a growing place for science but also for new forms of loyalty such as nationalism; American school texts on the nation's history were as fiercely partisan as those in France, while American teachers struggled also to identify a national tradition in literature and art. Both nations sought to align schools increasingly with commercial needs, introducing a variety of practical programs. The list of similarities is extensive.

Yet, obviously, differences abounded as well at every point in the nineteenth century. Some contrasts were massive: while the United States struggled to introduce organizational improvements, there was no hint of national centralization, the hallmark of the French system, at least in principle and to an increasing degree in fact. Teacher training and certification differed accordingly: the French set national rules for each level of training, while Americans by 1900 simply put teacher training and certification in states' control.

Other contrasts, though real, are more subtle. On the surface, the ongoing French battle over the church's role had no American counterpart. But in a larger sense, American school officials remained wedded to a substantial Protestant presence even in the public schools, while authorities in both countries—but perhaps particularly the United States—sought to maintain schooling as a source of discipline and a center for the inculcation of morality.

Gender differences require careful analysis. Americans were more comfortable than the French with introducing girls to new levels of education and particularly with coeducational schools. This reflected a distinctive American valuation of women — a greater emphasis on their moral qualities and their importance in educating young children; the French by 1900 were spending more time trying to persuade women simply to have more children. (Intriguingly, whereas American schools often dismissed married women lest they remind students of sexuality, French leaders, obsessed with population, urged their women teachers to marry.) At the same time, women made important educational strides in France as well, while American education reflected the continuing belief in the differences between the genders. Both societies placed great emphasis on training girls (but not boys) in domestic skills. Both set barriers that impeded women's advance into professional training. Both defined some educational fields as predominantly if not exclusively masculine. Americans balanced coeducation with their unusual emphasis on school athletics, which could heighten masculine swagger.

Nuanced analysis is clearly required in dealing with the two nations' approaches to mixing democracy with inequality in modern schooling. On balance, Americans placed a bit more emphasis on the democratic side, the French a bit more on the elite. Certainly France developed a firmer separation between the popular track — the primary schools, graced with a few options such as higher primary education and teacher training — and the elite level. The nation had yet to link the two systems fully by the early 1900s, though it would later move in that direction. American policymakers worked earlier and more thoroughly on the primary system (with the huge exception of the South and southern black education). The evolution of the high school, particularly as it won wider attendance and dropped formal entry tests, added to the American commitment to educational opportunity — though as late as 1914 only a minority of working-class boys were attending high schools even briefly. The spread of American secondary education was fueled by beliefs that schools could pave the way to better jobs and that society had a responsibility to provide more than basic training.

Nevertheless, the interest in separate opportunities for the middle classes ran strong as well in the United States. Private academies long provided a distinct, if quite haphazard, educational environment for those who could pay. Early high schools, particularly those devoted to classi-

Figure 8. An American school in the early twentieth century. As the teacher dissects a heart, children of both sexes gather about the table to watch.

cal training that might provide university entry, were elitist. Even as high schools expanded and classical curricula were downplayed, the notion of separate tracks for different kinds of students maintained the tension between democratic and elitist principles. Providence, Rhode Island, thus by 1914 had high school programs emphasizing manual arts, commercial training, and, still, the classical track. Working-class boys were almost entirely concentrated in manual arts, while the classical track had virtually no one from families lower than middle class. There was some social mixing in all this, but it was clearly limited. How different was this American system from the French mixture of superior primary schools, *collèges*, and *lycées*? American universities clearly differentiated by social origin, and the growing importance of university education for business management jobs simply heightened the significance of this division. The College Board's effort to provide better tests for entry into the most elite schools indicated a sincere interest in finding ways to identify worthy public school graduates, but also a definite commitment to divisions by talent. Elitism of various sorts, then, was a vital theme on the American side. It remained true that Americans found it harder than the French to create a fully elitist system, as opposed to haphazard and varied distinctions. The varied array and quality of colleges and universities, compared with France's more structured higher education, reflected American hesitation. By the same token, Americans found it harder to insist on uniform rigor and results from the schools that were, de facto, elite. Nothing like the demands of the *baccalauréat* examination awaited American students at any stage of their education, even when the new College Board system came into play in the early twentieth century.

Yet if they did not have a frankly elitist system, Americans tended over time to balance moves toward greater educational openness with some new efforts at separation. Primary schools, because they were largely built around neighborhoods, caused relatively little concern. Because neighborhoods tended to be separated by class, schools provided some social mixing but not beyond acceptable levels. The ongoing French efforts to provide distinct primary training for elite students had no clear echo in the United States. But the increasing openness of high schools, around 1900, drew quick qualification. By 1912, psychologists like Lewis Terman were introducing intelligence quotient (IQ) tests to various school systems; Terman first worked in districts around San Francisco. These tests, developed in France but far more widely used in the United States, purported to measure intelligence regardless of educational or environmental experience. American school officials were increasingly convinced that democratic pressures, in a period of rapid immigration particularly from southern and eastern Europe, risked overwhelming their systems with people of lower ability. Terman and others promised, at an extreme, to "identify the feebleminded," who could then be put in new institutions for the retarded. Beyond this, they sought to label different levels of intelligence that could be assigned to different school tracks. On this basis, systems such as that in Oakland, California, by 1915 were thoroughly tracked, with students assigned on the basis of IQ tests to high schools ranging from the vocational through the comprehensive to the college preparatory. Children of immigrant families were most commonly found deficient and assigned to one of the lower tracks. Schools officials blithely bandied about the resultant stereotypes: "The true difficulty is one of mental capacity, or general intelligence, which makes the Latins [mainly, Italians] unable to compete with children of North European ancestry." Another official asserted: "The children in our schools that are predominably [sic] foreign do not compare with the children of other schools either in progress thru school or in marks earned on tests of native ability." American schools thus differentiated, formally or informally, on the basis of "intelligence," though the systems changed frequently. Further, belief in the transcendence of middle-class, Protestant values also created a strong impulse to use schools to impose moral controls over inferior people. This theme, visible in 1840s Massachusetts as in early twentieth-century California, was less prevalent in France, in part because of firmer separation of educational levels. But the American impulse deserves comparison with the French interest in using nationalism to tame lower-class unruliness and the undeniable interest in changing certain lower-class habits to create better workers, mothers, and, by the 1880s, republicans.

Specific differences between the two systems warrant comparison as well, particularly when they reveal larger distinctions in educational values. France developed less enthusiasm than the United States did, by the early twentieth century, for aptitude tests. When the French tested, as with the *baccalauréat*, they relied on mastery of subject matter, in contrast to the American propensity, in the work of people like Terman and then later with the College Board's SATs, to seek "pure" intelligence, uncorrupted by educational background. Why the difference? Americans thought that finding aptitude was more democratic (though in fact the outcomes were often skewed by racial and ethnic prejudices). Testing of subject matter, in contrast, privileged those who had a better home background or who had afforded better schools up to that point. Aptitude testing also reflected American decentralization, where actual schools varied too widely to permit easy measurement of results. The French had greater confidence in their ability to monitor what schools taught and so to judge children by their learning results. It has also been speculated that Americans had less confidence in teachers than the French did and so wanted tests that would not be corrupted by teacher incompetence. The French were quite willing to assume that teachers did a fairly good job, so that testing subject mastery, often quite rigorously, was a fair way to measure student performance and to base assignments of future educational opportunities.

French schools continued to be more strictly regulated than those of the United States. There were fewer experiments with new methods of discipline, though corporal punishment did come in for criticism in both societies, and the French moved to eliminate it in the early nineteenth century, though without complete success. Many Americans embraced beliefs in children's innocence that the French did not, in the main, accept. French observers, indeed, commented on the freedom Americans allowed their children in family settings. Sheer docility and deference to authority were less important in the United States, though school officials in fact often liked to keep a careful watch on their charges. The French retained greater interest in drill exercises and experimented less with settings in which children might express themselves. They also retained more emphasis on boarding schools for children whose training was particularly important to the state. American interest in schools as centers of moralization led to some extensions of monitoring children that were less common in France. The French were certainly more content to have most children go home after a school day, to be taken care of by their families; they showed no particular inclination to stretch out school supervision through an array of extracurricular activities.

Certainly the French showed no interest whatsoever in schools as centers of sports competitions. Calisthenics classes for health were fine, but the amazing American array of athletic teams in schools and colleges, with playing fields and (increasingly) cheerleaders to match had no French echo. Why? Some observers believe that until recently the French had less cultural interest in formal exercise (as opposed, say, to simple walking) than developed across the Atlantic. The American mixture of genders may have prompted more interest in sports as a means of protecting and highlighting masculinity, which the French, separating girls and boys more firmly at school, did not require. American reservations about too much intellectualizing, which some observers find as a trait in the national culture by the nineteenth century, might contrast with a greater acceptance, at least by French officials, that schools began and ended with an academic role. But it may be the difference between conceptions of the schools' moral role that proved most telling, with Americans justifying their insertions of sports into schools by their belief in its character-building qualities. The French wanted schools to convey values: hence the special lessons for girls and the overall insistence on national loyalty. But their sense of the moral mission was more limited, and athletic exercise was evaluated in terms of physical benefit alone. Once sports were installed in American schools, of course, they tended to intensify, with coaches, facilities, and loyalties that needed ever more sports to keep the machinery oiled. The French simply avoided this spiral.

Finally, what about the larger picture: Did education play different roles in the two societies by 1900? Certainly any answer must be qualified, for parents, officials, and children in both societies shared so many educational goals. Two differences, however, are revealing—and revealingly complex. First, as the French built their system, mobility opportunities became tightly tied to educational success. People could and did rise from lower to upper class in France, but they usually started by rising in the school system, transcending the barriers between the mass and the elite tracks. Schools served mobility in the United States, but it was much easier to rise (particularly before 1945) without extensive education. This reflects, of course, the fact that American elite education was more haphazard and less carefully tied to government or business hierarchies than in France. Relatedly, the French continued to use boarding schools in many *lycées*, teacher training schools, and some *grandes écoles* after their use declined in the United States. This enabled the French more systematically to mold the kind of civil servants and teachers the state wanted.

At the same time, however, there is evidence to suggest that Americans (or at least middle-class Americans) placed more general faith in education than the French did. Their expectations about a particular type of school might vary, but they saw the principle of education in a slightly different light from the French. Americans tended to feel that schools stood at the center of society's obligations to its members. They did not believe this in 1800, but they came to believe it during the nineteenth century. If people had a chance at education, they could then fend for themselves (and if they failed, the fault was theirs—they had had a fair shot). There were obviously flaws in these assumptions—for example, the educational limits placed on ethnic groups, particularly blacks and Indians—but this does not mean that the basic faith was insincere. French observers, looking at schools for more limited personal and social gains, did not expect education to correct all social ills. They could admit that society might owe something to the poor, for example, even if it had provided educational opportunity; people could fail for reasons beyond their control, even if they had been educated. Of course, the fact that the

French placed more limits on mass education helped explain this different outlook. Correspondingly, as we have seen, Americans tended to look to schools for greater moral results than the French did.

These contrasts had wide implications in their effect on different judgments about what society had to do to be just. France, with an active socialist movement beginning in the late nineteenth century, clearly contained more people who articulated their sense of society's unfairness (even with a mass education system) than did the United States, where socialism was much more limited and the tendency to attribute poverty to personal fault much greater. The contrasts could also rebound on the educational system itself. Americans, with their commitment to education at least in principle, were willing to spend more on schooling overall, not only as taxpayers but also as parents supporting the rapidly growing number of college students. The French were more hesitant. Yet Americans' expectations could also make them readier than the French to criticize schools and teachers for shortcomings; Americans had a love-hate relationship with their schools that in many ways continues to this day.

Neither the French nor the American educational system was immune from further redirection by the early twentieth century. A number of fundamental shifts occurred amid further social change, as the twentieth century wore on, and some of them diverged from the patterns set by 1900. It remains true that, even at the end of the 1990s, differences between the two systems, and the assumptions behind them, that were so marked by 1900 continue to color the educational experience of these two Western nations.

Using the Sources Comparatively: France and the United States

WOMEN AND EDUCATION

France. French attitudes toward the education of women changed markedly during the nineteenth century, as did the actual education offered. In the first of the following passages, a Catholic statement at midcentury, traditionalist views come through clearly. The rise of republican sentiment brought with it a new rhetoric, along with new reasons for advocating educational access. The stirring second passage is by Jules Ferry, who ultimately shaped the republican school system. But pronounced gender separation remained, as the official statements shifted far more than did actual school content. In the third passage, selections are drawn from actual reading books assigned for girls' primary schools. How do the lessons given to girls compare with the traditionalist outlook that was widespread earlier in the century? How might girls actually have reacted to the gendered curriculum, as they gained greater literacy and more access to schools?

Gender issues in France might be compared with issues of social class. Here too, republicans talked a somewhat different game from what the schools actually implemented (see chapter 7). Was the separate treatment of girls more or less severe than that offered to the lower classes? Why did such gaps between rhetoric and reality emerge? In the case of gender, the rhetoric itself requires careful scrutiny (in the second passage): Does Ferry advocate equality? What kind of educational treatment do his arguments suggest girls should expect?

French gender issues demand comparison with those in other societies. Were the French distinctively laggard in relation to the United States? Which differed more, the official rhetoric or the actual curricula and educational opportunities offered to women? A sampling of American documents follows the French material, and then the comparison can be fairly joined.

Finally, the sources must be interpreted to help answer the intriguing question of why women's education advanced as rapidly as it did. In a society like France or the United States, where women were clearly regarded as inferior even by most "progressive" men, why did the primary schools increasingly embrace them?

MGR. DUPANLOUP

Traditionalist Views

1869

Young girls are raised for private life in private life. I urge that they not be admitted to the courses, examinations, and diplomas which prepare men for public life.

Mgr. Dupanloup, *M. Duruy et l'éducation des filles* (Paris: Ch. Douniol, 1869), 29.

The secondary education of young girls has generally remained religious, and the family, that shaken institution, owes to this teaching which purity it still retains; I urge that we not form free thinking women for our future.

JULES FERRY

Republican Rhetoric

1870

Seeking educational equality for all classes is only half the task; I demand . . . this equality for the two sexes. . . . The difficulty, the obstacle here is not cost, but custom; it lies above all in masculine bad faith. There are two kinds of pride in the world, pride of class and pride of sex; and this latter is much worse, much more persistent. . . . This is really a feature of French character, the blind spot that the most civilized among us carry on; let's not mince words, it's male pride.

I know that more than one woman may ask, what good are all these studies? I can answer: to raise your children, and this would be a good answer, but as it is trite I prefer to say: to raise your husbands. Educational equality means restoring unity to the family.

Today there is a silent but persistent struggle between the old society, the Old Regime . . . which does not accept modern democracy, and the society which issues from the French Revolution. . . . In this struggle, woman cannot be neutral. The optimists may imagine that the woman's role is negligible, but they do not realize the secret and persistent support that she brings to the old society, the society we wish to banish. . . . The bishops know this. Whoever wins women's loyalty, wins everything, because this affects both the child and the husband. This is why the Church wishes to keep women in its ranks, and this is why democracy must win women instead. Democracy must choose, as a matter of life and death: woman must belong to science or she must belong to the Church.

Jules Ferry, "Discours sur l'égalité d'education" (Salle Molière, 10 avril 1870), cited in Louis Legrand, *L'Influence du positivisme dans l'oeuvre scolaire de Jules Ferry* (Paris: M. Rivière, 1961), 235–37.

H. RAQUET

Readings on Domestic Economy for Farm Girls

c. 1900

The girl respects her parents, is submissive, full of good will in helping her mother in the work around the house . . . and garden. It's thus that a young girl gradually acquires the qualities of a good housewife. . . .

The good housewife is orderly; she is clean and active, thrifty and fore-sightful. She is also a good and honest woman, informed, obliging and devoted. . . .

Being orderly means having a place for everything, a time for each type of work. It means putting each thing in its place and devoting one-self to different tasks at appropriate times. Good order helps economize on time. . . .

Being clean means having no dust or dirt on or around oneself. Thanks to cleanliness, everything shines in the house; furniture, no matter how old, looks like it was just made; clothes are washed often and ironed with care. To achieve these results, the housewife must be active. The active house-wife works fast and well, talks little and works a lot.

H. Raquet, *La Première Année de ménage rural* 13th ed., (Paris: A. Colin, 1908), 5.

United States.   Gains in the schooling available for women form a vital part of the history of modern education, particularly in the United States. These gains were uneven, however, and often reflected distinctive views about women's roles and nature. The following documents suggest several approaches to women's education in the nineteenth and early twentieth centuries. The first, announcing the opening of a women's school in North Carolina, offers a reasonably clear definition of goals. It is not exactly traditional (compare, for example, the more restricted French Catholic approach), but it definitely argues for a particular focus. The second statement, offered by Emma Willard, an early feminist, to the New York state legislature, argues for more open education, but it too notes women's special needs. What kind of education would this approach imply? In the third passage, Charles Eliot, the president of Harvard, justifies new opportunities for women, but not full equality. How do his arguments compare with Emma Willard's? How do they compare with what French republican men were saying? Why were there still so many hesitations about women's education? Why, at the same time, did education expand as rapidly as it did? Finally, an inscription from Margaret Morrison College (now part of Carnegie Mellon) in Pittsburgh early in the twentieth century reminds us that even as more women entered higher education, they continued to encounter distinctive definitions. Slogans of this sort went along with the emphasis on liberal arts, librarianship, home economics, or social work for women, as opposed to the range of subjects open for men. At the same time, many women graduates went on to vigorous and diverse careers, not always in "female" fields; the women's education track remained complex.

RALEIGH REGISTER

A School for Women

1808

In conformity to the wishes of some respectable Patrons in this place and its vicinity, I purpose to open an Institution for Female Improvement, on the first day of January next. The course of Instruction intended to be pursued, is the result of observation and some experience, and will be adopted to the varied dispositions of genius of my Pupils, not losing sight of systematic Arrangement and Progression. My object not merely to impart words and exhibit things, but chiefly to form the mind to the labour of thinking upon and understanding what is taught.—Whether my plan is judicious, a short experience will decide; and by the event I am content to be judged. The domestic arrangement for an efficient accommodation of my Scholars, will be an object of primary concern, and placed under the immediate inspection of Mrs. Mordecai—believing it to be no small part of Education bestowed on Females, to cultivate a *Taste* for neatness in their Persons and propriety of Manners: they will be placed under a superintendence [*sic*] calculated as much as possible to alleviate the solicitude of Parents.—In my Seminary will be taught the English Language, grammatically, *Spelling*, Reading, Writing, Arithmetic, Composition, History, Geography, and the use of the Globes. The plain and ornamental branches of Needle Work—Drawing, Vocal and Instrumental Music, by an approved Master of distinguished talents and correct deportment.

Raleigh (North Carolina) *Register*, August 25, 1808.

Terms:—For Board, Washing, Lodging, and Tuition (Drawing and Music excepted) $105 per annum. An additional charge will be made for necessary Books, Paper, Quills, and Ink.

EMMA WILLARD

Address to the New York State Legislature

1819

The object of this Address, is to convince the public, that a reform, with respect to female education, is necessary; that it cannot be effected by individual exertion, but that it requires the aid of the legislature: and further, by shewing the justice, the policy, and the magnanimity of such an undertaking, to persuade that body, to endow a seminary for females, as the commencement of such reformation.

The idea of a college for males, will naturally be associated with that of a seminary, instituted and endowed by the public; and the absurdity of sending ladies to college, may, at first thought, strike everyone, to whom this subject shall be proposed. I therefore hasten to observe, that the seminary here recommended, will be as different from those appropriated to the other sex, as the female character and duties are from the male. . . .

If the improvement of the American female character, and that alone, could be effected by public liberality, employed in giving better means of instruction; such improvement of one half of society, and that half, which barbarous and despotic nations have ever degraded, would of itself be an object, worthy of the most liberal government on earth; but if the female character be raised, it must inevitably raise that of the other sex: and thus does the plan proposed, offer, as the object of legislative bounty, to elevate the whole character of the community.

Emma Willard, "Address to the Public, Particularly the Members of the Legislature of New York," in *Women and the Higher Education,* edited by Anna C. Brackett (New York: Harper, 1893), 84–87.

As evidence, that this statement does not exaggerate the female influence in society, our sex need but be considered, in the single relation of mothers. In this character, we have the charge of the whole mass of individuals, who are to compose the succeeding generation: during that period of youth, when the pliant mind takes any direction, to which it is steadily guided by a forming hand. How important a power is given by this charge! yet, little do too many of my sex know how, either to appreciate or improve it. Unprovided with the means of acquiring that knowledge, which flows liberally to the other sex—having our time of education devoted to frivolous acquirements, how should we understand the nature of the mind, so as to be aware of the importance of those early impressions, which we make upon the minds of our children?—or how should we be able to form enlarged and correct views, either of the character, to which we ought to mould them, or of the means most proper to form them aright? . . .

In some of the sciences proper for our sex, the books, written for the other [men], would need alteration; because, in some they presuppose more knowledge than female pupils would possess; in others, they have parts not particularly interesting to our sex, and omit subjects immediately relating to their pursuits. There would likewise be needed, for a female seminary, some works, which I believe are no where extant, such as a systematic treatise on housewifery.

DOMESTIC INSTRUCTION should be considered important in a female seminary. It is the duty of our sex to regulate the internal concerns of every family; and unless they be properly qualified to discharge this duty, whatever may be their literary or ornamental attainments, they cannot be expected to make either good wives, good mothers, or good mistresses of families: and if they are none of these, they must be bad members of society; for it is by promoting or destroying the comfort and prosperity of their own families, that females serve or injure the community. To superintend the domestic department, there should be a respectable lady, experienced in the best methods of housewifery, and acquainted with propriety of dress and manners. Under her tuition the pupils ought to be placed for a certain length of time every morning. A spirit of neatness and order should here be treated as a virtue, and the contrary, if excessive and incorrigible, be punished with expulsion. There might be a gradation of employment in the domestic department, according to the length of time the pupils had remained at the institution. The older scholars might then assist the superintendent in instructing the younger, and the whole be so arranged, that each pupil might have advantages to become a good domestic manager by the time she has completed her studies.

CHARLES W. ELIOT

Inaugural Address as President of Harvard

October 19, 1869

The attitude of the University in the prevailing discussions touching the education and fit employments of women demands brief explanation. America is the natural arena for these debates; for here the female sex has a better past and a better present than elsewhere. Americans, as a rule, hate disabilities of all sorts, whether religious, political, or social. Equality between the sexes, without privilege or oppression on either side, is the happy custom of American homes. While this great discussion is going on, it is the duty of the University to maintain a cautious and expectant policy. The Corporation will not receive women students into the College proper, nor into any school whose discipline requires residence near the school. The difficulties involved in a common residence of hundreds of young men and women of immature character and marriageable age are very grave. The necessary police regulations are exceedingly burdensome. The Corporation are not influenced to this decision, however, by any crude notions about the innate capacities of women. The world knows next to nothing about the natural mental capacities of the female sex. Only after generations of civil freedom and social equality will it be possible to obtain the data necessary for an adequate discussion of woman's natural tendencies, tastes, and capabilities. Again, the Corporation do not find it necessary to entertain a confident opinion upon the fitness or unfitness of women for professional pursuits. It is not the business of the University to decide this mooted point. . . . Practical, not theoretical, considerations determine the policy of the University. Upon a matter concerning which prejudices are deep, and opinion inflammable, and experience scanty, only one course is prudent or justifiable when such great interests are at stake—that of cautious and well-considered experiment. The practical problem is to devise a safe, promising, and instructive experiment. Such an experiment the Corporation have meant to try in opening the newly established University Courses of Instruction to competent women. In these courses the University offers to young women who have been to good schools as many years as they wish of liberal culture in studies which have no direct professional value,

Charles W. Eliot, Inaugural Address, quoted in Samuel E. Morison, *The Development of Harvard University* (Cambridge: Harvard University Press, 1930), lxx–lxxi.

to be sure, but which enrich and enlarge both intellect and character. The University hopes thus to contribute to the intellectual emancipation of women. It hopes to prepare some women better than they would otherwise have been prepared for the profession of teaching, the one learned profession to which women have already acquired a clear title. It hopes that the proffer of this higher instruction will have some reflex influence upon schools for girls—to discourage superficiality, and to promote substantial education.

Inscription on
Margaret Morrison College Rotunda,
Pittsburgh, Pennsylvania
c. 1920

These are women's high prerogatives to make and inspire the home—To lessen suffering and increase happiness—To aid mankind in its upward struggle—To ennoble and adorn life's work however humble.

SPECIAL FEATURES OF EDUCATIONAL INTEGRATION

Peasants in France.   One of the most important transitions in nineteenth-century French education involved the growing conversion of the peasantry to some appreciation of formal education. Peasants and schools did not easily mix: peasants had a lively oral, local culture and an extensive need for child labor. Both impeded an interest in schooling. But some peasants had turned to schools before the nineteenth century, and new reasons soon developed for others. Ultimately, of course, the French republic completed the process of pressing education on peasants, even in remote areas, in part to work toward greater political loyalty.

The following two passages both discuss the peasant-school relationship. The first, by a teacher in southern France in 1861, emphasizes some of the difficulties, though the teacher's account might well be biased against peasant culture. The second account, treating the post–World War I period, discusses how rural children actually encountered schools in Brittany, one of the more remote French areas, where the traditional language, Breton, was very different from French. Do the two passages show some consistent peasant reactions? What relationships do the passages suggest between actual peasant experience and the hopes of France's educational policymakers? What kind of signals did teachers provide for peasant students, besides explicit lessons, and how do these compare with other teacher-student settings (the education of U.S. immigrants, for example)? The great challenge for mass education in a country like France was to draw the peasants in, to relate to but also to change their culture. What do these documents show about how this process developed?

M. FABRE

A Teacher's Lament

1861

The children of our hamlets are slower . . . than those of the cities who . . . don't devote themselves after school to games and dissipation. Besides which, city students always hear French spoken at home, while in Provence, ours hear only dialect; and the priest requires school students to speak in dialect. In addition, city children don't miss school the way village children do—some coming only in the morning, missing the afternoon, others vice versa. Ours come, in other words, never at the set time and almost always straggle in, because parents order them to work in the fields, the woods, etc. Thus they come ordinarily only three or four months consecutively. . . . But if I try to put one of the students in a lower division after he returns, he will always shout that he's going away, that he'd prefer not to come than to be set back. What is the teacher to do? In order not to lose the student, he gives in . . . and the student barely advances.

M. Fabre, *Mémoire*, January 22, 1861 (Archives nationales, F17/11 758).

PIERRE-JAKEZ HELIAS

A Breton Peasant Remembers the 1920s

What everyone hoped was that I hadn't acted too simpleminded in front of Monsieur Le Bail [the local parliamentary deputy]. I admitted that he had spoken to me in French and that I hadn't been able to answer him. "That's why you have to go to school," they told me. Monsieur Le Bail apparently never tired of repeating that the Reds [republicans] had to be better educated than the Whites [Catholic conservatives]. Education was the only possession that fathers did not bequeath to their sons. The Republic offered it to everybody. Anyone could take as much of it as he pleased. And the more he took, the more he could free himself from the Whites, who were in possession of nearly everything else. . . .

"But all I ask is to stay here, Grandfather."

"Exactly. Because you still don't know any French. The day you speak it as well as Monsieur Le Bail, you'll want to go somewhere else."

"Then why does Monsieur Le Bail stay in Plozévet?"

"He doesn't always stay in Plozévet. He goes to Paris to make speeches in the 'Chamber.' He goes to defend people in the law court at Quimper. With French, you can go everywhere. With only Breton, you're tied on a short rope, like a cow to his post. You have to graze around your tether. And the meadow grass is never plentiful." . . .

Another problem was that its schools were located right at the center of the low end of town, wedged into a White neighborhood. I would therefore have to cross the square, walk all the way to the church, and then venture into enemy territory—the hangout of a gang of boys my own age who, even then, used to taunt us from time to time as they skirted the fields. There would be a daily war. Grandfather reassured me. "The schoolmasters will keep order among you. You'll be able to fight anywhere else if you like, but not there," he said. One other thing bothered me. The street in front of the big school was called "Shit Street," probably because it was covered with mud and filth. It wasn't nice. But Grandfather had an answer for everything. "Exactly," he said. "At school you'll be cleaned up in every way possible." . . .

One had to be a professed Red—and a very vivid Red at that—to dare to send one's daughter to the *communale* school. For there was another school run by the nuns under the patronage of the rector and his vicar. It was located below the level of the road that ran along the south end of the

Pierre-Jakez Helias, *The Horse of Pride: Life in a Breton Village* (New Haven: Yale University Press, 1978), 134–76.

church. There, the daughters of the Whites received a religious and taste-ful education which was suitable to making them into good lambs of the Lord. ... Families that lived under the domination of the Whites—in other words, who depended upon them for their jobs and their daily bread—were obliged to go there as well. More especially, if you sweated over a farm that belonged to a city White, from Quimper or Paris, or if you were forced to shelter your family under some White's roof, there was no question of having your daugh-ters educated anywhere but at the Nuns' School, under penalty of being requested to clear out by the next Michaelmas Day and to hang yourself somewhere very far away—as far away as possible—for you would be pur-sued by a curse. "Red head, wrong-headed, Revolutionary!" Even those who were known to be Red and who worked for Reds, and therefore owed absolutely nothing to the Whites, were exposed to constant harassment.... The great concern of the state teachers was to convince the tenant farmers who weren't under the thumb of any White and who claimed to be sympa-thetic to the Reds, yet didn't profess their allegiance to them. That was also the case of tradespeople whose customers were divided between the two clans. Bringing all such people to a decision was a matter of skillful calcula-tion. The most important consideration in favor of the *communale* school was a parent's ambition to see his or her daughter rise to the rank of a teacher or a postal clerk, since the Nuns' School trained girls mainly to be good Catholic housewives who would remain at home, unless they entered the Church. The priest and their allies counterattacked by loudly proclaiming that a state school was "the Devil's school," that one never learned any prayers there (and what, then, about eternal salvation?), that Christ on his cross was not admitted, and that the Red teachers corrupted youth and undermined the very foundations of society. The nuns' girls, who were both curious and frightened, would ask the Red children whether it was true that the Devil sometimes came in person to dance on the tables, with his horns and his horse's hooves. And the Red children never failed to reply that it was indeed true, adding that when Satan appeared, he was completely naked, from top to bottom, including the middle....

Since I was an only child at the time and the son of a mother who was fiercely determined to keep her good reputation, I was among those who were the least badly dressed. I even had a good pair of drawers under my trousers, which was not true of everyone—far from it. Underwear was rare. And none of us, of course, had a coat for the rainy season any more than our fathers or mothers did. The worst off were those who came from some distance—from Penhors, for example—who had to jog for two and a half miles in all kinds of weather. When they got wet, they would stay wet for the whole day, even though the classroom stove—if there was one—did its best. Then, on the way home, they'd get soaked again. Their old clothes, all covered with mud, would be spread out to dry in front of the fire. The next day they'd wear them again, still stiff with dirt, dry or not. Many of the children didn't have an extra pair of trousers or slippers....

But there was a teacher—luckily, only one—who, in his moments of rage, would let his temper get the better of him and strike you on the knuckles with a steel ruler if your work was bad. Your chilblains would burst and ooze. Discomfort and pain. He was also the one who, with two fingers, would grab you roughly by the hair on your temples and at the same time call you every unpleasant name he could dig out of his vocabulary. That one really went too far. On two or three occasions the strongest boys fought with him. And people say that one day a farmer whose son he had badly mistreated arrived in the schoolyard with whip in hand to thrash the torturer. We were all rushed back into the classroom, and apparently the matter was finally settled. . . .

We knew perfectly well that we were always on the lookout for an opportunity to do something foolish, being free little scoundrels. We also knew that our ears were made to be tweaked, that from time to time the blackboard pointer would be cracked down on our backsides. We knew that it was for our own good, or at least what others considered to be our own good. . . .

The first day of school was, of course, always approached with apprehension. We would have barely crossed the threshold and there we were, in another world. It was a little like going to church, but far more disconcerting. In church our parents were with us, but in school they didn't come in. . . . At school we heard nothing but French; and we had to answer with whatever French words we had picked up. Otherwise, we'd keep silent. We read and wrote in French. If at home we hadn't had our missals, our catechism book, and our hymnals—all in Breton—in addition to *The Lives of the Saints*, we would have had good reasons for believing that no one ever wrote or read Breton. The schoolmistresses didn't wear nuns' coiffes, but dressed in fashionable city clothes and even wore leather shoes during the week. The schoolmasters might have looked quite like ordinary men had it not been for their collars and ties hanging over ridiculous little single-breasted vests. (Rather often we saw them walking on wooden soles, which made them less intimidating.) And those men and women normally went about bareheaded, a thing our parents would never have dared to do, nor would we. As I said, we were told to remove our caps when we entered the classroom. Just as in church. But the lessons we had to learn were harder than the catechism lessons, and there were more of them. And we had to write all the time, wasting expensive paper. In the end, we would receive our elementary-school diplomas, which were much harder to earn than the first-communion certificates. . . .

It was in the schoolyard, during our supervised recreation, that we were in danger of being caught using full sentences in Breton while chatting in a covered corner of the yard. Once, at the height of a passionate discussion among the boys, one of the schoolmasters—who was in the habit of pacing up and down between the back of the town hall and the fence around the headmaster's garden—had walked stealthily up behind them.

In the lower grades we would, in such cases, get off with a slap, a bruised ear, and our promise never to do it again. But the older we grew, the more frequently punishment rained down upon us. And still for our own good. . . . How could we speak French to describe what was happening in our town, where no one spoke anything but Breton?

When the kids came back from school with their books in military haversacks, their fathers (and sometimes their mothers) would take fifteen minutes off to flip through, as best they could, the amazing tools which, as they well knew, were used to discover the world. Most of them—not all— had learned to read, but many had forgotten; they hadn't had any need or opportunity to develop their small skill, and so could barely make out the words. Every man to his trade, as they say. But all of them aspired to having their children sanctified by the elementary-school diploma, which would be framed and hung nobly on the front of the cupboards, between the pious images and the photographs of family weddings. . . .

There was another reason for our parents' resolute desire to have us learn the language of the bourgeoisie, even if it meant . . . to a certain extent, repudiating our mother tongue. It was that they themselves were humiliated because they knew nothing but their mother tongue. Every time they had to deal with a city civil-servant and every time they ventured into a city, they were exposed to sly smiles and to jeers of all kinds. . . .

Learning French at school did not turn out to be all that difficult. But arithmetic was something else again—from the four operations to sums about filling a bathtub, via surfaces and volumes. And there was another problem. Frenchmen didn't calculate the way Bretons did, which complicated life, to say the least. Our lessons began with a thick cord stretched across the classroom, in front of the teacher's desk, and on which empty spools were threaded, every tenth one painted red. With the tip of a long reed, the schoolmistress would separate them from each other, and we had to count them aloud, one by one or by groups. Those who made mistakes or who just stood there gaping were called to order by the tip of the reed, which was imperatively brought down on their heads. . . .

Actually, we made out rather well, perhaps because our parents were remarkably good at calculating in their heads, without resorting to any pencil at all. Alain Le Goff was a past master at it. When I asked him how he did it, he wasn't able to explain, but he looked at me with sparkling eyes and said: "We in our family have always been very poor. If we had been stupid as well, we would have starved to death. So we were condemned to using our minds in order to have some chance of staying alive. Now it's up to you to use yours." I wanted to stay alive, no doubt of that. . . .

As for the names of plants, I believe we, in fact, knew more than some of our schoolmasters because of having run through the fields and filled our bellies with everything that was edible, even though we got diarrhea from time to time. Besides, botany in school was always rather limited. Did your schoolmaster know about nothing but medicinal herbs? Would he have been able to find mouse-peas, silver-drops, snap-dragons, Virgin-eyes, devil-bells, dog-tails, crow-leeks, larkspur, groundnuts, and catnip? There were many other things he didn't know and about which even his books said nothing. But the very worst thing that could happen to country children was being closed in behind a door for five days a week in order to learn things which had nothing to do with their everyday lives, whereas man's real work, we thought, was outside. It was particularly unpleasant to remain seated on benches for hours while the springtime sun shed its light, ironically, on spelling mistakes and turned our nine-times-seven-equals, fifty-six [*sic*] into smoke. . . .

At school, our teacher's duty was to explain to us the mechanism of the elections, and the voting process was to be carried out in the classroom. That we might understand more clearly, he asked us to nominate candidates from among ourselves, after which, in a cardboard box set up on the desk, we would each place a piece of paper that we had folded in four behind the corner blackboard, which was to serve as a voting booth. We didn't have any envelopes either, but never mind. I was one of the two candidates chosen by the class. Of course, all my friends knew that I was a Red and my opponent a White. That was probably why we had to confront each other—to make it seem realistic. Since the Reds were a weak minority in the commune, I expected to be beaten. But to the amazement of the schoolmaster himself, I won hands down. What had happened? Had they voted for me because I was at the head of the class, the boy who did the best homework and who recited better than the others, hence the one best qualified to defend my constituents in the Paris Chamber and in front of the "Government Boys"? Had there been some obscure reasons for the fact that my opponent hadn't managed to rally the Whites around him for a unanimous vote? Be that as it may, I was nicknamed "deputy," and some of my schoolmates have been calling me that all my life. But the recreation period following the election was very stormy indeed. Single combats took place under the covered corner of the yard and also around the lavatory, which resulted in one of the doors being torn off. Soon the schoolmaster didn't know whom to slap first. . . .

Meanwhile, I was slaving away for the scholarship examinations. Not long before I was to take them, the rector came to see my mother at a quiet hour in the afternoon, taking advantage of the fact that my father was at work. He spent his time complimenting her on her son, who was so good in school that he would do brilliantly at a Christian college such as Saint-Gabriel in Pont l'Abbé or at the seminary. She was not to worry about the expenses involved, which were not within her means, because he himself and other generous patrons would see to them. My mother, as a good Christian, could not say no. She got out of it by saying that she would discuss it with her husband, who was the master. That was what all Bigouden women answered when they were in trouble. But it meant no. When my father was informed, he settled the matter, saying he had not brought up his son to be a priest; that was fine for the Whites. The only proper ambition for a Red was to be a teacher. "Anyway," my father added, "he'll go to the lycée in Quimper for nothing. Monsieur Gourmelon said that he'd have no trouble getting a scholarship if he would be a little careful with his arithmetic."

I personally should have really liked to become a carpenter or, if not that, a quartermaster in the Navy.

And to remain a Red, of course.

Long live the Republic!

Immigrants in the United States.   The sheer scope of immigration in American history makes the connection between immigrants and the schools a vital topic. The process of drawing the immigrants in and using schools to "remake" them in some respects was the American equivalent of the French peasant challenge. Indeed, many immigrants did come from peasant stock. Historians' attention has focused particularly on the years around 1900, when the huge wave of southern and eastern European immigrants arrived; but some key points apply to other periods of immigration, including the most recent decades. First, many immigrants benefited from schooling in their adaptation to a different society; some were able quickly to use education to begin a process of social mobility. Second, many American educators were deeply suspicious of immigrants and sought to segregate them (for example, by testing) or to impose new values on them. How do these characteristics combine in explaining what schooling did to and for immigrant children and their families? The documents that follow also suggest that the attitudes immigrants brought to education formed a crucial variable: some groups embraced the process with more enthusiasm than others, some children had more opportunities than others. Where, finally, does the immigrant experience fit into the larger history of American education? What distinctive features of the national approach to education were confirmed in dealing with immigrants, and what changes were introduced? Immigrants form a special case of the general issue of the tension between equality and inequality in modern education—how does American treatment compare, say, with French or Japanese approaches to lower-class groups that were also held to be somewhat different, possibly inferior, in culture?

LEONARD COVELLO

An Italian Immigrant's Experience around 1900

The Soup School got its name from the fact that at noontime a bowl of soup was served to us with some white, soft bread that made better spitballs than eating in comparison with the substantial and solid homemade bread to which I was accustomed. The school itself was organized and maintained by the Female Guardian Society of America. Later on I found that this Society was sponsored by wealthy people concerned about the immigrants and their children. How much this organization accomplished among immigrants in New York City would be difficult to estimate. But this I do know, that among the immigrants of my generation and even later *La Soupa Scuola* is still vivid in our boyhood memories.

Why we went to the Soup School instead of the regular elementary public school I have not the faintest idea, except that possibly the first Aviglianese to arrive in New York sent his child there and everyone else followed suit— and also possibly because in those days a bowl of soup was a bowl of soup.

Once at the Soup School I remember the teacher gave each child a bag of oatmeal to take home. This food was supposed to make you big and strong. You ate it for breakfast. My father examined the stuff, tested it with his fingers. To him it was the kind of bran that was fed to pigs in Avigliano.

"What kind of a school is this?" he shouted. "They give us the food of animals to eat and send it home to us with our children! What are we coming to next?"

By the standards I had come to know and understand in Avigliano, the Soup School was not an unpleasant experience. I had been reared in a strict code of behavior, and this same strictness was the outstanding characteristic of the first of my American schools. Nor can I say, as I had indicated to Vito, that a blow from Mrs. Cutter ever had the lustiness of my old teacher, Don Salvatore Mecca. But what punishment lacked in power, it gained by the exacting personality of our principal.

Middle-aged, stockily built, gray hair parted in the middle, Mrs. Cutter lived up to everything my cousin Vito had said about her and much more. Attached to an immaculate white waist by a black ribbon, her pince-nez fell from her nose and dangled in moments of anger. She moved about the corridors and classrooms of the Soup School ever alert and ready to strike at any infringement of school regulations.

I was sitting in class trying to memorize and pronounce words written

Leonard Covello, *The Heart Is the Teacher* (New York: McGraw-Hill, 1958), cited in *Education in the United States: A Documentary History*, vol. 4, edited by Sol Cohen (New York: Random House, 1974), 2174–75.

on the blackboard—words which had absolutely no meaning to me. It seldom seemed to occur to our teachers that explanations were necessary.

"B-U-T-T-E-R—butter—butter," I sing-songed with the rest of the class, learning as always by rote, learning things which often I didn't understand but which had a way of sticking in my mind.

Softly the door opened and Mrs. Cutter entered the classroom. For a large and heavy-set woman she moved quickly, without making any noise. We were not supposed to notice or even pretend we had seen her as she slowly made her way between the desks and straight-backed benches. "B-U-T-T-E-R," I intoned. She was behind me now. I could feel her presence hovering over me. I did not dare take my eyes from the blackboard. I had done nothing and could conceive of no possible reason for an attack, but with Mrs. Cutter this held no significance. She carried a short bamboo switch. On her finger she wore a heavy gold wedding ring. For an instant I thought she was going to pass me by and then suddenly her clenched fist with the ring came down on my head. . . .

I learned arithmetic and penmanship and spelling—every misspelled word written ten times or more, traced painfully and carefully in my blankbook. I do not know how many times I wrote "I must not talk." In this same way I learned how to read in English, learned geography and grammar, the states of the Union and all the capital cities—and memory gems—choice bits of poetry and sayings. Most learning was done in unison. You recited to the teacher standing at attention. Chorus work. Repetition. Repetition until the things you learned beat in your brain even at night when you were falling asleep.

I think of the modern child with his complexities and his need for "self-expression"! He will never know the forceful and vitalizing influence of a Soup School or a Mrs. Cutter. . . .

Silence! Silence! Silence! This was the characteristic feature of our existence at the Soup School. You never made an unnecessary noise or said an unnecessary word. Outside in the hall we lined up by size, girls in one line and boys in another, without uttering a sound. Eyes front and at attention. Lord help you if you broke the rule of silence. I can still see a distant relative of mine, a girl named Miluzza, who could never stop talking, standing in a corner behind Mrs. Cutter throughout an entire assembly with a spring-type clothespin fastened to her lower lip as punishment. Uncowed, defiant—Miluzza with that clothespin dangling from her lip. . . .

The piano struck up a march and from the hall we paraded into assembly—eyes straight ahead in military style. Mrs. Cutter was there on the platform, dominating the scene, her eyes penetrating every corner of the assembly hall. It was always the same. We stood at attention as the Bible was read and at attention as the flag was waved back and forth, and we sang the same song. I didn't know what the words meant but I sang it loudly with all the rest, in my own way, "Tree Cheers for De Red Whatzam Blu!"

But best of all was another song we used to sing at these assemblies. It was a particular favorite of Mrs. Cutter's and we sang it with great gusto, "Honest boys who never tread the streets." This was in the days when we not only trod the streets but practically lived in them.

MARY AUTIN

A Russian Jewish Immigrant's Experience
1912

Education was free. That subject my father had written about repeatedly, as comprising his chief hope for us children, the essence of American opportunity, the treasure that no thief could touch, not even misfortune or poverty. It was the one thing that he was able to promise us when he sent for us; surer, safer than bread or shelter. On our second day I was thrilled with the realization of what this freedom of education meant. A little girl from across the alley came and offered to conduct us to school. My father was out, but we five between us had a few words of English by this time. We knew the word school. We understood. This child, who had never seen us till yesterday, who could not pronounce our names, who was not much better dressed than we, was able to offer us the freedom of the schools of Boston! No application made, no questions asked, no examinations, rulings, exclusions; no machinations, no fees. The doors stood open for every one of us. The smallest child could show us the way.

This incident impressed me more than anything I had heard in advance of the freedom of education in America. It was a concrete proof—almost the thing itself. One had to experience it to understand it. . . .

The apex of my civic pride and personal contentment was reached on the bright September morning when I entered the public school. That day I must always remember, even if I live to be so old that I cannot tell my name. To most people their first day at school is a memorable occasion. In my case the importance of the day was a hundred times magnified, on account of the years I had waited, the road I had come, and the conscious ambitions I entertained.

I am wearily aware that I am speaking in extreme figures, in superlatives. I wish I knew of some other way to render the mental life of the immigrant child of reasoning age. I may have been ever so much an exception

Mary Autin, *The Promised Land* (Boston: Houghton Mifflin, 1912), 186–204.

in acuteness of observation, powers of comparison, and abnormal self-consciousness; none the less were my thoughts and conduct typical of the attitude of the intelligent immigrant child toward American institutions. And what the child thinks and feels is a reflection of the hopes, desires, and purposes of the parents who brought him overseas, no matter how precocious and independent the child may be. Your immigrant inspectors will tell you what poverty the foreigner brings in his baggage, what want in his pockets. Let the overgrown boy of twelve, reverently drawing his letters in the baby class, testify to the noble dreams and high ideals that may be hidden beneath the greasy caftan of the immigrant. Speaking for the Jews, at least, I know I am safe in inviting such an investigation.

Who were my companions on my first day at school? Whose hand was in mine, as I stood, overcome with awe, by the teacher's desk, and whispered my name as my father prompted? Was it Frieda's steady, capable hand? Was it her loyal heart that throbbed, beat for beat with mine, as it had done through all our childish adventures? Frieda's heart did throb that day, but not with my emotions. My heart pulsed with joy and pride and ambition; in her heart longing fought with abnegation. For I was led to the schoolroom, with its sunshine and its singing and the teacher's cheery smile; while she was led to the workshop, with its foul air, care-lined faces, and the foreman's stern command. Our going to school was the fulfilment of my father's best promises to us, and Frieda's share in it was to fashion and fit the calico frocks in which the baby sister and I made our first appearance in a public school-room.

I remember to this day the gray pattern of the calico, so affectionately did I regard it as it hung upon the wall—my consecration robe awaiting the beatific day. And Frieda, I am sure, remembers it too, longingly did she regard it as the crisp, starchy breadths of it slid between her fingers. But whatever were her longings, she said nothing of them; she bent over the sewing-machine humming an Old-World melody. In every straight, smooth seam, perhaps, she tucked away some lingering impulse of childhood; but she matched the scrolls and flowers with the utmost care. If a sudden shock of rebellion made her straighten up for an instant, the next instant she was bending to adjust a ruffle to the best advantage. And when the momentous day arrived, and the little sister and I stood up to be arrayed, it was Frieda herself who patted and smoothed my stiff new calico; who made me turn round and round, to see that I was perfect; who stooped to pull out a disfiguring basting-thread. If there was anything in her heart besides sisterly love and pride and good-will, as we parted that morning, it was a sense of loss and a woman's acquiescence in her fate; for we had been close friends, and now our ways would lie apart. Longing she felt, but no envy. She did not grudge me what she was denied. . . .

Father himself conducted us to school. He would not have delegated that mission to the President of the United States. He had awaited the day with impatience equal to mine, and the visions he saw as he hurried us over the sun-flecked pavements transcended all my dreams. . . . He had very little opportunity to prosecute his education, which, in truth, had never been begun. His struggle for a bare living left him no time to take advantage of the public evening school; but he lost nothing of what was to be learned through reading, through attendance at public meetings, through exercising the rights of citizenship. Even here he was hindered by a natural inability to acquire the English language. In time, indeed, he learned to read, to follow a conversation or lecture; but he never learned to write correctly, and his pronunciation remains extremely foreign to this day.

If education, culture, the higher life were shining things to be worshipped from afar, he had still a means left whereby he could draw one step nearer to them. He could send his children to school, to learn all those things that he knew by fame to be desirable. The common school, at least, perhaps high school; for one or two, perhaps even college! His children should be students, should fill his house with books and intellectual company; and thus he would walk by proxy in the Elysian Fields of liberal learning. As for the children themselves, he knew no surer way to their advancement and happiness.

ELLWOOD CUBBERLY

An Educator's View

1909

During the middle years of the nineteenth century, large numbers of English came, in all a total of about three and one-half millions having arrived since 1820. Still later, large numbers of Scandinavians arrived, these going largely to the agricultural sections of the Northwest. In all, nearly two millions of Scandinavians have come to our shores.

While these people frequently settled in groups and retained for a time their foreign language, manners, and customs, they were nevertheless relatively easy to assimilate. All except the Irish came from countries where general education prevailed, and where progressive methods of agriculture, trade, and manufacturing had begun to supersede primitive methods. All were from race stock not very different from our own, and all possessed courage, initiative, intelligence, adaptability, and self-reliance to a large degree. The willingness, good nature, and executive qualities of the Irish, the intellectual

Ellwood Cubberly, *Changing Conceptions of Education* (Boston: Houghton Mifflin, 1909), 13–15.

thoroughness of the German, the respect for law and order of the English, and the thrift of the Scandinavian have been good additions to our life.

About 1882, the character of our immigration changed in a very remarkable manner. Immigration from the north of Europe dropped off rather abruptly, and in its place immigration from the south and east of Europe set in and soon developed into a great stream. After 1880, southern Italians and Sicilians; people from all parts of that medley of races known as the Austro-Hungarian Empire, — Czechs, Moravians, Slovaks, Poles, Jews, Ruthenians, Croatians, Servians, Dalmations, Slovenians, Magyars, Roumanians, Austrians; and Slavs, Poles, and Jews from Russian persecution; and Greeks, Syrians, and Armenians from the south, have come in great numbers to our shores.

These southern and eastern Europeans are of a different type from the north Europeans who preceded them. Illiterate, docile, lacking in self-reliance and initiative, and not possessing the Anglo-Teutonic conceptions of law, order, and government, their coming has served to dilute tremendously our national stock, and to corrupt our civic life. The great bulk of these people have settled in the cities of the North Atlantic and North Central states, and the problems of proper housing and living, moral, and sanitary conditions, honest and decent government, and proper education have everywhere been made more difficult by their presence. Everywhere these people tend to settle in groups or settlements, and to set up here their national manners, customs, and observances. Our task is to break up these groups or settlements, to assimilate and amalgamate these people as a part of our American race, and to implant in their children, so far as can be done, the Anglo-Saxon conception of righteousness, law and order, and popular government, and to awaken in them a reverence for our democratic institutions and for those things in our national life which we as a people hold to be of abiding worth.

SARA O'BRIEN

English for Foreigners

1909

This is a tooth-brush.
It is my tooth-brush.
I take it in my hand.

Sara O'Brien, *English for Foreigners* (Boston: Houghton Mifflin, 1909), 24, 55, 76, 140, 149.

I dip it in warm water.
I shall brush my teeth.
I brush my teeth.
I brush my teeth with this tooth-brush.
I brush all of my teeth.
I brush them every day.

I take this thread.
I shall clean my teeth with it.
I clean between my teeth with it.
My teeth are clean and white.
I take care of my teeth.
I take good care of my teeth.

This is the family, in the sitting room.
The family is made up of the father, the mother, and the children.
The father is the husband.
That is the mother who is sewing.
The mother is the wife.
The father and the mother are the parents.
The sister is playing the piano.
The brother is standing beside her.
The family makes the home.
Copy: *There is no place like home.*

A gentleman knows how to dress well. He doesn't buy clothes which he can't afford. He knows it is cheaper to pay cash for his clothes than to buy on credit.

A gentleman always wears clean clothes. He changes his clothes often. He airs the clothes which can't be washed. He knows that he must wear clean clothes to keep in good health. Unclean clothes bring disease to him, and may also bring disease into his home.

A gentleman is neat in his dress. He does not dress in loud colors. He likes better the kind of clothes which do not attract attention. It pays to dress neatly, for often a man is judged by his clothes.

Are you a citizen of the United States? The United States takes care of all its citizens and gives them many rights. A citizen has the right to life, liberty, and happiness. He has the right to buy and sell, to have a home, and to help in making the government under which he lives a good government. These rights of citizenship must be paid for by the men who enjoy them. A true citizen pays for his rights by obeying the laws, paying his taxes, and taking part in protecting the government of the United States.

The law tells you what is best for you and for everybody else. You must obey the law, and you should help others to keep the law. A citizen obeys the laws because they are made by the people, for the good of all the people. A law-breaker not only hurts himself but others also. That is why the government must have courts of justice and jails. The only way to make good laws is by choosing the right men to make the laws.

A citizen pays his just taxes, and shares in the government of his city and country. He is interested in the public health, in education, and in all things that are for the good of the city and the state. He watches the work of all the City Departments, and knows how the public money is collected and spent. He earns his own living, and deals honestly with all men. He aids the poor and helpless, and does all he can to prevent cruelty to children and animals.

He is willing to pay for his rights even by giving up his life for his country, if necessary. Because he is a free citizen of his state and of the United States, he is ready at all times to serve his city, his state, and his country.

The American flag means liberty and justice for everybody. It is honored by all citizens on the land and on the sea. For it the soldiers of our army and the sailors of our navy are willing to fight and even to die.

The colors of the flag tell the story of the nation's freedom. Red is for bravery, white is for purity, and blue is for justice.

The stripes tell the number of the original states of the United States, and the stars tell the number of states now in the Union. How many stars has the flag now?

All Americans love the Stars and Stripes. Let us all respect the flag and be true to it.

Copy: *America is another word for opportunity.*

6

Modern Education in Japan, 1870–1950: Tradition and Change

A society with far different traditions from those of France and the United States, Japan inevitably encountered a distinctive set of problems and opportunities in forging its own impressive educational system. Serious work on educational reform began in Japan only in the 1870s. Of course, the nation had its vigorous preindustrial system, based on Confucianism, which helps explain why it turned to education quickly in its effort to respond to new challenges; and there had been earlier debates, such as those around the role of the "Dutch" school and translations of Western scientific works, that foreshadowed newer issues. But the full effort began late by Western standards, occurring only after the West had forced open the nation to foreign trade, following Admiral Perry's historic intrusion in 1853 and after the Japanese themselves had spent about fifteen years in intense internal strife over what course to adopt in light of Western interference.

Once the process was begun, aspects of modern Japanese education emerged very quickly; at points, the Japanese proved quicker in imitating European patterns, particularly in elite education, than the United States was. But the formative period of modern schooling in Japan extended well into the twentieth century, whereas both France and the United States had constructed basic frameworks by 1900 or soon thereafter. This chapter traces the Japanese building effort, before comparing it with the comparable stages in the West in the next chapter.

Timing was not the only difference in the framework for reform. Relationship to broader social change was another distinctive feature.

Modern education in the West emerged along with other changes, such as industrialization and increased political democracy. Education helped cause some of the broader societal shifts, but it also resulted from them. Japanese reformers saw educational change as a vital preparation for a larger restructuring, as they pondered how to reform a feudal, preindustrial society under the spur of new Western demands for access. Thus shifts in schooling began very early, and by Western standards very self-consciously and explicitly. Educational change was a fundamental feature of the Meiji era that began in 1868, as Japan jettisoned feudalism and began to restructure the economy. School reform was a planned effort, to a much greater extent than in the West, and it was designed to set other changes in motion. Of course, as time went on and Japan began to industrialize and to introduce new political forms, some of the same social and economic interactions occurred as in the West; education did not stand alone. It remains true that the Japanese attempt—which proved largely successful—to use education as a catalyst was different from the more haphazard model in the West.

In setting up its educational system, Japan dealt with many of the same issues as in the West, including questions of gender, the balance between elite and mass training, and so on. But the nation faced a mirror-imaged advantage and disadvantage that obviously differed from the initial conditions of modern education in either France or the United States.

The advantage was simple: once its leaders had resolved on major change, they could copy Western systems intact (for by the 1870s and 1880s it was pretty clear what the main Western framework was). There was less need for gradual or hit-and-miss experiments. This potentially allowed greater coherence in the whole process of change. Both France and the United States moved back and forth in emphases and institutions; Japan had less reason to do so because it had well-developed Western models to imitate. Of course there were hesitations and setbacks. Initial plans were overambitious, and initial Westernizers encountered conservative resistance, from the emperor on down, that forced modifications. Even centralization, intended to create a seamless system, had its lapses, though these were less noticeable than in France. In addition to internal issues, there was the not trivial question of what Western system to copy. Reform-minded observers sent to the West by the Japanese government in the 1860s and 1870s had a chance to look both at the United States and Western Europe. On the whole, European patterns made more sense as models than American ones. The United States at this point offered a less impressive structure for elite education, particularly in technical fields. American interests in women's higher education left the Japanese cold, for observers found American women treated with absurd deference — of the sort that should be reserved for one's elders. Nevertheless, the Japanese shopped around for different Western ingredients, a process that continued through the American occupation of Japan after World War II. Still, the chance for a systematic effort, based on imitation of reasonably mature educational patterns in the West, was unusual in world history to that point.

But the advantage brought an inevitable disadvantage: educational change had to be associated with massive incorporation of foreign culture. Unlike either France or the United States, Japan had to scrap its Confucian educational system (after agonizing debate) because the old system simply could not incorporate those aspects of Western learning, particularly in science, that seemed essential for a modern society. Developing new schools that could retain Japanese loyalty while convincing all people that education was personally and socially significant even though no longer traditional, even though it explicitly taught a generation values that their parents had not known, was an immense task. In practice, of course, the Japanese succeeded by maintaining important traditional elements or by inventing traditions that helped the society cohere. Not everything was new or Western. But the amount of change associated with schooling went well beyond what either the French or Americans had grappled with, when at most only very bounded imitations — such as ultimate American interest in European research universities — had been necessary.

THE REFORM CURRENT

Suggestions of reform began to emerge in the 1860s, before the Meiji restoration launched the nation clearly on the course of substantial change. It was during this decade that Japanese reformers, like Yukichi Fukuzawa, began visiting the West, paying particular attention to education. Many of these travelers later emerged as leaders in the Ministry of Education, though some of them had serious reservations about too much Westernization. Reformers urged the introduction of more science into Japanese training and more broadly sought to break the Confucian habit of looking to tradition. During the 1860s, Japanese missions to Europe or the United States typically gained only a broad overview of educational systems, though it was enough to convince some of the new leaders that Japan had serious restructuring to do. By the early 1870s, study trips were more focused, charged with inquiring into such issues as teachers' pay, administrative structures in the schools, and even school buildings. The Japanese took the task of learning from the West very seriously. Institutional changes began to occur as well. New foreign language schools sprang up, teaching in English, French, and Russian as well as Chinese and Dutch. In 1865 a Nagasaki school employed a Dutch instructor to teach physics and chemistry. In 1869 restrictions of social rank for entrance to certain colleges were removed; non-samurai could attend elite schools. By 1871 the government sent an official delegation to Europe and the United States, including a special commissioner for education. This was a larger and more formal effort than the previous trips by individual reformers. These changes were scattered, to be sure, and they took place in an atmosphere of caution. A new school of Japanese learning in 1868 articulated widely shared concerns: "Foreign learning must be made to subserve the interests of Japan. . . . It is incumbent on every citizen to understand the nature of the public institutions of his country, and to become familiar with the duties pertaining to his position in society." But at the same time, "useless styles of composition, and aimless discourses and discussions, ought to be abandoned . . . and the literary and military branches of learning ought to be so cultivated as to be mutually helpful."

In framing a new system of schooling, Japanese leaders had several important goals. First, they believed that an extensive system of education was essential for a modern state and a modern economy. This is why, beginning in 1871 with the establishment of a central Ministry of Education, they embarked on an almost entirely new school program. Second, relatedly, they assumed that education must be in government hands, because only the state could reorient teaching and afford the huge investments needed to build from scratch. A handful of private institutions and some foreign missionary operations existed, but they had limited significance. Government sponsorship helped Japan avoid the quarrels over religious domination that affected so many Western systems, and it reduced (without eliminating) debates about a special aristocratic role. Education was seen as something to be rationalized; it was secular and state-oriented, regarded mainly as a tool of government to train reliable and obedient citizens and give them the skills required by a modern society. It aimed at producing a literate labor and military force, a broad group of technicians, and a small leadership elite.

The new system meant unprecedented exposure to science. It meant mass schooling, rather than training for a large minority. It moved Japanese society from one in which functions were largely determined by birth to one in which they were set largely by education—creating new mobility opportunities in the process. The system also lent itself to indoctrination. In that regard, a feature of state-controlled education in the West was pressed further in Japan, though the comparison must be made carefully: primary schooling became a way to teach people what to think, with tremendous emphasis on rote. National obedience and uniformity thus were key products of this new system.

The first decisive move occurred with the ambitious Education Code of 1872, a far more sweeping measure than any Western country had introduced at a single juncture. The law set up a national education system, with 8 university districts, each with 32 middle-level districts, each of these in turn with 210 primary schools—for a total in principle of 54,000 primary schools. The twin goals were a highly centralized system—the Japanese were particularly taken with the centralization of French education, at a point when they were trying to strengthen as well as to modernize their own government—and universal coverage. A key provision of the Education Code was that: "learning is no longer to be considered as belonging to the upper classes, but is to be equally the inheritance of nobles and gentry, farmers and artisans, males and females."

This was an extraordinary commitment. Influenced by its earlier educational heritage but also by the pressing need to catch up economically and militarily with the West, Japan decided that a rapid transformation of education was a fundamental component. The result was a much greater collective, and ultimately personal, devotion to schooling than that achieved in any other society, including the West. In turn, Japan's educational strides undergirded the nation's extraordinary success over the next century, producing skills and loyalties essential to industrialization, political change, and (for a key period) military commitment, without huge social upheavals.

The 1872 code was followed by a number of important specific steps. The Ministry of Education began to open public libraries, initially including only Japanese and Chinese books but then adding Western works as well. It also began to expand teacher training colleges, for the new program vitally depended on redressing the massive shortage of skilled teachers; indeed, the lack of competent personnel was a problem for several decades. This was one of the costs of trying to build a whole system in one fell swoop. In 1875 the first normal school for female teachers was set up; like the West, but more abruptly, Japan discovered that new uses of women were essential to staff a mass education system. Developments during the 1870s were a high-water mark of Western influence in Japanese schooling. In 1873, an American adviser, David Murray, was brought in from Rutgers University. Hundreds of American and European readers were translated wholesale into Japanese. Teacher training and vocational education also widely copied Western models. As many as five thousand foreign experts were employed by the educational system. And in 1876 Japan sent a massive display about its educational plans to an exposition in Philadelphia (though it was at pains to emphasize its impressive earlier achievements).

Yet change did not proceed as rapidly as the early planners had hoped. The initial goal of four years of schooling for everyone had to be scaled back to three. Even by 1900, only two state universities had been established (instead of the eight recommended), and only 27,000 instead of 54,000 primary schools opened — an impressive achievement, but short of the mark. Many schools were badly housed in inappropriate buildings. Teachers' competence remained a sore point; in 1880, only 10 percent of them had been formally trained. Pay was low.

One of the problems was money. Japan was a poor society. The government had hoped to rely on local taxes and tuition payments for most of the educational budget, but these proved inadequate. Many people could not afford any fees, and indeed these were finally abolished in 1900. (In 1907, as the Japanese system strengthened and the economy began to advance, the schooling requirement, with no fees, was raised to six years.) Equally important, before about 1900, was the considerable peasant resistance to the whole idea of education, at least as the government presented it. Elements of this reaction were similar to resistance in the West. Many peasants depended on child labor, by age ten if not before. They did not like outside authorities interfering with their control over their children. Incompetent, sometimes brutal teachers added to the tensions. The Western-style education being offered seemed particularly irrelevant to many Japanese. After all, in contrast to the West, the first wave of modern schools made few bows to traditional religious or family values, which inevitably reduced their appeal. A number of popular rebellions occurred in the 1870s against government-mandated change, including the schools. Many peasants believed that the government simply intended education as a conduit into obligatory military service, which they also resented. The gap between peasants and education was gradually narrowed, partly because peasants came to see practical advantages in acquiring some basic skills and in giving their children a chance at mobility; even becoming a teacher could seem a massive step upward. By the early 1900s universal education was a reality—an amazing accomplishment in a mere thirty years.

In the process, however, educational goals veered away from the straightforward Westernization suggested in the 1870s. Conservative objections to undue change forced new complexity, but this also made schools somewhat more recognizable in the eyes of many people. Western advisers like David Murray suggested some concessions to popular discontent, including more local autonomy and a reduction in corporal punishment. By 1879 there was also a move to provide more domestic training in the schools for girls; sewing classes were one result. But the emperor and conservative advisers around him believed that the crucial adjustments must go further, through the reintroduction of key Confucian values, without which schooling would merely create moral disorder. During the 1880s the educational establishment became something of a battleground, with ministers often fired and rehired depending on the faction in power. Particular opposition developed to American-influenced ideas about local school autonomy and what was seen as the more general Western impulse toward using schools to promote individualism.

The Emperor Meiji toured the nation in 1878 and was distressed by some of the educational developments he saw. He instructed his Confucian lecturer, Motoda Eifu, to compose a statement on the "great principles of education," which was published as an imperial rescript in 1879 and became a pillar of the conservative counterattack. The rescript implied that Westernization in education had gone too far. A moderate official, Hirobumi Ito, objected to the sweeping attack, arguing that what was sapping morals in Japan was the excessiveness of change in general, not just school reform, and that educational policies would still produce long-term gains. Ito's efforts were rewarded by dismissal, and a new conservative ordinance was issued in 1880.

The basic conservative goal was to place moral training at the center of the school curriculum. The 1881 Memorandum for Elementary School Teachers proclaimed: "In order to guide people, make them good, give them wide knowledge, and to do this widely, teachers must particularly stress moral education to their pupils. Loyalty to the Imperial House, love of country, filial piety toward parents, respect for superiors, faith in friends, charity toward inferiors, and respect for oneself constitute the great path of human morality. The Teacher himself must be a model of these virtues in his daily life, and must endeavor to stimulate his pupils along the path of virtue." From 1880 onward, use of foreign books on morality was prohibited, and officials began to inspect textbooks; several were banned as likely to promote social disorder. New books were prepared to teach morality, and teacher autonomy was curbed in favor of state supervision.

While conservatives took the lead in this new emphasis, many reformers and progressives joined in. They too wanted moralization and national unity, talking of the use of "moral suasion" to reshape popular habits. Even more than in France (where quarrels over the church often dominated debate), various factions in Japan could agree on the need for nationalism; as in France, and indeed the United States, the need to teach good character was not at this point a partisan issue. Reformers in Japan thus helped write some of the new imperial edicts and participated in the new note of caution about incorporating Western values.

In the mid-1880s a more flexible conservative, Arinori Mori, became minister of education. Mori, like the conservatives, opposed Western individualism and materialism, which he believed he had seen in visits to Paris and elsewhere. But he also realized that Western-style skepticism about received wisdom had produced vital benefits in science and technology. He saw his task as a blending of the latter approach, to help Japan build a modern, science-based economy, with Japanese nationalism and political absolutism, to provide a docile population. In principle, by Western standards, he sought to reconcile the irreconcilable, though many Western systems also found ways to promote open inquiry in science while working for religious or at least political loyalties in mass schooling. Determining how different Japan was, in its own policies, is a crucial comparative issue; to an extent, Japanese officials simply struggled more publicly with problems that Westerners hid under rhetorical covers, because of the specific Japanese problem of identifying and dealing with foreign educational imports.

Mori's solution, which in a sense lasted until after World War II, involved drenching the primary school system in nationalism and moral exhortation, while creating an elite university sector that was granted remarkable academic freedom. Mori believed that the small numbers involved in university study made a different approach tolerable, an approach essential to upgrade Japan's scientific and technical base. Thus not only the primary schools but also the teacher training establishments emphasized loyalty to the emperor and the fundamental obligation of citizens to the collective well-being of the state. Normal schools highlighted character training, not academic subjects. Each teacher college had six hours of military drill each week, and many of the principals were regular army officers. Loyalty and obedience were stressed as essential virtues. Primary schools offered some technical training along with the moral lessons, but this was designed to fit people for their station in society. Thus women were prepared for housewife roles or low-level jobs, peasants for labor in the field. Western-style technical instruction was slow in coming, in part because of a shortage of trained teachers but also because Confucian conservatives worried about the implications of such training for social stability. The Japanese found an alarming shortage of technicians during their mid-1890s war with China (which the nation nevertheless won handily), and this prompted further change. The Vocational Education Law in 1894 set up schools at the lower secondary level, feeding into technical schools that graduated engineers, accountants, and other professionals. These practitioners lacked the prestige of university graduates. As in many societies, technical education remained a bit of an outlier; but economic and military needs for middle-level personnel were increasingly satisfied.

In these initial decades, women's education, not surprisingly, remained somewhat ambiguous. Rapid expansion of factory jobs, and the growth of clerical jobs, helped motivate attendance at primary schools, where girls and boys participated in almost equal numbers and where, thanks to American influence, coeducation prevailed. Women also had oppor-

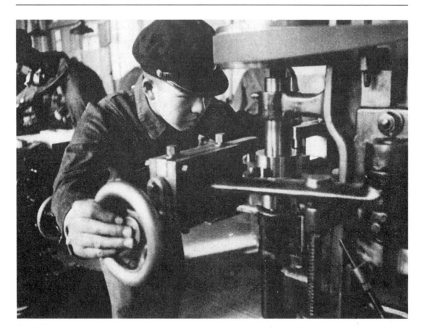

Figure 9. Technical training in Japan in the interwar years: a key focus of Japanese education.

tunities in teaching. But aside from limited teacher training, other outlets beyond primary school were slow to develop, because Japanese leaders were unsure of women's roles and eager to maintain a considerable emphasis on family functions. It was also judged essential to keep males and females separate after the primary grades. In 1899 the Higher Girls' School Law was passed, aimed at providing one secondary school for females in each district. In 1908 there were 159 secondary schools for women, compared with more than 300 for men. By 1900 women could take examinations to become doctors, and the first medical school was opened for females. In 1901 the Japanese Women's University was founded, though it operated at an academic level below other universities. The Tohoku Imperial University, established in 1906, admitted some women students. But women's access to higher education remained very limited until after World War II.

Around 1900, emphasis on the "good wife, wise mother" theme was particularly intended for upper-class girls in the higher schools. Lower-class women were expected to remain in productive labor, and gender-specific advice seemed less necessary for them despite the novelty of women's educational gains. With time, however, attention to wider inculcation of domestic emphases gained ground, spurred not only by conservatives but also by progressives who hoped to protect working women from exploitation and who worried about the quality of Japanese child-rearing. It was in this vein that, as late as 1937, staff members of the Tokyo Higher Normal School for Women put out educational materials stressing that "home life occupies, and has occupied throughout the ages, the most important sphere in the life of the Japanese woman. It will do so tomorrow, and for all the days to come." Adding that this goal must orient education for women, along with subsidiary attention to other "social roles," the materials noted that "this is a special Japanese characteristic, for our people have unified love of country with love of home."

The special attitudes toward women's education spilled over into the perception of women teachers. Links between women and men teachers were much less developed than in France (where many teachers were unionized in common) or the United States (where coeducation was extensive). Women teachers continued to gain ground in Japan, particularly at the primary level, if only because they accepted low salaries and inferior assignments; but their numbers lagged behind those in Western countries. A 1920 survey of male teachers praised women's ability to follow orders and deal with detail; but the men worried about women's presumed inability to do research, administrative ineptitude, and undue affection toward children. The steady increase of women teachers was thus also widely lamented, even by women convinced that their gender should remain in the home.

Japan's basic educational structure, as it developed around 1900, presented a number of important features. Coverage was one, as nearly universal participation was being achieved; this had, among other things, the predictable result of virtually 100 percent literacy among both men and women in the younger generations—another massive achievement in a short time. Commitment to education showed in the sheer amount of attention the government paid to the subject (including, of course, its intense debates about goals). It showed also in an unusually long school year, running more than two hundred days, at least in principle. Education was serious business. Styles of teaching emphasized rote learning, particularly in the primary grades. Students needed certain skills; they

Debating the Past
Individualism and Japanese Education

One of the standard judgments about Japanese education involves its effort to substitute collective identities for individualism, in its version of moral training. Plausible arguments that not only Confucianism but also Japanese feudalism promoted group loyalties, which were then transferred to and reinforced by modern education, underlie this approach. Japanese officials, from the 1880s onward, were explicit about their distaste for the individualism they saw in Western school systems and about their insistence on a national alternative. Other Japanese comments, often from people more sympathetic to the West, reflected a sense that the schools did in fact constrain individual identities. Thus a Japanese feminist, Shidzue Ishimoto, looking back on her schooling early in the twentieth century, described "the most agonizing maze of rules" involved in the elaborate training in manners and memorization. She called her education "a most circumscribed way of living." Western historians and observers have been even more systematic in their often critical comments about Japanese antiindividualism. American occupation forces after World War II used terms like "lack of autonomy," "rote learning," and lack of attention to the needs of the child, claiming that authoritarian pressure increased during the war to the extent that schools "frequently resembled small military installations."

Clearly, the evidence mounts, requiring careful assessment of individual experiences in Japanese schools. But a few cautions are in order. Was Japanese education really so uniform and so structured that individualism would necessarily be crushed? Would a peasant, or a girl, gaining education for the first time, even amid strong group pressures, not also gain some possibility of new individual awareness? Certainly, autobiographies more commonly mention the excitement of going to school than the confining effects. The frequent experience of upward mobility through education in Japan and the intensely competitive examinations also contain complexities, for both emphasized individual achievement. The balance between individual and group identity may well have been distinctive in Japan, but despite the frequent characterizations of Japanese group-mindedness the individual element cannot be neglected.

There is also the problem of the comparative standard. Many comments on Japanese education (including some by Western-minded reformers) imply that individualism in the West is easily identified.

How did Western schools promote individualism, as they were actually conducted? Did school discipline (with often harsher physical punishments than in Japan), moral and sanitary regulations, teacher attitudes, and methods of learning clearly promote the individualism that educators in France and the United States undeniably boasted of? What were the actual differences between individual and group identities in Western compared with Japanese school systems? Do we need a more subtle comparative approach?

needed discipline; they should be urged to avoid unduly independent inquiry, which might smack of foreign-style individualism. Teachers, who themselves had little voice over subject matter, set students to memorizing vocabulary (a difficult task in Japan because of the use of Chinese words and characters) as well as factual material in geography and history. Textbooks prevailed, and libraries were typically limited. Examinations, vital for advancement, stressed factual retention, reinforcing the overall emphasis on memory and repetition. Deep respect for the teacher's authority reflected the kinds of values Japanese education was meant to instill.

Higher education for men formed the final piece in the Japanese educational pattern before World War I, and again there were complexities. Some commitment to open access warred with the sheer cost of advanced training and a strong elitist tradition. Many of the same debates that occurred at the primary level played out in higher education as well between the 1870s and the 1890s; the parallelism was not surprising since the Japanese were trying to create a single basic system.

A utilitarian, antitraditional emphasis dominated the approach to higher education during the 1870s, under the influence of Westernizers like Yukichi Fukuzawa. The purpose of education was practical, not ethical, designed to provide new technical competencies for Japanese society and the possibility of personal advancement for individuals. Fukuzawa and others urged "enlightenment," as opposed to what they saw as the older, Confucian approach: "Learning does not mean useless accomplishments, such as knowing strange words, or reading old and difficult texts, or enjoying and writing poetry." Even the 1872 Education Code picked up these sentiments, criticizing the samurai because they "indulged in poetry, empty reasoning, and idle discussions, and their dissertations, while not lacking in elegance, were seldom applicable to life." The code assumed that secondary and university education should be open to talent, stimulating individuals to improve their economic and social positions; hence rigorous competitive examinations were designed to determine admissions beyond the compulsory primary level.

This trajectory encountered numerous obstacles. The government was able to found only one university, in Tokyo, before 1897, which hardly met the national demand. A number of private colleges and technical schools partially filled the gap, but the results were haphazard and only the prestigious Tokyo institution—with an enrollment of merely 340 students by 1880—really assured access to top government jobs. Even at the secondary level, the practical emphasis required massive use of European and American teachers, who paid scant attention to ethics. Many ambitious young people, including provincial samurai, sought access to the new training, but they were often unruly and, in government eyes, politically dangerous. Classrooms were crowded, relations with foreign teachers tense. An atmosphere of disorientation prevailed because of poor facilities, lack of collective purpose, and the strangeness of the new approach. Narrow ambition was often openly touted, as against not only moral standards but also rounded training. The Tokyo English Academy (one of many foreign-language preparatory schools) vaunted this expediency in 1875: "What the student desires most is to graduate as quickly as possible so that he may move on to the various technical fields in the university. Hence, this school should . . . encourage and advance career ambitions." In the context of Japanese traditions, this bald ambition was too much to accept. Furthermore, foreign teachers too often instilled mere parroting of English or German phrases in place of any real understanding. By the 1880s, calls for reform began to multiply, for the goal of material progress seemed inadequate. Police started to break up student meetings, while a broader effort to instill a common ethic of responsibility in the group being trained as a future elite gradually took shape.

Initial conservative reformers often focused on individual secondary schools, seeking, as one put it, to regain "the virtues of loyalty, filial piety, honor and duty, which had been cultivated for several centuries. . . . If today we want to develop moral education on national principles, we should take the former education as our model." Moral training was crucial.

Beyond changes in individual schools, which included reinstating traditional literature and philosophy taught by Japanese, the Ministry of Education began to replace foreign faculty and break from "exclusive dependence on Western teaching methods." A regulation of 1881 defined secondary education as "the obligation of those who are placed above the middle level [of society]." Innovations continued, including extensive instruction in English (along with Chinese and, sometimes, German). This was elite education, very different from the strictly Japanese language attainments of the primary school majority, but it was not a return to the old samurai approach. At the same time, better regulation of student life and new attention to physical fitness sought to bring greater order to the students themselves. Under Arinori Mori, minister of education between 1885 and 1889, this rebalancing was solidified at the national level. Education for "individual success" was redirected to training for "national interest." The hierarchy in the Japanese system was reemphasized: primary schools were designed to provide training so that the young would "understand their duties as Japanese subjects," whereas secondary and higher schools were intended to educate "gentlemen."

The Middle School Ordinance of 1886 divided secondary schooling into a five-year ordinary school, for students age twelve to seventeen, and a more prestigious higher middle school for students age seventeen to twenty. While the lower tier was locally funded and largely practical in orientation, the higher schools were maintained by the national government with a much different orientation. They also continued to charge fees. Graduates might enter business or government directly or go on to university, but in either case they were, in Mori's words, "headed for the upper crust: men worthy of directing the thoughts of the masses . . . the wellspring for those who wield the power of future Japan."

The result was a substantial network of schools beyond the primary level, presenting various options to the minority talented and wealthy enough to afford to pursue them. Normal schools trained teachers, both male and female. Vocational schools focused on technicians and engineers, while the lower-level middle schools produced practical managers. A variety of private schools added to the mix. The higher schools focused above all on the perfection of character, including rigorous inculcation of morality and a "code of respectability." Education officials defined the goal of "cultivating the gentleman" as "a man who, regardless of wealth, status, or occupation, elevates his will-power and keeps his thoughts clear and pure." Schools in this category were fenced off, almost monastic in their seclusion from the temptations of the outside world (including females). Students were encouraged to form close bonds with each other, developing institutional loyalties that would translate into a higher "national devotion." School flags and distinctive uniforms and exercises promoted this group spirit. Specialized training in law, medicine, engineering, literature, science, agriculture, or commerce provided some curricular focus, but the emphasis was on liberal arts training based on Japanese and Chinese literature, theoretical science, and literary English and German. Though criticized as being insufficiently practical, this largely humanistic approach fit well with the goals of gentlemanly training. Moderate fees helped discourage the masses, again contributing to the elite orientation of this echelon. As one headmaster put it, "Our school must never be satisfied with the mere pursuit of higher learning; we must always recognize our responsibility to cultivate national spirit through moral training. . . . Our [school] flag inspires us to expose our bodies, if necessary, to cannon smoke and a rain of bullets. It is, therefore, no different from a military flag." Most graduates intended to go on to university, which is where more empirical subjects—particularly law, immensely popular for those desiring government positions—would be encountered, but only after the rigorous group ethic had been formed.

The leaders who shaped the higher school approach had often experienced training in the West, finding it inadequate. One reformer, for example, criticized what he saw as the excessive rationalism of French higher education, which promoted too much political speculation and resultant instability. Far better would be a focus on institutional loyalties and good manners, which would produce a cultivated and coherent upper class.

With all this stratification, access to the higher schools was not reserved for the aristocracy. Examinations provided the key criterion, and students prepared for them zealously. Mere birth did not suffice. Requirements and fees put the higher schools beyond the reach of workers and peasants—in contrast, for example, to the trickle of access possible in France. But people in various ranks of the growing middle classes pressed in. Students with samurai backgrounds represented over half of higher school enrollments still in the early 1890s, but their percentage declined rapidly in favor of the sons of businessmen, rural landlords, and government bureaucrats. The competitive examinations encouraged efforts at personal advancement and mobility, through schools which, ironically, taught many traditional values and the kind of nationalism that urged self-effacement in light of the higher good of the state.

Emphasis on the gentlemanly ideal contributed to the sense of crisis about technical education that emerged in the 1890s. By this point the higher schools were eating up a full third of the budget for the Ministry of Education, which roused some bitter complaints in the Japanese parliament. From one standpoint, a huge investment in a mere 4,500 students, with a philosophy of moral cultivation that had little connection to the nation's productive capacity, was hard to defend. The new information about technical deficiencies that emerged in preparation for the war with China prompted the ministry to pledge new support for applied science and industrial engineering. The Higher School Ordinance of 1894 dealt with this issue, calling for revitalization of technical courses as the core of the higher schools' curriculum. Here, in unusually explicit fashion, was a standard issue in the development of modern education, faced by France and the United States as well. Technical training was increasingly needed, but somehow it did not quite fit expectations of what the real elite of society should know, and the disparity was difficult to resolve. In fact, having sketched a radical, technocratic response, the Japanese immediately pulled back, leaving the higher schools with their moral, liberal arts focus. Technical schools, as in France, were separated into a distinct, somewhat inferior academic track beyond the primary level. Higher school students themselves were manifestly averse to much technical exposure, and the prestige of the schools by this point gave them considerable autonomy from official government directives.

During the years after 1900 the elite secondary and university systems continued to evolve, but along lines by now firmly established. The higher schools developed a growing commitment to some student self-governance, which followed from the idea of building leaders with pronounced group and institutional loyalties. Along with self-government, for example in the dormitories, came frequent intimidation of dissident students, including some tragic hazing operations and even beatings. Gang fights, called "storms," frequently pitted older students against freshmen; attackers, clad only in loincloths and headbands, beat the freshmen with sticks and brooms and poured cold water on them. As one freshman reported, "What a terrible sight it was after the storm! The broken glass was scattered everywhere. . . . My bedding was soaking wet, and certainly

I could not sleep in it that night. My potted plant had been pulled up by the roots, and my friend had had his stomach stepped upon." Some student protest also occurred around 1900, less over political issues than over enforcement of group norms and self-government.

The elite higher schools also developed more formal rituals designed to cement loyalty to the group. Physical training blossomed into a variety of organized sports. Japanese higher schools resembled American schools in aspects of their sports enthusiasms. Exercise was held to be good in itself, and the idea of team spirit may have received even more attention in Japan than in the United States. But there was a similar sense that sports could serve a vital role in moral training and the formation of character—"uniting the public heart," as one educational authority put it. Higher schools even developed baseball teams, having copied the sport from American visitors. In 1896 to the great delight of the Japanese, one school administered a series of one-sided defeats on an American team that even included some visiting sailors.

If elements of the elite atmosphere suggested features of American higher education in the same period—the sports, camaraderie, and superior attitudes of the leading private universities in New England, for example, along with devotion to the moral values of the liberal arts—the hierarchical structure of the Japanese system was more similar to the French. Only about 10 percent of the boys graduating from primary school tried for any higher education. Moving from the basic middle school to the higher school was even more difficult, as there were places for only about 7 percent of all graduates. Finally, about half of the higher school graduates could find their way into the main, imperial universities (a total of at most 3 percent of the total population in the age group). Even among the universities there was a pecking order; like the *grandes écoles* in Paris, the universities of Tokyo and Kyoto, particularly their law faculties, constituted the pinnacle of success; other options were distinctly less valued. Of course there were some circumventions, like private schools or the possibility of studying abroad, that picked up a bit of the slack. But competition for the brightest opportunities was fierce, forcing rigorous study in preparation for the decisive examinations at each stage of the process. To be sure, failed examinations could be retaken by the higher school students—one reward of elite status—but getting into the higher schools in the first place was an unbuffered challenge. The result—again as in France, but supplemented by the special rituals that created even more group solidarity in Japan—was the formation of a proud, easily identified national leadership group, based on educational performance. For, by 1900, once a man entered a leading university, he was virtually assured a top government post. It took a bit of time, given the initial prominence of older samurai and even some self-made business magnates, but increasingly education shaped the Japanese upper class. In 1903, only about 20 percent of the national elite came from the ranks of university graduates; by 1938 the figure had reached 39 percent, and it was 50 percent and rising by 1941. By 1964, as the process continued, 83 percent of the national elite came through the competitive educational route, displacing traditional aristocrats and landowners unless they, too, met the educational challenge. Again as in France, schooling, mobility, and social structure increasingly intertwined.

MOBILIZING THE SYSTEM, 1920–1945

While key educational debates seemed resolved by around 1900, as the basic school structure and definitions of goals were achieved in Japan, important rebalancing occurred during the difficult years between the world wars, and then again as a result of Japanese defeat. These in a sense completed the establishment of a viable framework, though only after several revealing twists and turns.

The most obvious development in the 1920s and 1930s was the insertion of increasingly strident nationalism into the school system at all levels. Japanese leaders, already concerned about Western influence, grew increasingly resentful of the West after the turmoil of World War I and the peace settlement and as aspects of Western culture such as fashions and cosmetics gained new influence. There was rising concern also about popular loyalties, after the establishment of universal male suffrage in 1925. A conservative leadership sought new ways to ensure mass obedience even as rapid economic change, and considerable dislocation, continued. For all these reasons, more vigorous authoritarian groups gained ground, and they saw education as a vital target. Many historians have argued that Japanese culture lagged well behind the pace of social and economic change, which inevitably made education a crucial battleground. (This could be an issue in Western education as well, but it is possible that Western culture moved more smoothly in tandem with other developments such as advancing industrialization.) The Japanese had already established the importance of moral and political indoctrination in the schools, so it was small wonder that education was again singled out. As one group proclaimed, "We plan a fundamental reform of the present educational system, which is copied from those of Europe and America; we shall set up a basic study of a national education with origins in our national polity. Thereby we anticipate the further development and improvement of the wisdom and virtue of the [Japanese] race."

More than a nationalist surge was involved. The Ministry of Education had attempted, under the impact of World War I, to improve science teaching, even in the primary schools. During the earlier conservative reaction in the 1880s, science courses had become highly generalized at this level, with injunctions to teach children some facts about nature and purely useful knowledge, rather than larger, rationalistic scientific principles. Rising levels of military and industrial competition made it clear that more focused training in physics and chemistry was needed. A 1917 directive urged improvement in teaching methods, "with particular emphasis placed on experiments. Excessive adherence to method and indoctrination should be avoided as much as possible; efforts should be focused rather on . . . the cultivation of a creative and spontaneous spirit." New needs, in other words, were promoting innovations in the direction of critical thinking and apparent Westernization.

As in the nineteenth century, conservative reaction was vigorous, though tempered with pragmatism. In contrast to educational policy in Nazi Germany, there was no effort to fight science and technology. Rather, these were to be combined with a new apotheosis of the "Japanese spirit," including emperor worship, nationalism, and, increasingly, militarism. Science, urged many policymakers, could be combined with Confucian traditions in linking Western rationalism with spirituality, or with what a 1937 report called "the culture peculiar to Japan."

In 1937, a Bureau of Educational Reform was established, with responsibility, among other things, for what was called "thought supervision planning." The government took over direction of activities associated with education, such as scout groups. Textbooks were standardized even further, with emphasis on absolute loyalty to the state. Military training was combined with gymnastics courses: "military arts in the physical training course shall be cultivated for the purpose of training both body and mind and also of fostering the samurai spirit." Emphasis on women's family obligations, already vigorously ensconced in lessons and reading materials, was also intensified. Regulations in 1941 stressed that the goals of women's schooling were to produce "good wives and wise mothers."

Adult courses were set up "in order to elevate the character of mothers who take charge of the important duties of the house and to foster their just and rightful views." Yet with this combination of traditionalism and new nationalism, attention to science persisted, leaving the Japanese not only exceptionally well educated, by world standards, but well attuned to technical requirements. Time allocated to science courses slipped just slightly, but acknowledgment of the importance of Western science was maintained. As the 1941 regulations noted, "a faculty for analytical and logical observation must be fostered. . . . Common sense regarding national defense must be cultivated by drawing attention to the fact that national defense depends a great deal on scientific progress." A mixture of traditional, Western-derived, and military purposes kept Japanese commitment to education strong. Until military spending began to escalate, in fact, in 1932, Japanese expenditure on schooling long surpassed the outlays for the army and navy.

Observers inside and outside Japan have often tried to analyze how such a well-educated population could allow its political system to be taken over by militarists, its school system bent (though not entirely converted) to warlike, authoritarian ends. Obviously, Japan was not unique in this pattern; Germany, the West's best-educated nation, underwent an even more startling transformation in the same period. But specifically Japanese patterns played a role. The effort to use education both to introduce foreign ideas, particularly but not exclusively associated with science, and to instill a sense of tradition and group loyalty left the system vulnerable to further nationalist manipulation. The role of the state in centralizing the school system helped generate rapid educational progress but also, inevitably, enhanced lessons about state authority— in contrast to more mixed systems in places like the United States and even France that qualified the state's more sweeping claims. The need to borrow scientific knowledge from the West (and often to learn it partly in a Western language) and the emphasis on factual testing and drill discouraged, though they did not prevent, critical thinking. Education risked becoming merely a matter of passing memorization examinations. Vivid divisions between the successful elite and the more clearly manipulated masses, though not unique to Japan, also promoted tolerance for the conversion of moralization efforts into educational preparations for war. During the 1920s and 1930s, the military aspects of physical training in the higher schools increased—often to the delight of the elite students, who found them "great fun"—even as propaganda and exercise combined at the primary level.

No education system can resist the demands of modern, total warfare, so the embrace between Japanese schools and the military effort of World War II should not be exaggerated. Nevertheless, schools and militarism did mix, and then Japan lost. Inevitably, the education system was thoroughly reevaluated, by the Japanese themselves as well as the American occupation forces, after 1945.

The resultant reforms emphasized several major changes as they were worked out mainly by 1949. First, textbooks were thoroughly revised to eliminate militaristic and nationalistic references and invocations of emperor worship. Similar changes occurred in teacher training materials; the reformers targeted such notions as "total subservience of individual toward the state." Local parent-teacher associations were formed, becoming more active than their American counterparts and giving women new public roles. Exclusions at the higher educational level were attacked, as the reformers sought to extend the egalitarian principles already present in the primary system. Secondary and higher schools were made coeducational to bring fuller access to women. The cherished higher schools, that product of the 1880s synthesis, were abolished, extended into a much greater number of four-year universities (some, to be sure, of dubious prestige). American phasing was introduced: six years of primary school, three years of middle school, three years of secondary school, and then, for a small but growing minority, the possibility of university. Obligatory schooling was extended to nine years, and secondary schooling was to be open to as many as wished to attend—a figure that rapidly became nearly universal.

The results of these final formative changes modified but did not fully revolutionize Japanese schooling. Some of the changes built on trends already at work. The people's commitment to education itself was well established. Attending for nine years (at least) rather than six caused no problems. Secondary education had become increasingly open to non-samurai, even during the 1930s. Losing the higher schools was a major shift, but the idea of educational access made sense to Japanese in many groups. The basic educational challenge of combining Western with Japanese notions was redefined by the pressures of American occupation, but it was by no means new. At the same time, Americanization was inherently incomplete. Merely extending coeducation, for example, did not mean that education for women in Japan came to mean the same thing as in the West. Greater attendance at universities actually increased the pressure to study for examinations and pass competitive tests—more of the population was involved than ever before. Further, the fact that reforms came under foreign guidance gave the Japanese government the opportunity, by the 1950s, to undo some of the American-sponsored changes, with popular support, confirming centralized control over the basic system in the process. What the postwar changes and counterthrusts did, in essence, was complete the construction of Japan's modern system, much of which had already been built, both before the distortions of militarism and even during the years of extreme nationalism.

There was a final irony. American-aided reform pressures, combined with earlier developments, produced one of the world's most meritocratic educational systems. American occupiers urged principles of equal opportunity that they firmly believed in but that by no means constituted reality back home. Japan already had an egalitarian, centralized primary setup; it was already committed to competitive tests for the higher reaches of the system. Now, with the expansion and greater openness of the secondary system, accidents of birth counted for less, in education and through education in social mobility, than ever before—and less than in the United States.

Using the Sources: Japanese Education

RECOLLECTIONS OF SCHOOLING IN JAPAN IN THE MEIJI DECADES

The following passages (two from autobiographies, one from a novel about Meiji Japan) offer insights into the ways students experienced education at the turn of the century. They speak to levels of commitment, the role of social class, the nature of teaching, and the mixture of Western and traditional subjects—all vital issues in the history of Japanese education. Each passage is atypical in some respects—the one by Tokutomi deals with a Christian secondary school, for example—and the variety of settings is a useful reminder that even Japanese education was hardly uniform. While drill and memorization are mentioned, for example, they are not stressed as much as general accounts of Japanese teaching methods might suggest. The first selection is from a memoir by Jun'ichiro Tanizaki (1886–1985), one of Japan's leading twentieth-century authors. The second, by Kenjiro Tokutomi, is from a novel originally published in 1901 and modeled after the work of Charles Dickens. It was one of the most popular novels in modern Japan, based on the author's own boyhood in the 1880s and 1890s. The recollections of Baroness Ishimoto in the third selection suggest some special features of education for women. But her school was one reserved for peeresses, set up by the emperor in the 1870s to help preserve the traditional upper class. Ishimoto, though later a leading feminist, was from a samurai family. It is inevitable that memoirs disproportionately reflect special attainments or positions; but how can they be used to suggest some of the more widely shared features of Japanese schooling? Ishimoto's memoir was written after World War II, but it evokes schooling early in the twentieth century; the author was born in 1887.

None of these passages is comparative, but they certainly evoke comparative issues. What was distinctly Japanese about the school experiences they suggest? How much do these accounts differ from what one would expect to find in Western recollections or reconstructions from the same period? How, for example, does the rural account compare with a French peasant's recollections? The issue of Westernization is crucial: How much was "Western" about the Japanese schools, and how much — including the need to assimilate some very unfamiliar ways, but also the need to protect a special identity — was distinctively Japanese?

JUN'ICHIRO TANIZAKI

Recollections about Primary School in the 1890s

The teachers usually wore Western-style suits; but one sometimes saw Japanese dress too. They wore their Western clothes very badly; they might have stiffly starched collars and cuffs, but as likely as not there would be a gap between their vests and their trousers revealing an expanse of white shirt. Many of the teachers dispensed with suspenders or leather belts and wore instead a narrow waistband of blue, white, or purple crepe de Chine; and some wore traditional sandals instead of shoes. Mr. Inaba

Jun'ichiro Tanizaki, *Childhood Years: A Memoir,* translated by Paul McCarthy (Tokyo: Kodansha International, 1988), 39–40, 146–48.

was more careful in his dress than many, but he, too, often combined a suit with sandals. (I remember he lived in Tamachi, Shiba, preferring to walk all the way to school each morning rather than take the horse-drawn trolley available from Shimbashi.) He liked Japanese clothing, and in later years wore it more and more often. He wore a *hakama* divided skirt very correctly over a silk kimono; but I never saw him in a formal *haori* coat. Whenever he appeared in Japanese dress, he had sandals on his bare feet, which were rather larger than average—perhaps ten or ten and a half inches long. In fact, the little toe of each foot projected beyond the sandal's rim and onto the road surface. . . .

The students all wore Japanese dress. The boys' kimonos had to be narrow-sleeved, though *haori* coats could be worn over them. In Shitamachi schools at any rate, *hakama* skirts were not part of the students' outfit. The girls wore nothing over their kimonos while the boys had a kind of apron to protect their clothes from dirt. Japan was not as sanitary a place then as it is now, and there were often many children with discharges from the ears and runny noses. (There were actually some teachers who would suck up the mucous running from their pupils' noses!) The boys' kimonos were for the most part made of cotton, either solid dark blue or with a splash, with sons of richer families wearing silk, including especially thin silk in the summer. . . .

Mr. Inaba was no longer the inexperienced teacher fresh from normal school who failed me four years before, but he was still young and energetic, full of enthusiasm and with many dreams he hoped to fulfill. . . .

The range of his reading was very broad, from the works of ancient Chinese sages and Buddhist (particularly Zen) philosophical texts, to Japanese poetry and romances from the ninth century on. He brought slim Japanese-style volumes that slipped easily inside his kimono, or occasionally just ten or twenty sheets of rice paper on which he had carefully copied in brush and ink passages from the ancients that he particularly admired. . . .

From what I observed, Mr. Inaba's knowledge of classical Chinese was considerably greater than that of the average primary-school teacher of those days—and standards then were of course higher than they are today in the same subject. He was apparently not very good at English, the normal vehicle for the acquisition of knowledge of Western culture at the time; but there were doubtless partial translations of, and introductions to, Plato and Schopenhauer available in Japanese, and he must have come to know those philosophers through such secondary or tertiary sources.

What he most frequently talked of, though, and with most fervor, were Buddhist works and ideas. . . .

With a teacher like Mr. Inaba, the pedagogical method used in the classroom was by no means standardized or formalistic. He believed in free, living education and refused to be bound by textbooks, taking advantage of whatever opportunities presented themselves from day to day; and this was true not only in the hours of moral-ethical instruction, but also during reading and history lessons as well. As a result, he would occasionally go off on a tangent totally unrelated to the textbook or curriculum. One winter day, for example, as the lesson was about to begin, the weather suddenly turned much colder and large flakes of snow began swiftly to fall. Mr. Inaba immediately stood up and, taking a piece of chalk, wrote on the blackboard that well-known Japanese poem:

Snow and sleet and hail are separate
Yet, melting,
All become water
Flowing in the valley stream.

KENJIRO TOKUTOMI

On Meiji Schools

1901

I went on attending primary school as before. The school was a small thatched building, standing among paddy-fields about half a mile from our cottage. It was not much different from the old temple-schools of feudal times, our valley being so out of the way; though we did have slates, along with old-fashioned fixed ink-slabs. In summer we went to school while it was still dark and practiced writing by candle-light—Morning Penmanship, it was called—while in winter, as there was no heating in the school building, at the beginning of term each of us would carry his own tiny charcoal brazier with him to school, and keep it there till the holidays. That's how primitive things were then. Not only were we remote from the capital; the walls of our valley rose steeply on every side, as if we were living on the bottom of a giant stone bowl. If it was to reach us at all, modern civilization had to sweat its way over the mountain passes in straw sandals—so it was pretty slow in coming, like the doctor who doesn't hurry to a poor patient. As for the Tokyo newspapers, only one copy penetrated to our town, one single paper for the whole community. The thirty or forty citizens who formed the local "intelligentsia" passed it round among themselves from house to house, with the result that this globe of ours had rolled round sixty

Kenjiro Tokutomi, *Footprints in the Snow,* translated by Kenneth Strong (Tokyo: Charles E. Tuttle, 1970), 59–60, 181–82.

times or more before it reached the last reader—long enough for quick-tempered Frenchmen to stage half-a-dozen revolutions, or throw out twice that number of cabinets. Consequently we were not very well up in the way things were going on in the country as a whole. But such was the constant stream of reforms and changes of all kinds in those early years of the Emperor Meiji's reign that even with us there was always a feeling of instability in the air.

At school we were first divided into ten graded classes, then into six, then finally into three—upper, middle, and lower. As a result we found ourselves taking the same examinations over and over again—even in some cases graduating several times over from the same school. We would start off with a Wordbook and a First Geography Reader, but the textbooks would change abruptly two or three times a year, and some of the poorer children had to give up school altogether because they couldn't afford so many books. I hated arithmetic and calligraphy, but got on splendidly with history, composition, geography, not to mention general mischief, managing to keep at the top of the class in spite of losing marks on my sums and copy-writing. Looking back from this distance, I can see the teacher must have let me off lightly now and then (he was a fine old fellow, short-sighted and devoted to his pipe; he could not have been kinder to me, though everything he taught was wrong. Lenience was his creed, and Masumi, I think, his name—Teacher Masumi, that's it). I can't have done too badly, though. An Inspector from Tokyo who was visiting schools all over the country praised me when he came to our school (you can't imagine what a heroic figure this visitor from the capital seemed in our eyes—and how Teacher Masumi must have trembled as he took him around!). I was clever, they said, as well as being a rich man's son; and at school I gave myself airs accordingly. . . .

The first sight I had of the College when I arrived from Uwajima nearly knocked me over. (I was still a country bumpkin, don't forget.) The site, to start with: up in the foothills, away from Kobe City proper, with the Rokko mountains behind and over to the right the panorama of Awaji Island and the ships strung out across the Bay of Osaka, like toy boats on a tray—this was overwhelming enough, and on top of it the fine array of buildings: classroom block, dormitories, dining-hall, and chapel, all standing on their own—it struck me as much too good for a school. Later, when a fellow-student assured me Doshisha College in Kyoto was more splendid still, and Tokyo University many times grander even than Doshisha, I could only gape. (It didn't take much to set me gaping in those days!) The students who studied in such surroundings must all be paragons, the teachers great scholars, the Principal a genius of learning and wisdom. A hick like myself would never have a chance, I told myself in despair before I set foot on the campus.

But thanks to the Reverend Shizu's letters of introduction, both the Secretary and Professor Shimizu treated me very kindly. The dreaded examinations too, including my special bogey, the sweat-producing algebra, I managed to survive with an average of seventy per cent, which I thought wasn't doing too badly, though I say it who shouldn't. It was English (conversation, not reading) I was most afraid of. Miracles do happen, though. I was sitting waiting in the examination room when the door opened portentously. Enter the foreign examiner.

Ohs and Ahs of astonishment from us both, and we shook hands, the examination (for the moment) forgotten. For my examiner was none other than Mr. Wilkie Brown, for whom I had so stumblingly interpreted at Uwajima Police Station. A coincidence worthy of a novel! After we had talked about how I came to be trying for the College, he went on to the examination proper; but meeting him so unexpectedly had given me such courage, I rolled out the most unpronounceable words without a tremor. A poor enough performance it must have been, even so, but he took pity and gave me a generous 7—and capped it with an invitation to come to his home for evening conversation practice twice a week after term began. I was truly grateful for such kindness.

So much for the examination. I paid my registration and first month's tuition and board, and was entered in the third year. The Secretary found me a job as a cleaner in the classroom block, with two rooms to swab out each day, one before school and one after.

BARONESS SHIDZUE ISHIMOTO
Women's Upper-class Schooling

At the age of twelve [in 1909], I finished the primary course in the Peeresses' School and entered the high school in the same compound, which was supposed to correspond to the boys' middle school. In reality there was a distinct difference between the two in the standard and character of learning. Boys were taught and trained to be "great personalities"; girls were first and foremost taught to become obedient wives, good mothers, and loyal guardians of the family system. This discrimination was not calculated to encourage girls to independent thinking. Women were not expected to be pioneers in any enterprise.

The five years' education in the girls' high school was looked upon as the

Baroness Shidzue Ishimoto, *Facing Two Ways: The Story of My Life* (Stanford: Stanford University Press, 1984), 53–56.

Figure 10.   Training in calligraphy in a girls' high school around 1900.

grand finishing course, so that few girls remained at school for postgraduate work. Arithmetic, algebra, Euclid, physics, chemistry, national and foreign geography and history were taught, but we were only allowed to peep into the world of science and did not spend much time or energy on any one of the more approved subjects. Japanese literature, both classical and modern, covered the largest part of class assignments, for as a matter of fact well-educated Japanese citizens had to learn at least four or five thousand Chinese ideographs, most of which are pronounced in three or four different ways and written in at least three styles. A vast amount of attention had to be bestowed on these. Besides this strenuous memory work, penmanship, painting, drawing, music, sewing, embroidery, and cooking were taught in both the Western and the Japanese manner. The girls were kept quite busy.

Even penmanship for the Japanese is no trifle. A woman cannot marry into a good family if she reveals a sign of low breeding in her handwriting. And men will experience disadvantages in getting positions unless their handwriting is good. . . .

At school, therefore, we spent hours and hours bending over our desks and white sheets of rice paper, in our hands big and small brushes which we dipped in India ink, writing Japanese characters, stroke by stroke, trying to present graceful and dignified ideographs. . . .

Another lesson, rather unpopular among the girls, was ethics. In this class we were taught that loyalty and filial piety are the chief and fundamental morals, that our concern should be directed to expressing our sense of gratitude to the Emperor as obedient subjects, and to parents and ancestors as faithful daughters. At the Peeresses' School, the girls recited these precepts every morning before the lessons, saying, "We girls in the Peeresses' School shall respect the imperial family, and try to be model subjects loyal to the Emperor and the Empress. . . ."

This ethics class at our school was relied upon for character building. Its substance lay in the Confucian teachings emphasizing loyalty to the ruler and duty to parents. We were brought up to think frequently of our obligations to our elders and to the Emperor. We were taught what "we ought to do and to be," but never did we discuss questions of personal freedom and independent thinking or the right to be guided by one's own conscience. A familiar proverb said "Good medicine is bitter to the mouth: so is good advice to naughty ears." Naturally the girls disliked these preachings, pounding again and again on tired ears.

To reinforce these moral obligations we were given lessons in "manners and etiquette," that we might be disciplined in modesty and reverence. Our school had a separate house, built in pure Japanese style, for instruction in etiquette. It had a mat floor and an alcove in which the essential ornaments were placed in strict accordance with the prescriptions of the Ogasawara School of Etiquette. We took off our shoes before we entered the house and sat rigid on the mats. We learned formality of every possible kind, such as wedding and funeral ceremonies in both Shinto and Buddhist styles, the reception of guests, and entertaining or being entertained at table. The complexity of this instruction was such that we had to practice, for instance, sitting and standing positions, and three forms of bowing: to elders, to equals, and to inferiors.

INTENSIFIED NATIONALISM IN JAPANESE SCHOOLS, 1930s

The movement toward nationalism in Japanese education reached its apogee with the publication by the Ministry of Education of *Fundamentals of Our National Polity* (Kokutai no hongi) in 1937. This short work, which eventually sold more than two million copies, was designed to set the ideological course for the Japanese people, beginning with the schools as the cornerstone of national culture. Study groups were formed to discuss its content, schoolteachers were given special commentaries, and the government made a determined effort to reach ideological uniformity under its rubric.

Figure 11. Japanese children take turns every morning hoisting the national flag (1930s).

What problems with Western influences was this document designed to resolve? How was Japanese nationalism defined, and how much change was involved from earlier educational content in Japan (also compare chap. 8, where nationalism in postwar Japan is discussed). All modern nations used education for nationalist indoctrination; how did the Japanese approach resemble, and how did it differ from, that of the United States or France? How did the Japanese effort to use nationalism to counterbalance individualism compare with the uses of nationalism in the West? The rhetoric was clearly different, as Japanese nationalism was presented as an antidote to Westernisms; but were the real tensions so distinctive?

MINISTRY OF EDUCATION

Fundamentals of Our National Polity

1937

The various ideological and social evils of present-day Japan are the results of ignoring the fundamental and running after the trivial, of lack of judgment, and a failure to digest things thoroughly; and this is due to the fact that since the days of Meiji so many aspects of European and American culture, systems, and learning have been imported, and that, too rapidly. As a matter of fact, the foreign ideologies imported into our country are in the main ideologies of the Enlightenment that have come down from the eighteenth century, or extensions of them. The views of the world and of life that form the basis of these ideologies are a rationalism and a positivism, lacking in historical views, which on the one hand lay the highest value on, and assert the liberty and equality of, individuals, and on the other hand lay value on a world by nature abstract, transcending nations and races. . . .

Yet even in the Occident, where individualism has formed the basis of their ideas, when it has come to communism, they have found it unacceptable; so that now they are about to do away with their traditional individualism, and this has led to the rise of totalitarianism and nationalism and to the springing up of Fascism and Nazism. That is, it can be said that both in the Occident and in our country the deadlock of individualism has led alike to a season of ideological and social confusion and crisis. . . .

Loyalty means to reverence the emperor as [our] pivot and to follow him implicitly. By implicit obedience is meant casting ourselves aside and serving the emperor intently. To walk this Way of loyalty is the sole Way in which we subjects may "live," and the fountainhead of all energy. Hence, offering our lives for the sake of the emperor does not mean so-called self-sacrifice, but the casting aside of our little selves to live under his august grace and the enhancing of the genuine life of the people of a State. . . .

In our country filial piety is a Way of the highest importance. Filial piety originates with one's family as its basis, and in its larger sense has the nation for its foundation. Filial piety directly has for its object one's parents, but in its relationship toward the emperor finds a place within loyalty. . . .

Ryusaku Tsunoda, W. T. de Pary, and Donald Keene, eds., *Sources of Japanese Tradition* (New York: Columbia University Press, 1958), 2:278–88.

The life of a family in our country is not confined to the present life of a household of parents and children, but beginning with the distant ancestors, is carried on eternally by the descendants. The present life of a family is a link between the past and the future, and while it carries over and develops the objectives of the ancestors, it hands them over to its descendants. . . .

And then, this harmony is clearly seen also in our nation's martial spirit. Our nation is one that holds *bushido* in high regard, and there are shrines deifying warlike spirits. . . . But this martial spirit is not [a thing that exists] for the sake of itself but for the sake of peace, and is what may be called a sacred martial spirit. Our martial spirit does not have for its objective the killing of men, but the giving of life to men. This martial spirit is that which tries to give life to all things, and is not that which destroys. That is to say, it is a strife which has peace at its basis with a promise to raise and to develop; and it gives life to things through its strife. Here lies the martial spirit of our nation. War, in this sense, is not by any means intended for the destruction, overpowering, or subjugation of others; and it should be a thing for the bringing about of great harmony, that is, peace, doing the work of creation by following the Way. . . .

To put it in a nutshell, while the strong points of Occidental learning and concepts lie in their analytical and intellectual qualities, the characteristics of Oriental learning and concepts lie in their intuitive and aesthetic qualities. These are natural tendencies that arise through racial and historical differences; and when we compare them with our national spirit, concepts, or mode of living, we cannot help recognizing further great and fundamental differences. Our nation has in the past imported, assimilated, and sublimated Chinese and Indian ideologies, and has therewith supported the Imperial Way, making possible the establishment of an original culture based on her national polity. . . .

The same thing holds true in the case of education. Since the Meiji Restoration our nation has adapted the good elements of the advanced education seen among European and American nations, and has exerted efforts to set up an educational system and materials for teaching. The nation has also assimilated on a wide scale the scholarship of the West, not only in the fields of natural science, but of the mental sciences, and has thus striven to see progress made in our scholastic pursuits and to make education more popular. . . . However, at the same time, through the infiltration of individualistic concepts, both scholastic pursuits and education have tended to be taken up with a world in which the intellect alone mattered, and which was isolated from historical and actual life; so that both intellectual and moral culture drifted into tendencies in which the goal was the freedom of man, who had become an abstract being, and the perfecting of the individual man. At the same time, these scholastic pursuits and education fell into separate parts, so that they gradually lost their synthetic coherence and concreteness. In order to correct these tendencies, the only course open to us is to clarify the true nature of our national polity, which is at the very source of our education, and to strive to clear up individualistic and abstract ideas. . . .

Our present mission as a people is to build up a new Japanese culture by adopting and sublimating Western cultures with our national polity as the basis, and to contribute spontaneously to the advancement of world culture. Our nation early saw the introduction of Chinese and Indian cultures, and even succeeded in evolving original creations and developments. This was made possible, indeed, by the profound and boundless nature of our national polity; so that the mission of the people to whom it is bequeathed is truly great in its historical significance.

AMERICAN ASSESSMENT OF JAPANESE EDUCATION

The United States occupation of Japan in 1945 provided an extraordinary opportunity for one society to evaluate and revise another society's educational system. American authorities were understandably concerned about the militaristic and ultranationalist content of Japanese education over the preceding two decades, but their concerns reached further. What additional features of Japanese education needed attention, in their judgment? Did they offer a fair assessment of Japan's modern educational history?

The following selection, citing reports of 1945 and 1946, comes from an extensive set of recommendations and assessments issued in 1948. The selection provides answers to the basic questions about the American reform approach and about wider comparative issues as well.

What about the relationship of the American assessments to actual systems in the United States? Did the reformers accurately reflect the way United States education worked, or did they try to force Japan to move further toward ideals that even the United States itself had not managed to realize?

A number of basic reforms were introduced. Given Japanese culture and educational tradition, which of them would have been most likely to encounter resistance? How would you expect Japanese officials to reinstitute some cherished features of their own educational values?

SUPREME COMMANDER FOR THE ALLIED POWERS

Education in the New Japan
1948

"The Japanese government shall remove all obstacles to the revival and strengthening of democratic tendencies among the Japanese people. Freedom of speech, of religion, and of thought, as well as respect for the fundamental human rights, shall be established."
—Potsdam Proclamation, 26 July 1945.

"A system of education should be so organized as to encourage the fullest development of which each individual—boy or girl, man or woman—is capable as an intelligent, responsible, and cooperating member of society. . . . Freedom of inquiry, rather than exclusive memorization of factual knowledge for examination purposes, should be emphasized."
—Report of the United States Education Mission to Japan, (p. 18), 30 March 1946.

"Education should be looked upon as the pursuit of truth, as a preparation for life in a democratic nation, and as a training for the social and political responsibilities which freedom entails. . . . Measures should be taken as rapidly as possible to achieve equality of educational opportunity for all."
—Directive of the Far Eastern Commission, 27 March 1947.

. . . In any long range policies and plans for the democratization of Japan, education necessarily plays a fundamental role. For the implementation of those policies, as far as education is concerned, major responsibility was assigned by the Supreme Commander for the Allied Powers to the Civil Information and Education Section of General Headquarters. . . .

The ideology of militarism and ultranationalism was faithfully mirrored in the school curriculum of the immediately prewar and wartime period. This was especially true of courses in history, geography, morals, music, and physical education. History was exploited in two ways for the accomplishment of this purpose, by treating Japanese legends and mythology

Supreme Commander for the Allied Powers, General Headquarters, Civil Information and Educational Section, Education Division, *Education in the New Japan* (Tokyo: Supreme Commander for the Allied Powers, May 1948), 1:7, 36–37, 39, 189, 191, 387–89.

as if they were history, and by interpreting the facts of history from an ultranationalistic point of view. The morals course, which had long been an important element of the curriculum, was aimed at indoctrinating the student with the principles of the ideology of disciplined subordination to the state, and of the iconography of Japanese tradition. Geography, in its turn, became the study of geopolitics and the justification for overseas expansion. Likewise in the music courses songs were utilized skillfully. From 1941 on, approved music texts were avowedly militaristic, glorifying war and battle. Language, too, was made a study in tradition; the Japanese language was extolled as a medium through which the Imperial and national principles could be understood, a symbol of Japanese spirit and unity.

After 1925, military training had come to absorb more and more of the time devoted to physical education, until eventually that course was almost completely militarized. . . .

The National School Plan [1941] was a clear and frank crystallization of the new philosophy of education. Its avowed purpose was to create an "original educational system" that would train the Japanese "to obey the Imperial Rescript on Education in order to guard and maintain the prosperity of our Imperial Throne" and to eliminate the idea that "the main object of education is to develop individuality." Until the end of the War, educational activities were an implementation of the policies formulated in this plan. . . .

Features of the New Program

The plan of the tentative curriculum . . . eliminates the Japanese traditional approach of organizing children's experiences around knowledge and skills which adults thought children should possess, and centers the program around the interests, needs, and aptitudes of children. It reduces the number of courses, thus making it possible for student energies to be more wisely and effectively expended. Finally it constitutes a real effort on the part of the Ministry of Education fundamentally to change Japanese education.

In addition to listing the program of studies at the various grade levels, the Curriculum Committee reached two decisions which had far-reaching effects for the schools: (1) there would in general be no special courses nor special textbooks for girls; (2) in basic courses (language, social studies, etc.) all types of schools at the same grade level would use the same courses and basic texts. These decisions meant that the complex system of education at the secondary level, which operated undemocratically and discriminated educationally against various types of students, was so modified that those discriminations were eliminated as far as the curriculum was concerned. This in itself constituted a fundamental reform in Japanese education. . . .

A few details of the new program stand out when it is compared with the old. All military subjects have been out of the schools since early in the Occupation. The separate courses in morals, geography, and history which handled subject-matter material without relating it to problems and topics which were meaningful to pupils replaced by an integrated course in social studies. . . . Materials were related to the interests and social activities of the children. The course in Chinese classics, which heretofore was required through five years of the middle schools, was made an elective. It has occupied approximately the position in Japanese education that Latin occupied in the past in American schools. In the new curriculum, work in Chinese classics is available for the student who wants it or needs it but it is not forced upon all upper secondary level students. The course in calligraphy, which was given through the entire school program, has been reduced to two years of fundamentals at the lower secondary level with elective courses in the subject available at other years beyond. While this was a tradition-shattering move, it was justifiable in a curriculum designed for the needs of the children attending school.

Domestic science formerly was required of girls throughout eight of the 11 years in the elementary schools and the girls' high schools. Under the new program it will be required for two years in the elementary school, offered in the new lower secondary school as one of several vocational courses of which each pupil will choose one, and offered as an elective course in the three years of the new upper secondary school. In the lower secondary school it is expected that almost all girls will choose home economics to fulfill the requirement of four hours weekly in a vocational course. Thus the same number of years as before is available if a girl desires a great deal of training in homemaking, but is not required for all these years. Girls who wish to go on to higher education have greater opportunity than heretofore to prepare for advanced work, while girls who wish as much domestic science as possible may obtain the same amount as before.

SUMMARY

What have been the tangible results after two and a half years of the Occupation of Japan by Allied Forces?

1. Ultranationalistic and militaristic elements and influences—personnel, textbooks, curricula—have been removed from the school system. . . .

4. Free compulsory education has been extended from six years to nine years, covering the elementary and lower secondary school periods, thus insuring a greater degree of educational opportunity for all children.

5. Structural reorganization of the entire educational system on a simplified plan of six years of elementary education, six years of secondary education, and four years or more of higher education (6-3-3-4 plan) has been authorized legally as the basic system for the country. . . .

7. Coeducation has been authorized at all levels, affording to girls and young women greatly increased educational opportunities on a basis of equality with those available to boys and young men.

8. Marked decentralization of control of education from national to local governmental units has been achieved and further plans for decentralization are in progress. . . .

17. Extensive revisions of curricula and courses of study have been carried on at all educational levels.

18. Important steps have been taken to democratize administration and supervision and to give administrators and supervisors a consciousness of their obligations and opportunities as educational leaders.

19. Classroom teachers have been given a new vision and stimulus for the development and use of improved teaching methods, emphasizing initiative, originality, and pupil participation.

7

Comparing Schools and Societies: An Analytical Challenge

Not surprisingly, the United States, France, and Japan all ended the formative decades of their educational systems with a number of unanswered questions. Japan's questions were the most obvious as well as the most recent. By the late 1940s, the issues of how to blend new forms with well-established educational interests (some dating from before the Meiji era) were inescapable. Nothing like defeat in war and an extended occupation challenged the United States or, at least to the same extent, France. But France by the 1920s faced unavoidable tensions about the linkage between the mass primary system and the elite secondary and university tracks. The United States had yet fully to confront the gap between professed devotion to educational opportunity and the separate and inferior treatment of most African Americans or, more generally, the challenge of relating universal schooling to the impulse to separate students by social background and ability. All three societies, of course, would also confront further challenges, if only because the requirements of technical competence for a modern labor force steadily escalated.

Yet in dealing with problems and challenges, all three societies relied heavily on the institutions and educational principles established in the formative decades. There is a natural tendency to replicate educational patterns from one generation to the next, because policymakers hearken back to their own schooldays even when they think they are pushing for change. Educational organizations are not necessarily more conservative than other groups, but they often shift gears slowly. Furthermore, each nation had devised an educational system that to some extent corresponded to more basic national institutions and values (or at least those of some key dominant groups). And each nation had achieved considerable educational success, by the early to mid-twentieth century, which

153

additionally reduced the impulse to experiment too radically. Before turning to the most contemporary history and to undeniably important shifts in recent decades, it is time to venture a fuller comparative assessment of the systems that had been formed.

Each modern educational apparatus—in France, the United States, and Japan—presented crucial, distinctive features. It is tempting to seek some national character expressed in and furthered by the schools. Japan's group consciousness, the greater democratic commitment in the United States, and France's centralization and deliberate secularization might provide appropriate labels. There are distinctive national details as well:

— While both France and Japan dealt with minority groups in forming their new educational structures, only the United States faced a situation as complex as the legacy of slavery. The general trend in modern education was toward homogenization of minority groups; this was France's approach to minority languages, and it characterized the American use of schools to inculcate "national" political and family values in immigrant groups. But African Americans, especially in the South, were kept apart. They often sought and gained education, but the emphasis on segregation was unusual, particularly given the nation's democratic rhetoric.

— Japan stood out for its complex grappling with foreign educational values and, ultimately, its particular use of nationalism and emperor worship.

— France alone faced a pitched battle between church and state, yielding its unusually politicized, secular tone by 1900.

— Somewhat more subtly, Americans incorporated a rather unusual culture of childhood in building their nineteenth-century schools. Increasingly convinced that children were innocent, somewhat delicate creatures, middle-class Americans spent more time than their French or Japanese counterparts in trying to ensure appropriate physical space for schools. They pressed harder for modifications of traditional discipline, though all countries gradually reduced corporal punishment. Certainly by the late nineteenth century they were trying to incorporate a wider variety of activities in the schools—dances, sports, extracurricular clubs—in an effort to ensure that education applied to the whole person, not just the academic side, and that children had fun. By the same token, too much school pressure on children probably worried Americans more than was the case elsewhere—hence, among other things, the American avoidance of a rigorous examination system comparable to the French *baccalauréat* or the Japanese hurdles on the way to the higher schools.

A number of stark national differences can be cited. On the whole, however, a more rigorous comparative approach is most fruitful, taking more complex contexts into account and incorporating similar trends as well as contrasts, old and new. When one seeks to make useful comparisons, it is important to avoid sweeping generalizations. The observer must look beneath apparent differences to recognize consistent themes. A devotion to the classics, for example, whether the Latin works in Europe or texts of Chinese Confucianism in Japan, indicates similar tendencies in their supporters. Many of the changes in France, the United States, and Japan stemmed from shared processes as well as direct imitation. The problems, however, were at times both unique and unavoidable in the swift current of massive educational change.

Everywhere, for example, education extended the power of the state, moving into areas once reserved for family, community, and church. This extension might be eagerly pursued, as in Japan and France where education fed into a larger centralizing process, or more reluctantly and haphazardly applied, as in the federal United States. Nowhere, however, could policymakers refrain from intruding the state, not only as provider of basic skills but as shaper of moral codes. Degree of centralization did make a difference—as when Japan escalated its educational manipulation in the 1930s—but even local systems confronted families with challenging new pressures. Was social control via the schools less in the United States, where localism and middle-class values dominated, than in Japan or France around 1900? Everywhere, lower classes faced new, state-enforced demands for personal hygiene, book learning, and national loyalty.

Education in all three countries both challenged and confirmed marked social stratification. Established elites struggled to preserve their hold, by means of new and traditional school forms, against both mass pressure and the technical needs of industrializing societies. A trilateral pull—among old elites, mass schooling, and new technical elites (including those upwardly mobile from lower or lower-middle classes)—occurred in all three countries, though the ultimate balances varied somewhat.

The need to provide some education for everyone emerged over several decades in the United States and France, while it was the clearest principle in Japan's educational reform of 1872. Basic school skills seemed essential for economic advance—literacy and numeracy, but also less tangible skills like punctuality and ability to deal with strangers. And the chance to try to indoctrinate the masses with love of nation was too great to resist. At the same time, however, most systems drew clear divisions between mass schooling and subsequent educational opportunity. The policies of most secondary schools—whether private academies, as in the early-nineteenth-century United States, or fee-charging *lycées* or higher schools as in France and Japan—limited opportunity for a while. France and Japan then constructed systems where demanding tests, as well as costs, kept the lower classes separate—though France allowed scattered individuals to advance. When the economy demanded mid-level technical skills, these were provided by changes to the primary system, creating genuine but limited mobility opportunities, not by opening up the elite track. Japan rejected a technical redefinition of the elite track directly, France did so in effect. The United States, with a less explicit class system; struggled more with boundaries, creating the institution of the high school, which became more democratic but within which tests and tracking established distinctions. The greatest inequalities in the United States involved the maintenance of some private secondary schools and a host of private universities, some of which clearly recruited and perpetuated elites; but since they were private, rather than state-sponsored, they did not force a decision about the conflicts with the nation's democratic values. Middle- and upper-class people maintained special schools for themselves in all three countries, though they could not close entry from below; methods varied, depending on larger ideas about social justice.

Definitional issues occurred within the middle and upper classes as well. Industrial economies created growing needs and opportunities for technical expertise, yet all three industrial countries refused to equate this expertise with peak educational success. Engineering graduates might do well economically, though the majority reached the center of the middle class at most; but the most prestigious schools stressed a somewhat more traditional curriculum, and it was from these schools that top government and professional leadership was drawn. Classical *lycées* in France, the higher schools in Japan, the academic tracks in American high schools and then the top colleges all stressed some version of a broader liberal arts education, often including exposure to classical languages like Latin or Chinese. These educational experiences, open only to a small minority, provided a sense of separation and distinction. They often inculcated hard work and self-discipline. And they may, as their proponents claimed (and claim still today), have taught broader, more humane values than a more technical orientation could provide. The result, however, was a complex educational stratification that created tensions within the middle and upper classes themselves and that complicated any definition of the most desirable modern knowledge. Science and technology advanced in the cultures of the West and Japan, but their triumph was neither swift nor complete.

Yet even a partially traditional curriculum did not prevent some real social mobility to the top, as people from the lower reaches of the middle class and sometimes below managed to translate academic talent into a radical improvement in personal status. Older upper-class groups, like the samurai or the New England Brahmins, declined only gradually, but they did decline, as people from lower social origins rose to power and as the significance of newer kinds of knowledge increased. Japan's system, thanks to the rigorous examinations, may have been more open to educational mobility than was its American counterpart, where the Ivy League universities were so long dominated by an established upper class; this was one reason American mobility was less tied to education. Even in this case, however, there was change; the establishment of the College Board signaled a desire of the top schools to recruit from public high schools as well as leading private academies. Education preserved older values and older groups, but it was on balance a force for social change. And in all three countries, the appeal of possible mobility was a key reason for growing commitment to the education of one's children. American immigrants and the French or Japanese youths who aspired to be teachers — quite apart from the few who might really imagine gaining access to the *grandes écoles* or the University of Tokyo — looked on education as a source of hope. School systems and curricula that deliberately tried to encourage ordinary people to stay in their place did not produce mass mobility, but they inevitably created more instability—more striving and more changes in rank—than some of their proponents wished.

The complex balance between change and continuity certainly applied to women. Women's education created open anxiety in all three countries, particularly when it moved beyond the primary level. Ideas about women's inferiority, the widely felt need to keep women in the home, and new worries about masculinity in an industrial age all pushed for limitations and separate curricula. Schools sometimes intensified their domestic message in reaction to women's entry into new jobs—a pattern visible at points in all three countries. At the same time, women did gain ground educationally, and the extent of change was impressive. Even conservative policymakers saw advantages in educating women as mothers. Modern education itself demanded new roles for women in the ranks of schoolteachers. Rapid progress in women's schooling is actually harder to explain than the continued reservations, but key factors—including ubiquitous imitation, in Japan's case—can be identified. Some new skills were needed for the women who worked, and even leaders who thought of women primarily in terms of motherhood recognized that some formal education applied here as well. Finally, as with all the main educational trends, national variants loom large. While all three nations debated and hesitated, Japan definitely held back on women's education beyond primary schools, while the United States moved most rapidly toward coeducation in high schools and increasingly in state universities. These differences reflected distinctive values concerning women's roles and potentials, even as women's education everywhere advanced, and they contributed to ongoing differences as well—including variations in the numbers of female teachers.

Along with the complex interaction between stabilizing and innovative social consequences, the establishment of modern educational systems also involved fascinating tension between moral and academic content. The two tensions were related, of course. Conservatives who were skeptical about educating the masses or women often insisted that whatever reading material was offered emphasize family, obedience, and morality. But liberals pushed in this direction too. Even in the United

States where, outside the South, there were few outright opponents of mass schooling, reformers like Horace Mann urged the moral goals of education above all.

The moral emphasis might seem unexpected. After all, if education was mainly designed to prepare workers and the skilled elite for the demands of an industrial economy, or even if schools were seen primarily in terms of instilling the benefits of modern science, one would expect primary attention to academic subject matter. Japanese reformers in the 1870s indeed reflected this emphasis, wanting Confucian morality to be replaced by science and mathematics, along with technical subjects. This is what, on first glance, the Japanese thought they saw in the West. But even reformers quickly had to admit the need for a broader view. Similarly in France, the republicans who attacked Catholic schools argued that Catholic morality was narrow and out of date—but they did not in the main claim that morality was not a primary educational purpose. Occasionally, they might talk of schooling in terms of reason and science; but usually they tried to make sure that republicanism had a moral code too. Morality was quite obviously urged in the primary grades: the masses must be taught docility, good personal habits, and (for women) domestic devotion. But schools for the elite emphasized moral values as well. This was a dominant facet of the environment of the Japanese higher schools and persisted also in American universities even as these undertook more abundant research and technical training. American interest in extracurricular activities, particularly sports, was justified especially in terms of their moral service in building character, initiative, and group spirit. Emphasis on morality followed from schools' role in partially replacing families and churches, the earlier sources of ethical instruction. It also resulted from a widespread sense that, in a period of rapid industrial and political change, people needed very explicit moral guidance if society was not to split asunder. This guidance applied to the masses, who were taught to maintain virtuous families and to work diligently, but it also informed the elite, whose character was still more important than their technical training.

By the late nineteenth century, the morality being urged in education was not purely traditional. Earlier reading primers in the United States, filled with simple Protestant virtues, were replaced with more secular ones, though habits like thrift and family loyalty still loomed large. Catholic definitions of morality lost ground in the French schools. New moral ingredients included growing attention to cleanliness and bodily discipline, adherence to modern virtues such as punctuality and efficient use of time, and of course nationalism. Specific definitions of morality varied from one country to the next. The Japanese emphasis on group loyalty and a militaristic version of nationalism unquestionably differed from the somewhat milder American nationalism, which was also blended with greater commitment in principle to individualism. French national loyalty had its military aspect, but it also included a high regard for skepticism and rational analysis that gave it a distinctive tone as well.

In all three countries curriculum reflected the tension between subject matter emphasis and moral exhortation. How much should students memorize simply because memorization was good mental discipline and easy to test, how much should they be encouraged to master the ability to question materials and come up with answers? How much should education consist primarily of authoritative textbooks? Rules and regulations played a vital role as well: even schools that professed commitment to freedom of thought, as in American lessons about national political ideals, might seek to regulate students' lives so fully that the actual lessons proved quite different. American schools around 1900, for example, often emphasized teaching immigrants good personal habits and subjecting many students to adult supervision through team sports and other activities, while insisting on teacher authority in the classroom. They were, in sum, trying to teach more docility than educational policymakers acknowledged. Again, there were national differences in the style and implications of control: Japanese commitment to memorization seemed unusually great (and successful); the French left students quite free from school supervision outside the classroom (except in the secondary schools that boarded students).

Adding up the differences, amid common trends and problems, is no easy task. Japan used education as part of a vast set of social changes, yet it continued to enforce somewhat more subservience on women in the schools and tried to form a new kind of group loyalty that recalled elements of traditional Confucianism. Americans wrestled more with democracy in education than the Japanese did; this shows up in distinctive American attitudes to female education and in the idea that children should be left some initiative. Yet for many individuals, the common experience of redefining childhood in terms of classroom time, of emphasizing national loyalty, or of providing new hopes for mobility and new horizons beyond the family was the main point, whatever the specific national system.

Did the educational systems succeed by the time their formative decades drew to a close? Different measurements produce different assessments—a not surprising result since the goals of education were sometimes contradictory themselves. All three countries unquestionably managed to use their educational advances to support growing industrialization. There were worries, of course: Japan had to beef up technical training in the 1890s, while the French encountered criticism that their approach to science and technology education was too abstract and rationalistic. And it is not clear how much effect education had on early industrialization in France or the United States. By the late nineteenth century, however, Japan's educational surge helped provide growing numbers of skilled workers, literate clerical personnel, and engineers as a basis for industrial progress. The expanded need for service workers in the United States and France was satisfied directly by mass education and special commercial courses, including those for women. France trained key managerial groups in its technical schools, where not only expertise but habits of hard work and group loyalty paid off. By 1900, the United States was beginning to rely on trained researchers to generate new products and inventions; the age of the tinkerer-inventor was passing, and corporations increasingly formed professional research and development groups.

Education also generated new nationalist loyalties. Japan does not stand alone here. The French soldiers who enthusiastically went to war in 1914 clearly reflected nationalist passions learned in the schools of the republic. Even socialist workers, in principle opposed to nationalism, found it hard to ignore the siren call they had first heard in school. Americans who, after World War I, decided that their nation should stand alone in its isolated superiority and resist foreign influence also reflected generations of classroom exposure to the idea of a special national mission. Modern schools were intended to transfer attachments, and they did.

Did the moral lessons pay off? Schooling may have helped make people become more orderly. Many observers have noted that random fights and violence declined in the United States and France toward the end of the nineteenth century. Student riots declined, at least in the United States and, later, Japan. Schools did not stand alone in promoting more disciplined habits—not just orderliness, but also personal hygiene—but they surely played a role. Other features of the schools' moral message were less clearly received, however. While some girls may have seen their interest in families and marriage confirmed by their special lessons, others chafed against this aspect of their schooling and vowed to find other ways to express themselves and use their new academic skills; increased education unquestionably fueled new women's activities, despite the common attempt to link it with domesticity. This was true, at least for individual women, even in Japan. Families themselves did not become more stable merely because schools preached familial values. Education had diverse, sometimes unpredictable results, partly because its overall implications were not always clear-cut; some of the actual results of modern schooling—including the rival authority of the teacher—could reduce family cohesion. And other social developments, some of which were destabilizing, could counter the values preached in schools.

Education sometimes had a definite but perverse impact. Modern schooling, especially in the West and Japan, encouraged women to have fewer children by giving them a sense of new goals and an awareness of alternatives. The same pattern has emerged more recently in other parts of the world. French and some American policymakers around 1900 hoped that education would encourage higher, not lower, birthrates (at least by the "right sort" of people, socially and ethnically); they were, quite simply, wrong—another indication of the importance but complexity of educational results.

Education did not automatically create the kind of uniform political base that some policymakers sought. Industrial unrest grew widespread around 1900, for example, and no amount of school-based inculcation of national loyalty or of belief in individual opportunity turned the tide. Only Japan's massive dose of educational indoctrination in the 1920s and 1930s may have reduced political protest, along with other factors including severe police tactics.

Nor did education generate uniform national cultures and aspirations—though here the confusion rested partly within the educational goals themselves. Because educational systems did not systematically promote open opportunity, often trying to teach the lower classes to respect their place, large segments of the lower classes, including many immigrant groups in the United States, maintained different kinds of educational expectations from those of the middle and upper classes. Schooling provided some essential skills, and its requirements were increasingly unavoidable; but some people sought to end their exposure as quickly as possible, seeing no way to use it really to change their lot in life. Truancy and school discipline issues continued to reflect some students' sense that education was largely irrelevant. Yet education allowed some individuals in all groups to think about new prospects and to use school success to move up the social ladder. Modern education, in sum, tended to persuade most people of its value, but the definitions of value varied and the extent of persuasion was not uniform.

Results, not surprisingly, must be measured in comparative terms, since national systems differed on key points. It is not surprising, for example, that education produced more tension among American women about domestic versus wider roles than among their Japanese counterparts. American schooling helped trigger a greater enthusiasm for sports and formal exercise (at least in principle) than existed in France until very recently. French education must be measured in part in terms of the national conflicts over the role of the church, and while French schools did not convert the entire population to secularism the trends did move in that direction, as religious practice declined steadily after about 1890. Schools in the United States sought to Americanize immigrants, and while they did not homogenize cultures as much as some educators intended, they unquestionably had some effect, as second-generation immigrants, shaped by schools, moved away from many of their parents' habits, values, and even language. Japanese schools succeeded in their special task of combining economic change with political loyalty, even beyond the defeat in World War II.

Schooling was not the only factor guiding modern history in industrial societies. As it redefined childhood, exposing children to unprecedented experiences with lessons and classroom discipline, it clearly cast a wide influence. By the same token, when schools differed—by nation, or in their interactions with various social classes, with minority races, or with women—their impact would help shape ongoing differentiations as well.

Using the Sources Comparatively: France, the United States, and Japan

STYLES OF SCHOOL REFORM

French approaches to education and equality.   The French Revolution and the early years of Napoleon tossed up many reform ideas. In the first of the following passages, from a pamphlet by the philosopher Destutt de Tracy, a leading early-nineteenth-century theorist traces one view of the state's new responsibility in education. His argument is not complex, reflecting thinking that was shared by Napoleon and by many French educational leaders and promoting ideas that continued to influence French policy later. The second passage, from a speech to French teachers in an 1878 conference, reflects some similar thinking about education and social class. How do these ideas compare with educational approaches in Japan and the United States? Why, in one of the most revolutionary societies in the world during the nineteenth century, would a divided approach to education retain such vigor? Note that the second passage occurs at a point when debates between Catholics and republicans about control of education were heating up; which side does the passage represent? How does this approach to moralization compare with approaches current in other countries during the nineteenth century? Finally, however, the class system was debated. In the third passage, Jules Ferry, the republican leader, states the need to replace class with democracy, though in fact his later educational reforms fell short of this ambitious goal. His speech occurred before he had actually entered government and defined a more moderate republicanism.

DESTUTT DE TRACY

Observations on Public Education

1801

I must first remark that in every civilized society, there are necessarily two classes of men: one which supports itself by the work of its hands, and another which lives on earnings from property or by performing certain

Destutt de Tracy, *Observations sur le système actuel d'instruction publique* (Paris, year IX [1801]), 2–6.

functions, in which the work of the mind has a greater role than that of the body. The first is the working class; the second is what I will call the knowledge class.

People in the working class need the work of their children; the children themselves need early to learn the habits of the difficult work which is their destiny. They cannot spend a long time in school. They need only a summary education, though complete for its type, which they can get in a few years, so that they can soon enter the production shops or take up domestic or rural duties. They must also have schools where they get this abbreviated education without leaving their father's house.

Those in the knowledge class, on the other hand, can give more time to their studies; and they must give more, for they have more things to learn to fulfill their destiny, things that one cannot grasp without sufficient maturity and some previous mental development. They must leave home and move to school. They must have specialized teachers in the schools, for the type of study they need requires teachers to supervise and direct the work that should follow the lessons they receive; otherwise the lessons will have no utility.

These are arrangements that depend on no human will; they derive from the nature of man and society; no one can change them. . . .

Let us thus conclude that every well-run State, which gives enough attention to the education of citizens, should have two complete systems of instruction, which have nothing in common with each other. . . . I regard it as a great mistake to believe that primary schools can be linked to the central schools or serve as their point of entry.

Speech to Teachers by a Regional School Inspector
1878

Deep in the human soul there are some simple truths that primary instruction should draw out. . . . Take a few of your oldest and most serious students some evening, a bit outside the last house of the village, at the time when the noises of work and life are fading; and have them lift their eyes to the star-filled sky. They have never seen it. They have never been taken with the thought of the innumerable worlds and of the eternal order and

Archives nationales, Ministry of Education Department Reports, 1878 (Vosges Department).

movement of the universe. Awaken these new ideas in them, show them this spectacle of the infinite before which the first shepherds of Asia prostrated themselves and before which the genius of Pascal still trembled.

. . . You know nothing about astronomy? So what! It's not a matter of science, but rather instilling in the souls of these children something that you feel. I don't know what things you'll say to them, but I know that the tone you use is important; I know that, long after you've stopped speaking, they'll think about what you said, and from that day forward you'll be something more than a spelling or arithmetic teacher in their eyes.

. . . In these delicate regions of religion and politics, amid these greater moral notions, fundamental to human education, there are two parts to distinguish.

The first is as old as humanity, innate, anchored in all consciences, inseparable from human nature, clear and evident to every person: this is the domain of intuition.

The other is the result of study, of reflection, of discussion, and of science. It contains no less respectable truths than the first domain, but they are not as striking, not as simple, not accessible to every mind. And this domain is subject to controversy and passion, and in any case it requires specialized, long, and deep study; it doesn't belong in popular education; don't touch it. But the other domain does belong to you, and your students demand it.

JULES FERRY

Democratic Education

1870

Inequality of education, from the social standpoint, is one of the most striking and harmful results of the accident of birth. With educational inequality I defy you to have equality of rights—not in theory, but in real practice— yet this equality is the foundation and essence of genuine democracy. . . .

In a society which takes as its main charge the formation of liberty, there's a pressing need to suppress class distinctions. I ask you in good faith—you who have received various educational degrees—if there is no more class distinction in our society? I say that there is one such distinction, the most difficult to uproot—the difference between those who have

Jules Ferry, *Discours sur l'égalité d'éducation*, delivered April 10, 1870, *Journal officiel,* April 10, 1870.

obtained education and those who have not. Gentlemen, I defy you to form an egalitarian nation from these two classes, a unified nation with shared fraternal ideas who constitute the strength of real democracies if, between these two classes, a basic cohesion has not developed, an initial fusion that results from the mixture of rich and poor on the benches of the same school.

Educational reform in the United States. Horace Mann (1796–1859) was the leading educational reformer in the United States toward the middle of the nineteenth century. The following passages, taken from various annual reports he issued in his capacity as head of the Massachusetts Board of Education between 1839 and 1846, lay out some of his fundamental thinking about education.

What does he see as the primary purposes of education and the relationship between moral and intellectual training? On what bases might some people at the time have disagreed with his orientation, defining education in other ways, and what groups might particularly have disagreed? Why have some recent historians rated Mann's approach as a form of social control? Are there inconsistencies within Mann's views as to the best ways to raise up free citizens—for example, in the relationship between discipline and individualism? What are his views on discipline and on the nature of childhood? How much of Mann's basic thinking still pervades American education? Is his approach part of a durable American style? Mann and his fellow reformers can be seen as causing a distinctive national culture concerning education; did they also reflect unusual values and needs among key elements of the population?

HORACE MANN

The Goals of Education

The preservation of order, together with the proper despatch of business requires a mean, between the too much and the too little, in all the evolutions of the school, which it is difficult to hit. When classes leave their seats

Horace Mann, *On the Education of Free Men* (New York: Columbia University Press, 1987), 49–59.

for the recitation-stand, and return to them again, or when the different sexes have a recess, or the hour of intermission arrives;—if there be not some order and succession of movement, the school will be temporarily converted into a promiscuous rabble, giving both the temptation and the opportunity for committing every species of indecorum and aggression. In order to prevent confusion, on the other hand, the operations of the school may be conducted with such military formality and procrastination:—the second scholar not being allowed to leave his seat, until the first has reached the door, or the place of recitation, and each being made to walk on tiptoe to secure silence,—that a substantial part of every school session will be wasted, in the wearisome pursuit of an object worth nothing when obtained.

When we reflect, how many things are to be done each half day, and how short a time is allotted for their performance, the necessity of system in regard to all the operations of the school, will be apparent. System compacts labor; and when the hand is to be turned to an almost endless variety of particulars, if system does not preside over the whole series of movements, the time allotted to each will be spent in getting ready to perform it. With lessons to set; with so many classes to hear; with difficulties to explain; with the studious to be assisted; the idle to be spurred; the transgressors to be admonished or corrected; with the goers and comers to observe;—with all these things to be done, no considerable progress can be made, if one part of the wheel is not coming up to the work, while another is going down. And if order do not pervade the school, as a whole, and in all its parts, all is lost; and this is a very difficult thing;—for it seems as though the school were only a point, rescued out of a chaos that still encompasses it, and is ready, on the first opportunity, to break in and reoccupy its ancient possession. As it is utterly impracticable for any committee to prepare a code of regulations coextensive with all the details, which belong to the management of a school, it must be left with the teacher; and hence the necessity of skill in this item of the long list of his qualifications.

The government and discipline of a school demands [sic] qualities still more rare, because the consequences of error, in these, are still more disastrous. What caution, wisdom, uprightness, and sometimes, even intrepidity, are necessary in the administration of punishment. After all other means have been tried, and tried in vain, the chastisement of pupils found to be otherwise incorrigible, is still upheld by law, and sanctioned by public opinion. . . . The discipline of former times was inexorably stern and severe, and even if it were wished, it is impossible now to return to it. The question is, what can be substituted, which, without its severity, shall have its efficiency.

In the contemplation of the law, the school committee are sentinels stationed at the door of every schoolhouse in the State, to see that no teacher ever crosses its threshold, who is not clothed, from the crown of his head to the sole of his foot, in garments of virtue; and they are the enemies of the human race,—not of contemporaries only, but of posterity,—who, from any private or sinister motive, strive to put these sentinels to sleep, in order that one, who is profane, or intemperate, or addicted to low associations, or branded with the stigma of any vice, may elude the vigilance of the watchmen, and be installed over the pure minds of the young, as their guide and exemplar. If none but teachers of pure tastes, of good manners, of exemplary morals, had ever gained admission into our schools, neither the school rooms, nor their appurtenances would have been polluted, as some of them now are, with such ribald inscriptions, and with the carvings of such obscene emblems, as would make a heathen blush. Every person, therefore, who endorses another's character, as one befitting a school teacher, stands before the public as his moral bondsman and sponsor, and should be held to a rigid accountability. . . .

One of the highest and most valuable objects, to which the influences of a school can be made conducive, consists in training our children to self-government. . . . So tremendous, too, are the evils of anarchy and lawlessness, that a government by mere force, however arbitrary and cruel, has been held preferable to no-government. But self-government, self-control, a voluntary compliance with the laws of reason and duty, have been justly considered as the highest point of excellence attainable by a human being. No one, however, can consciously obey the laws of reason and duty, until he understands them. Hence the preliminary necessity of their being clearly explained, of their being made to stand out, broad, lofty, and as conspicuous as a mountain against a clear sky. There may be blind obedience without a knowledge of the law, but only of the will of the lawgiver; but the first step towards rational obedience is a knowledge of the rule to be obeyed, and of the reasons on which it is founded.

The above doctrine acquires extraordinary force, in view of our political institutions,—founded, as they are, upon the great idea of the capacity of man for self-government,—an idea so long denounced by the state as treasonable, and by the church as heretical. In order that men may be prepared for self-government, their apprenticeship must commence in childhood. The great moral attribute of self-government cannot be born and matured in a day; and if school children are not trained to it, we only prepare ourselves for disappointment, if we expect it from grown men. Every body acknowledges the justness of the declaration, that a foreign people, born and bred and dwarfed under the despotisms of the Old World, cannot be transformed into the full stature of American citizens, merely by a voyage across the Atlantic, or by subscribing the oath of naturalization. If they retain the servility in which they have been trained, some self-appointed lord or priest, on this side of the water, will succeed to the authority of the master they have left behind them. If, on the other hand, they identify liberty with an absence from restraint, and an immunity from punishment, then they are liable to become intoxicated and delirious with the highly stimulating properties of the air of freedom; and thus, in either case, they remain unfitted, until they have been morally acclimated to our institutions, to exercise the rights of a freeman. But can it make any substantial difference, whether a man is suddenly translated into all the independence and prerogatives of an American citizen, from the bondage of an Irish lord or an English manufacturer, or from the equally rigorous bondage of a parent, guardian, or school teacher? He who has been a serf until the day before he is twenty-one years of age, cannot be an independent citizen the day after; and it makes no difference whether he has been a serf in Austria or in America. As the fitting apprenticeship for despotism consists in being trained to despotism, so the fitting apprenticeship for self-government consists in being trained to self-government; and liberty and self-imposed law are as appropriate a preparation for the subjects of an arbitrary power, as the law of force and authority is for developing and maturing those sentiments of self-respect, of honor, and of dignity, which belong to a truly republican citizen. . . . Now, for the high purpose of training an American child to become an American citizen,—a constituent part of a self-governing people,—is it not obvious that, in all cases, the law by which he is to be bound should be made intelligible to him; and, as soon as his capacity will permit, that the reasons on which it is founded, should be made as intelligible as the law itself?

Educational reform in Japan: Yukichi Fukuzawa.   The following passages were written by Japan's leading educational reformer, Yukichi Fukuzawa (1834–1904). Fukuzawa quickly realized the educational implications of Japan's new position in the world after Perry opened Japan to world markets in 1853. As early as 1860, he began to travel to the United States and Europe. His many books and articles about the West won a wide audience in Japan. Fukuzawa was no blind Westernizer; he criticized many aspects of the West, including what he viewed as the inappropriate place of women and the wasteful debates in Western parliaments. But he saw clear advantages in key aspects of Western education and devoted his life to installing them in Japan. In the first passage, from his *Autobiography*, published in 1899, he describes his principles. What Western emphases did he seek?

But the second passage reveals a somewhat different side. In an 1878 letter to a leading Confucian scholar, a close friend of the family, Fukuzawa states his position more cautiously and reveals a desire for a merger of principles. His correspondence with Nakamura Ritusen was published by the Ministry of Education and provoked lively discussions. What aspects of Confucianism does Fukuzawa here profess to cherish? Do his views seem merely tactical, compared with the more strident tone in the *Autobiography*, or is he actually clearer here on his larger educational goals? Note that this letter focused on primary education; might this help explain its tone? Which aspect of Fukuzawa's approach, the compromiser or the ardent Westernizer, turned out to characterize modern Japanese education more generally?

The issues Fukuzawa dealt with obviously differed greatly, in specifics, from those faced by Western reformers. Yet there are some obvious similarities with people like Horace Mann. What are they, and how can they be explained?

YUKICHI FUKUZAWA

Autobiography

1899

In my interpretation of education, I try to be guided by the laws of nature and I try to co-ordinate all the physical actions of human beings by the very simple laws of "number and reason." In spiritual or moral training, I regard the human being as the most sacred and responsible of all orders, unable in reason to do anything base. Therefore, in self-respect, a man cannot change his sense of humanity, his justice, his loyalty, or anything belonging to his manhood even when driven by circumstances to do so. In short, my creed is that a man should find his faith in independence and self-respect.

From my own observations in both Occidental and Oriental civilizations, I find that each has certain strong points and weak points bound up in its moral teachings and scientific theories. But when I compare the two in a general way as to wealth, armament, and the greatest happiness for the greatest number, I have to put the Orient below the Occident. Granted that a nation's destiny depends upon the education of its people, there

Eiichi Kiyooka, trans., *The Autobiography of Yukichi Fukuzawa* (New York: Columbia University Press, 1966), 214–17.

Figure 12. Training in everyday manners in a girls' high school around 1900. What were the explicit and implicit lessons in this kind of training for teenaged women?

must be some fundamental differences in the education of Western and Eastern peoples.

In the education of the East, so often saturated with Confucian teaching, I find two things lacking; that is to say, a lack of studies in number and reason in material culture, and a lack of the idea of independence in spiritual culture. But in the West I think I see why their statesmen are successful in managing their national affairs, and the businessmen in theirs, and the people generally ardent in their patriotism and happy in their family circles.

I regret that in our country I have to acknowledge that people are not formed on these two principles, though I believe no one can escape the laws of number and reason, nor can anyone depend on anything but the doctrine of independence as long as nations are to exist and mankind is to thrive. Japan could not assert herself among the great nations of the world without full recognition and practice of these two principles. And I reasoned that Chinese philosophy as the root of education was responsible for our obvious shortcomings.

With this as the fundamental theory of education, I began and, though it was impossible to institute specialized courses because of lack of funds, I did what I could in organizing the instructions on the principles of number and reason. And I took every opportunity in public speech, in writing, and in casual conversations, to advocate my doctrine of independence. Also I tried in many ways to demonstrate the theory in my actual life. During my endeavor I came to believe less than ever in the old Chinese teachings. . . .

The true reason of my opposing the Chinese teaching with such vigor is my belief that in this age of transition, if this retrogressive doctrine remains at all in our young men's minds, the new civilization cannot give its full benefit to this country. In my determination to save our coming generation, I was prepared even to face single-handed the Chinese scholars of the country as a whole.

Gradually the new education was showing its results among the younger generation; yet men of middle age or past, who held responsible positions, were for the most part uninformed as to the true spirit of Western culture, and whenever they had to make decisions, they turned invariably to their Chinese sources for guidance. And so, again and again I had to rise up and denounce the all-important Chinese influence before this weighty opposition. It was not altogether a safe road for my reckless spirit to follow.

YUKICHI FUKUZAWA

Letter to Nakamura Ritusen

1878

In the elementary schools today, the curriculum is not perfect; the only thing they do is to teach children how to read, write, and count, and that under a regimented rule as in the army and never in an atmosphere congenial to true education. All this is due to the lack of qualified teachers. It is not that the schools do not look for such teachers; they do, but there are not enough of them.

When there are no qualified men among the teachers, no matter how much the school curriculum is improved or whatever textbooks are pub-

Yukichi Fukuzawa, *Yukichi Fukuzawa on Education: Selected Works*, translated by Eiichi Kiyooka (Tokyo: University of Tokyo Press, 1985), 113–17.

lished, no great results can be expected. Especially, the moral education of filial piety and brotherly harmony cannot be taught by formal instruction. It has to be transmitted to the pupils informally or unawares through the personality of the teachers. If there were an ideal personality who was truly capable of being a teacher, even under the present school system, with the same books and the same curriculum, this teacher would certainly be able to influence his pupils in the ways of filial piety and brotherly harmony. There are even examples in which there was not even a book to read and yet good education was provided. Therefore, one may safely assert that the present deficiency in elementary school education is due not to the faults in the system of instruction but to the lack of qualified teachers. Such has been the general trend of education since the [Meiji] Restoration.

Without question, I do not make light of the teaching of filial piety and brotherly harmony. Since my childhood to this day, I have believed it to be an essential element in the morals of human nature. And I am sure that I am not alone in my beliefs: a large number of people will share the same beliefs. . . .

You also wrote that if I had decided that the moral doctrine of filial piety and brotherly harmony was too narrow to be taken seriously, that would be going against the will of my late father, and you hinted that this would be unfilial toward my father. I am always driven to shivers at the simple mention of undutifulness to parents. . . .

I trust that you, too, will acknowledge the love I have for my father. If you regard my father as a person who endeavored to follow and study Confucianism and was assiduous in literary activities, then I am the son of that very person, and I earnestly admire and believe in his words and deeds.

I went into Western studies while I was still young, and I have not been able yet to delve deeply into the inner philosophy of Confucianism. Moreover, being of shallow intellect and of simple reasoning, I do not yet know what exactly is the true way. But should my forebears' words and deeds be truly in accord with Confucianism, then I, too, am a believer in Confucianism with no vestiges of doubt.

I think there is a reason for your believing that I am against Confucianism. When I first began studying Western learning some twenty years ago, it was very much against the times, and very few relatives and friends approved my choice. Only with the approval of my late mother and late brother was I secretly able to begin my studies, and after much hardship, just as I was beginning to grasp an understanding of Western learning, the slogan "Drive Out the Foreigners" was raised. . . .

It was impossible at that time to discuss anything with adversaries. And we simply chose to stay away from them.

Therefore, I wish to state that I was not against the Confucian doctrine;

I was simply avoiding the Confucian advocates. Or rather, I was afraid of them, and I simply kept away from them. These probably are the circumstances for my reputation as anti-Confucian. All that belongs to the past now, and I no longer need to point out the differences. Western and Confucian teachings have now grown into one, and no contradiction is seen. This is a fortunate outcome for society.

Very respectfully,
Yukichi

January 25, Meiji 11th year (1878)

EDUCATION FOR MORALITY

Reading and morality in France: change and continuity. Using schooling to combine basic skills with moralization was a vital impulse in nineteenth-century education, not only in France. The French did face some special problems in the combination, however, as republicans sought to define a morality different from that of the church as part of their campaign against Catholic influence. The following passages, beginning with a manual on reading instruction from 1832 that made its moral lessons quite explicit, suggest how educators struggled to define morality. Even in the manual, designed to orient teachers in terms of their goals with students, some important issues surface, such as the relationship between general principles and a code more specifically addressed to the lower classes to keep them in their place. With the later triumph of secular education in France, new complexities developed. The second selection, from the 1880s, reflects republican views, as does the 1897 manual by Jules Payot, a school administrator. Passages from the liberal republican politician Ferdinand Buisson are from the years when the church's role had been greatly reduced. Policymakers sought to define a new moral code that would create "modern" outlooks. What did they mean by this? How much would this new code differ in practice from traditional standards? What would parents think of efforts to use schools to instill new values in children? And, of course, the comparative context adds further questions. How did French school morality, particularly as it was redefined for a secular republic, compare with the republican virtues sought by educators in the United States?

A. PEIGNÉ

"On Duties": From an Instruction Manual

1832

The first duty for a child is to love and respect his father and mother. He owes everything he is and possesses to them, and he can repay so many benefits only with sincere gratitude, full submission, and lively tenderness. . . . When you become adult, you will occupy a place in society. Your first duty then will be to love your country and obey its laws. You may be rich: in this case, don't forget that the noblest, most useful employment of wealth is to solace the poor. . . . If you are poor, never lose sight of work, that sure resource against indigence. Be honest; there is nothing so beautiful and respectable as that virtue which stands firm even amid misery. Be careful not to envy the rich, but the rich are not as happy as one might think. If they have goods in abundance, they also have abundant cares and griefs.

If you are artisans, work hard, be faithful and honest. If you are farmers, respect the property of others . . . treat the people attached to your service well, and don't mistreat animals. . . . Finally, if you are in commerce, remember that the best qualities of the merchant are honesty and intelligence. So be honest, keep your business orderly and scrupulously fulfill your contracts.

A. Peigné, *Méthode de lecture, ouvrage adopté par la société pour l'instruction élémentaire* (Paris: L. Colas, 1832), 69.

M. TOLAIN

Republican against Catholic Morality

1881

You [Catholics] understand morality differently from us. If you see a poor person, you want to help him in the form of charity, acting like a kind of Providence so that he will be attached to you by gratitude and obligation. . . .

M. Tolain, Senate debate, June 4, 1881, *Journal officiel,* 780.

We have a different way of understanding morality, we want to use education to establish solidarity with each child. . . . We tell the child: not only does he have the right to primary instruction but also, as soon as we are able to provide it, the right to an integral education such that, progressively, letters, sciences, arts, all the branches of human knowledge become the common domain of all citizens. . . .

[We no longer want] passive obedience, acceptance of revealed truth, failure to use one's reason to discuss what is good and what is bad. . . . I say that the first act of a teacher from a religious order is to accept revealed truth, since you declare the Church infallible. . . . I say that this is the negation of reason and conscience. . . .

When a man begins by abandoning his highest qualities, the exercise of his reason, he is in my judgment incapable of teaching. . . . I [also] refuse the monk the right to teach because he is submitted to a discipline and rule that I find anti-human, because you have imposed celibacy upon him. . . . It is due to this rule . . . that you produce all the scandals that daily fill honest men with horror and indignation.

FERDINAND BUISSON

The Benefits of Modern Education

1883

Go, little missionary of modern ideas, little primary school student. Leaving school, show your parents what you bring with you: your books, your notes, your pictures, the work you've begun in shop, tell them the stories, the moral tales you've been told; they'll quickly understand the changes that are occurring, the benefits of modern education . . . they'll say, if only we had been raised this way, and they'll kiss you to conceal their emotion. In this kiss are more promises for the Republic than many electoral victories.

Ferdinand Buisson, speech to the Association Polytechnique, 1883, reprinted in Ferdinand Buisson, *La Foi laique* (Paris: Hachette, 1912), 23.

FERDINAND BUISSON

Educating a Citizen of the Republic

1903

To make a republican, you must take a child, an adolescent, a young woman, the most uneducated man, the worker most overwhelmed with work, and give him the idea that he must think by himself, that he owes neither faith nor obedience to anything, that it's up to him to seek out the truth and not to receive it from some master or chief, whether temporal or spiritual. . . . Believing is the easiest thing in the world, but thinking is the most difficult. To judge by oneself, according to reason, requires a long and detailed apprenticeship, it requires years, it requires a prolonged and methodical exercise. It's a question of creating a free spirit. . . .

There is no liberal education where one does not place the student's intelligence amid contrary opinions, diverse claims . . . saying: compare and choose yourself. There are of course incontestable truths, such as mathematical truths, the laws based on the experience of all branches of science. The State teaches these not as dogmas, but as demonstrated truths which everyone can prove. As to beliefs and opinions, religious convictions, the State does not teach them, but it wishes to grant none of them a privileged position or the right to stifle contradiction.

Ferdinand Buisson, speech at a Radical Party congress, 1903, reprinted in Ferdinand Buisson, *La Foi laique* (Paris: Hachette, 1912), 178–79.

JULES PAYOT

The Education of the Family

1897

We don't pay enough attention to the education of the family by the child. In the less desirable families, the presence of the child makes the parents more reserved, more respectful of each other. The child who receives moral lessons in school clearly indicates his disapproval of

Jules Payot, *Aux Instituteurs et institutrices, conseils et directions pratiques* (Paris: A. Colin, 1897), 96.

anything at home that contradicts this teaching. A lower tone makes him suffer, and this suffering is often the point of departure of a superior moral life.

Reading and moralizing in the United States. The following passages are taken from widely used nineteenth-century American readers. They all illustrate the belief that moral education was a fundamental goal in primary school and that teaching reading, spelling, and pronunciation should further this end while advancing basic skills. What kind of moral virtues are advocated? Did they change from the 1820s to the 1850s? How do they compare with the moral lessons emphasized in American education today? Have American schools lessened their moral advocacy since the nineteenth century or simply changed its focus? How do you think different groups of students—from different social classes or religious backgrounds, for example—would have reacted to nineteenth-century moralism? Might some parents have objected to these moral pressures? Were the moralists working for or against social change and personal mobility (or were they divided on these points)?

The passages invite comparisons. All nineteenth-century school systems included moral training—this was true, clearly, in France and Japan. Some of their moral targets were shared, such as the urgent efforts to install patriotism and family loyalties. Are there, however, some more distinctive American virtues being pushed as well? How can they be defined? How would a Japanese observer of the 1880s, beginning to worry about too much "individualism" in Western education, react to these lessons?

LINDLEY MURRAY

Murray's *Reader*

1829

Many selections of excellent matter have been made for the benefit of young persons. Performances of this kind are of so great utility, that fresh productions of them, and new attempts to improve the young mind, will

---

Lindley Murray, *The English Reader*, Preface (Cooperstown, N.Y.: Phinney, 1829).

scarcely be deemed superfluous, if the writer make his compilation instructive and interesting, and sufficiently distinct from others.

The present work, as the title expresses, aims at the attainment of three objects: to improve youth in the art of reading; to meliorate their language and sentiments; and to inculcate some of the most important principles of piety and virtue.

The pieces selected, not only give exercise to a great variety of emotions, and the correspondent tones and variations of voice, but contain sentences and members of sentences, which are diversified, proportioned, and pointed with accuracy. Exercises of this nature are, it is presumed, well calculated to teach youth to read with propriety and effect. A selection of sentences, in which variety and proportion, with exact punctuation, have been carefully observed, in all their parts as well as with respect to one another, will probably have a much greater effect, in properly teaching the art of reading, than is commonly imagined. In such constructions, everything is accommodated to the understanding and the voice; and the common difficulties in learning to read well are obviated. When the learner has acquired a habit of reading such sentences, with justness and facility, he will readily apply that habit, and the improvements he has made, to sentences more complicated and irregular, and of a construction entirely different.

The language of the pieces chosen for this collection has been carefully regarded. Purity, propriety, perspicuity, and, in many instances, elegance of diction, distinguish them. They are extracted from the works of the most correct and elegant writers. From the sources whence the sentiments are drawn, the reader may expect to find them connected and regular, sufficiently important and impressive, and divested of everything that is either trite or eccentric. The frequent perusal of such composition naturally tends to infuse a taste for this species of excellence; and to produce a habit of thinking, and of composing, with judgment and accuracy.

That this collection may also serve the purpose of promoting piety and virtue, the Compiler has introduced many extracts, which place religion in the most amiable light; and which recommend a great variety of moral duties, by the excellence of their nature, and the happy effects they produce. These subjects are exhibited in a style and manner which are calculated to arrest the attention of youth; and to make strong and durable impressions on their minds.

The Compiler has been careful to avoid every expression and sentiment, that might gratify a corrupt mind, or, in the least degree, offend the eye or ear of innocence. This he conceives to be peculiarly incumbent on every person who writes for the benefit of youth. It would indeed be a great and happy improvement in education, if no writings were allowed to come under their notice, but such as are perfectly innocent; and if on all proper occasions, they were encouraged to peruse those which tend to inspire a due reverence for virtue, and an abhorrence of vice, as well as to animate them with sentiments of piety and goodness. Such impressions deeply engraven on our minds, and connected with all their attainments, could scarcely fail of attending them through life, and of producing a solidity of principle and character, that would be able to resist the danger arising from future intercourse with the world.

NOAH WEBSTER

The American Spelling Book

1831

Additional Lessons.
Domestic Economy,
Or, the History of Thrifty and Unthrifty

There is a great difference among men, in their ability to gain property; but a still greater difference in their power of using it to advantage. Two men may acquire the same amount of money, in a given time; yet one will prove to be a poor man, while the other becomes rich. A chief and essential difference in the management of property, is, that one man spends only the *interest* of his money, while another spends the *principal*. I know a farmer by the name of *Thrifty,* who manages his affairs in this manner: He rises early in the morning, looks to the condition of his house, barn, homelot, and stock—sees that his cattle, horses, and hogs are fed; examines the tools to see whether they are all in good order for the workmen—takes care that breakfast is ready in due season, and begins work in the cool of the day—When in the field, he keeps steadily at work, though not so violently as to fatigue and exhaust the body—nor does he stop to tell or hear long stories—When the labor of the day is past, he takes refreshment, and goes to rest at an early hour—In this manner he earns and gains money.

When *Thrifty* has acquired a little property, he does not spend it or let it slip from him, without use or benefit. He pays his taxes and debts when due or called for, so that he has not officers' fees to pay, nor expenses of court. He does not frequent the tavern, and drink up all his earnings in liquor that does him no good. He puts his money to use, that is, he buys more land, or stock, or lends his money at interest—in short, he makes his money produce some profit or income. These savings and profits,

Noah Webster, *The American Spelling Book* (Lexington, Ky.: W. W. Worsley, 1831), 53–57.

though small by themselves, amount in a year to a considerable sum, and in a few years they swell to an estate—*Thrifty* becomes a wealthy farmer, with several hundred acres of land, and a hundred head of cattle.

Very different is the management of UNTHRIFTY: He lies in bed till a late hour in the morning—then rises, and goes to the bottle for a dram, or to the tavern for a glass of bitters—Thus he spends six cents before breakfast late, when he ought to be at work. When he supposes he is ready to begin the work of the day, he finds he has not the necessary tools, or some of them are out of order,—the plow-share is to be sent half a mile to a blacksmith to be mended; a tooth or two in a rake or the handle of a hoe is broke; or a sythe or an ax is to be ground.—Now, he is in a great hurry, he bustles about to make preparation for work—and what is done in a hurry is ill done—he loses a part of the day in getting ready—and perhaps the time of his workmen. At ten or eleven o'clock, he is ready to go to work—then comes a boy and tells him, the sheep have escaped from the pasture—or the cows have got among his corn—or the hogs into the garden—He frets and storms, and runs to drive them out—a half hour or more time is lost in driving the cattle from mischief, and repairing a poor old broken fence—a fence that answers no purpose but to lull him into security, and teach his horses and cattle to be unruly—After all this bustle, the fatigue of which is worse than common labor, *Unthrifty* is ready to begin a day's work at twelve o'clock.—Thus half his time is lost in supplying defects, which proceed from want of foresight and good management. His small crops are damaged or destroyed by unruly cattle.—His barn is open and leaky, and what little he gathers, is injured by the rain and snow.—His house is in a like condition—the shingles and clapboards fall off and let in the water, which causes the timber, floors, and furniture to decay—and exposed to inclemencies of weather, his wife and children fall sick—their time is lost, and the mischief closes with a ruinous train of expenses for medicines and physicians.—After dragging out some years of disappointment, misery, and poverty, the lawyer and the sheriff sweep away the scanty remains of his estate. This is the history of UNTHRIFTY—his principal is spent—he has no interest.

Not unlike this, is the history of the Grog-drinker. This man wonders why he does not thrive in the world; he cannot see the reason why his neighbor *Temperance* should be more prosperous than himself—but in truth, he makes no calculations. Ten cents a day for grog, is a small sum, he thinks, which can hurt no man! But let us make an estimate—arithmetic is very useful for a man who ventures to spend small sums every day. Ten cents a day amounts in a year to thirty-six dollars and a half—a sum sufficient to buy a good farm-horse! This surely is no small sum for a farmer or mechanic—But in ten years, this sum amounts to three hundred and sixty-five dollars, besides interest in the mean time! What an amount is this for drams and bitters in ten years! it is money enough to build a small house! But look at the amount in thirty years!—One thousand and ninety-five dollars!—What a vast sum to run down one man's throat. . . .

TABLE XIII
LESSONS OF EASY WORDS, TO TEACH CHILDREN
TO READ, AND TO KNOW THEIR DUTY

Lesson I

No man may put off the law of God:
My joy is in his law all the day.
O may I not go in the way of sin!
Let me not go in the way of ill men.

II

A bad man is a foe to the law:
It is his joy to do ill.
All men go out of the way.
Who can say he has no sin?

III

The way of man is ill.
My son, do as you are bid:
But if you are bid, do no ill.
See not my sin, and let me not go to the pit.

IV

Rest in the Lord, and mind his word.
My son, hold fast the law that is good.
You must not tell a lie, nor do hurt.
We must let no man hurt us.

V

Do as well as you can, and do no harm.
Mark the man that doth well, and do so too.
Help such as want help, and be kind.
Let your sins past put you in mind to mend.

VI

I will not walk with bad men, that I may not be cast off with them.
I will love the law and keep it.
I will walk with the just and do good. . . .

VIII

A bad life will make a bad end.
He must live well that will die well.
He doth live ill that doth not mend.
In time to come we must do no ill. . . .

XI

He who came to save us, will wash us from all sin; I will be glad in his name.
A good boy will do all that is just; he will flee from vice; he will do good, and walk in the way of life.
Love not the world, nor the things that are in the world; for they are sin.
I will not fear what flesh can do to me; for my trust is in him who made the world.
He is nigh to them that pray to him, and praise his name.
Be a good child; mind your book; love your school, and strive to learn.
Tell no tales; call no ill names; you must not lie, nor swear, nor cheat, nor steal.
Play not with bad boys; use no ill words at play; spend your time well; live in peace, and shun all strife. This is the way to make good men love you, and save your soul from pain and woe. . . .

XIII

A good child will not lie, swear, nor steal. — He will be good at home, and ask to read his book; when he gets up he will wash his hands and face clean; he will comb his hair, and make haste to school; he will not play by the way, as bad boys do.

XIV

When good boys and girls are at school, they will mind their books, and try to learn to spell and read well, and not play in the time of school.

WILLIAM HOLMES McGUFFEY

McGuffey's Reader

1848

Mr. Lenox was one morning riding by himself; he alighted from his horse to look at something on the roadside; the horse got loose and ran away from him. Mr. Lenox ran after him, but could not overtake him. A little boy, at work in a field, heard the horse; and, as soon as he saw him running from his master, ran very quickly to the middle of the road, and catching him by the bridle, stopped him, till Mr. Lenox came up.

William Holmes McGuffey, *McGuffey's Newly Revised Third Eclectic Reader* (Cincinnati: Winthrop B. Smith, 1848), 33–34.

Mr. Lenox. Thank you, my good boy, you have caught my horse very cleverly. What shall I give you for your trouble?

Boy. I want nothing, sir.

Mr. L. Do you want nothing? So much the better for you. Few men can say as much. But what were you doing in the field?

B. I was rooting up weeds, and tending the sheep that were feeding on turnips.

Mr. L. Do you like to work?

B. Yes, sir, very well, this fine weather.

Mr. L. But would you not rather play?

B. This is not hard work; it is almost as good as play.

Mr. L. Who set you to work?

B. My father, sir.

Mr. L. What is your name?

B. Peter Hurdle, sir.

Mr. L. How old are you?

B. Eight years old, next June.

Mr. L. How long have you been out in this field?

B. Ever since six o'clock this morning.

Mr. L. Are you not hungry?

B. Yes, sir, but I shall go to dinner soon.

Mr. L. If you had sixpence now, what would you do with it?

B. I do not know, sir. I never had so much in my life.

Mr. L. Have you no play things?

B. Play things? What are they?

Mr. L. Such as nine-pins, marbles, tops, and wooden horses.

B. No, sir. Tom and I play at foot-ball in winter, and I have a jumping-rope. I had a hoop, but it is broken.

Mr. L. Do you want nothing else?

B. I have hardly time to play with what I have. I have to drive the cows, and to run of errands, and to ride the horses to the fields, and that is as good as play.

Mr. L. You could get apples and cakes, if you had money, you know.

B. I can have apples at home. As for cake, I do not want that; my mother makes me a pie now and then, which is as good.

Mr. L. Would you not like a knife to cut sticks?

B. I have one; here it is; brother Tom gave it to me.

Mr. L. Your shoes are full of holes. Don't you want a new pair?

B. I have a better pair for Sundays.

Mr. L. But these let in water.

B. I don't mind that, sir.

Mr. L. Your hat is all torn, too.

B. I have a better hat at home.

Mr. L. What do you do when it rains?

B. If it rains very hard when I am in the field, I get under the tree for shelter.

Mr. L. What do you do, if you are hungry before it is time to go home?

B. I sometimes eat a raw turnip.

Mr. L. But if there are none?

B. Then I do as well as I can without. I work on, and never think of it.

Mr. L. Why, my little fellow, you are quite a *philosopher*, but I am sure you do not know what that means.

B. No, sir. I hope it means no harm.

Mr. L. No, no! Were you ever at school?

B. No, sir; but father means to send me next winter.

Mr. L. You will want books then.

B. Yes, sir, the boys all have an Eclectic spelling book and Reader, and a Testament.

Mr. L. Then I will give them to you; tell your father so, and that it is because you are an obliging, contented little boy.

B. I will, sir. Thank you.

Mr. L. Good by, Peter.

B. Good morning, sir.

QUESTIONS

What service did this little boy perform for the gentleman? Would he take any pay for it? What did the gentleman think of the boy? What do you suppose made him so contented with his condition? Why should we always be contented with such things as we have? What note is that which is placed after all the questions in this lesson? What stop is that after the last word "sir"?

JOHN BONNER

A Child's History of the United States

1859

I have tried to recount how a few straggling bands of poor wanderers, seeking a scanty living on the wild sea-coast of America, have grown to be one of the greatest nations of the earth. It is a beautiful and a wonderful sub-

John Bonner, *A Child's History of the United States* (New York: Harper, 1859), 2:319–20.

ject to write about, and I wish, for your sake, that I had written the story with more skill.

No other people, since the world began, ever grew out of so small a beginning to so towering a height of power and prosperity in so short a time. If you seek to know why your countrymen have outstripped all the nations of the earth in this respect, the reason is easily found. The founders of this nation were honest, true men. They were sincere in all they said, upright in all their acts. They feared God and obeyed the laws. They wrought constantly and vigorously at the work they had to do, and strove to live at peace with their neighbors. When they were attacked they fought like men, and, defeated or victorious, would not have peace till their point was gained. Above all, they insisted, from the very first, on being free themselves, and securing freedom for you, their children.

If you follow the example they set, and love truth, honor, religion, and freedom as deeply, and, if need be, defend them as stoutly as they did, the time is not far distant when this country will as far excel other countries in power, wealth, numbers, intelligence, and every good thing, as other countries excelled it before Columbus sailed away from Spain to discover the New World.

Ongoing debate over education and its moral functions: Japan. The following two passages suggest some of the continuing issues as Japan's leaders tried to define the structure and purposes of education. In the first, a leading advocate of parliamentary, constitutional government, Okuma Shigenobu, challenges the centralized school system, in speeches of 1901 and 1913. Okuma had helped found the independent Waseda University in 1882 and argued for a pluralistic approach to education generally. How does his notion of pluralism relate to his definition of the purposes of schooling? Where would Okuma stand on the issue of Westernization versus Japanese tradition? How would the government most probably react to his views?

The second passage is drawn from Emperor Meiji's rescript on education issues in 1890. The imperial rescript was heavily influenced by Confucian advisers and reflects a neo-Confucian moral approach recast in the form of modern nationalism. "Japanism" is here contrasted with Westernization. The document was a foundation of Japanese education for some time, until repudiated in 1948. It served as the basis for indoctrinating schoolchildren, who were often required to memorize it. The imperial approach contrasts with Okuma's statement of values. How would you define the key differences? Is there any overlap? Would typical Western education officials have disagreed with the emperor's statement of purpose, aside from flowery language and specific references to the imperial throne? Where do you see the most important differences?

OKUMA SHIGENOBU

Pluralism in Japanese Education
1901, 1913

Although the State expends a great deal of effort for common education, it is extremely doubtful whether it is beneficial to carry out higher education in state-maintained institutions. The State has the power to do so, but there are times when the aims of the State are actually those of the government in power and they are not truly representative of the aims of the people. There may also be times when the aims of the State are in error.

If a state is the creation of an aggregation of people, it is difficult to maintain that it will not on occasion fall into error. Thus, I feel that all kinds of schools are necessary — governmental, public, and private. And as they vie with each other in the search for truth, they will illuminate the truth and will in the end bring forth new doctrines. It is my belief that Waseda University will develop to a greater or lesser degree its own characteristics in comparison with the Imperial University and other institutions and will, in the competition for study and research, exert a wholesome influence over education in general.

The true aims of education of Waseda University are the realization of the independence of study, the practical application of study, and the cultivation of model citizens. As Waseda University considers independence of study its true aim, it has emphasized freedom of investigation and originality of research with the hope that it might contribute to the world's scholarship. As the practical application of study is also one of Waseda University's aims, it has taught, along with the study of theory for its own sake, ways to apply theory in practice. It hopes thereby to contribute to progress.

Ryusaku Tsunoda, W. T. de Pary, and Donald Keene, eds., *Sources of Japanese Tradition* II (New York: Columbia University Press, 1958), 189–91.

As the making of model citizens is also an aim of Waseda University, it expects to cultivate good, loyal subjects of our constitutional empire who will be self-respecting, promote the welfare of their own families, prove useful to state and society, and who will participate widely in world affairs. . . .

Japan today stands at the point of contact between the civilizations of the East and the West. Our great ideal lies in effecting the harmony of these civilizations and in raising the civilization of the Orient to the high level of that of the Occident so that the two might co-exist in harmony. We must strive toward the realization of this ideal. In order to realize it we must, first of all, make our principal aim independence of study and the application thereof; we must strive to prosecute original research and then practically apply the results of such studies. Those who would engage in such a pursuit must respect their own individuality, strive for the welfare of their families, work for the benefit of their state and society, and participate in world affairs. . . .

In general there are not many students who can go to college. They constitute a minority. It is this small minority of students who set the example for the nation at large. They are the leaders of the nation. They are the strength of the nation. They form the foundations for the steady progress of the nation. They are the ones who become the vanguards of civilizing enterprises. In order to become a model citizen, knowledge alone is not sufficient; the building of a moral personality is necessary. And he must aspire to make a contribution not only to himself, his family, and his nation, but also to the world. If I may explain this in terms of an ancient Chinese [Confucian] expression, it is "the cultivation of the personality, regulating of the family, ordering of the country, achieving of peace in the world." . . .

Morality and ethics find their source in family life. Customs of behavior also spring from the family. Thus, the fundamental principle of education must be the cultivation of character. Man becomes self-seeking if he strives only to acquire specialized knowledge.

Imperial Rescript on Education
1890

Know ye, Our subjects:

Our Imperial Ancestors have founded Our Empire on a basis broad and everlasting, and have deeply and firmly implanted virtue; Our subjects

---

Ryusaku Tsunoda, W. T. de Pary, and Donald Keene, eds., *Sources of Japanese Tradition* II (New York: Columbia University Press, 1958), 139–40, 189–91.

ever united in loyalty and filial piety have from generation to generation illustrated the beauty thereof. This is the glory of the fundamental character of Our Empire, and herein also lies the source of Our education. Ye, Our subjects, be filial to your parents, affectionate to your brothers and sisters; as husbands and wives be harmonious, as friends true; bear yourselves in modesty and moderation; extend your benevolence to all; pursue learning and cultivate arts, and thereby develop intellectual faculties and perfect moral powers; furthermore advance public good and promote common interests; always respect the Constitution and observe the laws; should emergency arise, offer yourselves courageously to the State; and thus guard and maintain the prosperity of Our Imperial Throne coeval with heaven and earth. So shall ye not only be Our good and faithful subjects, but render illustrious the best traditions of your forefathers.

The Way here set forth is indeed the teaching bequeathed by Our Imperial Ancestors, to be observed alike by Their Descendants and the subjects, infallible for all ages and true in all places. It is Our wish to lay it to heart in all reverence, in common with you, Our subjects, that we may all attain to the same virtue.

8

Paths to Contemporary Education

Change and continuity are the historian's basic analytical tools, easy to cite and often difficult to balance. With modern educational systems set by the early to mid-twentieth century, it was not surprising that France, the United States, and Japan all preserved important features into subsequent decades—those features shared and those distinct. In addition to outright continuities, a number of changes preserved the imprint of past patterns. But there were larger shifts as well, partly because each nation sought to deal with problems resulting from its own prior formulations and partly because all faced some new challenges associated with further advances in the industrial economy and in democratic politics. Industrialization, for example, demanded ever higher levels of skill and literacy; new features of democracy included pressures for greater educational equality (for African Americans, in one key example) and for more ample opportunities for women. Before turning briefly to specific national patterns, we will sketch this combination of continuity, modified continuity, and outright change.

Japan and France, not surprisingly, preserved their taste for rigorous examinations, such as the *baccalauréat*. The United States, though introducing some new results testing to measure school performance, continued to shy away from sweeping tests and preferred more open-ended aptitude measurements for deciding on tracks or college admissions. Basic outlines of educational organization persisted. France made only minor modifications in its highly centralized apparatus. Japan quickly restored central government control after American occupation ended. In both cases, the attractions of systematic organization and state power, established earlier, continued to be hard to resist. In contrast, the United States maintained its more local flavor, with some changes. Individual states took growing roles in setting educational policies—determining textbook choice in some cases, curricular standards in most; localities could no longer fund their whole systems, and state resources began to account for about half of all spending, which meant new policy determination as well. But the federal government continued to play only a modest role. From World War II onward, it did provide research funding and training support at the university level; federal assistance to students attending college, beginning with postwar veterans' benefits, also promoted expanded enrollments. And specific policies, such as requiring colleges to pay more attention to women's sports (from the 1970s onward), had impact. Overall, however, particularly below the university level, the national government was not a major player. Efforts even to offer federal advice about education were frequently rejected. Only through the federal courts, which began to regulate educational opportunity, was there a significant central effort, and this was loose; there was no national system.

Other continuities included Americans' delight in massive sports activities; the nation's definition of appropriate school functions continued to be distinctive. The sports apparatus intensified—many universities ran essentially professional operations, particularly in football and basketball—simply continuing in established directions. France was still willing to identify a portion of the population destined for working-class jobs and to educate them distinctively. Tests and school performance directed about a quarter of the student population, by age fourteen to a mixture of secondary school classes and vocational apprenticeship in the mature French system. While this was an expansion of opportunities beyond the turn-of-the-century level, it continued to reflect a certain degree of comfort with, or realism about, educational inequality. Japan, as it regained control over its system in the 1950s, reinstalled a predominant emphasis on group cohesion. In contrast to the more helter-skelter kindergartens in the United States, for example, Japanese kindergartens emphasized group loyalty among students above all—even above the authority of teachers.

Nationalism continued to burn bright in the schools. Japan eliminated its military emphasis, a crucial change from interwar policies. But the stress on the special glories of Japanese culture and the pride in distinctive contemporary achievements continued. Nationalism persisted with even less modification in many American schools. In the late 1930s a history textbook reformer, Harold Rugg, introduced new materials that traced the role of economic inequality in the nation at various points in the past; his efforts were blasted by critics as treasonable. As one attacker put it, "All the old histories taught my country right or wrong. That's the point of view we want our children to adopt. We can't afford to teach them to be unbiased and let them make up their own minds." The Rugg materials were speedily replaced with more consistently favorable presentations of the nation's past. Again in the 1990s, efforts to teach history in a way that dealt with problems in the nation's past, such as racial injustice, were met with massive conservative attack. One major presidential candidate in 1995 said, quite simply, that the purpose of history courses was to teach students that the United States was the greatest nation on the face of the earth. Authors of nationalist primers in the late nineteenth century would easily have recognized these sentiments.

The list of continuities is considerable. Because prior educational policies had seemed successful and because they reflected deep national values while also creating such values, many policymakers maintained established guidelines. Change within continuity was an even more important pattern than continuity outright. Educational gains for women persisted, for example, in all three countries. More women gained access to higher education, and secondary schools in France and Japan opened widely. In France and the United States, women also began to enter professional schools such as law and medicine in massive numbers from the 1960s onward. This was no minor modification of prior trends. Older attempts to define a special, domestic focus for women, by preaching family obligations and setting up gender-specific programs in home economics, virtually disappeared. But women and men did not become educationally the same. Prior traditions and informal barriers continued, for example, to reserve the majority of slots in engineering schools for men. Women still predominated in the ranks of primary school teaching. In general, the notion that women did less well in educational areas requiring rigorous mathematics, reflecting older beliefs in differences in rational power, continued to affect educational choice and performance—including the confidence of female students themselves. Further, key national differences in women's effective access to education were also maintained. Japan, though changing, still reflected greater inequality in educational choices between males and females than did the Western countries.

Modified continuity showed also in the use of schools to teach morality. The rhetoric of the nineteenth century, with its direct invocations of children's obligations to obey their parents and shun sin, began to disappear, even to seem quaintly or shockingly repressive. But schools still tried to moralize. In the United States, program after program tried to teach children not to smoke or to use drugs and pressed for sexual abstinence. Japanese schools, eager to maintain the moral value of older traditions, set up a crash program to teach children how to use chopsticks properly after the government learned that customary manners were deteriorating in favor of the greater speed of knife and fork. All three nations enforced more rigorous standards of hygiene and health. Not all the moralization efforts worked, but the attempt unquestionably persisted in new guises.

Special national characteristics also affected the pattern of modified continuity. American educators and families found new ways to reflect the older belief that children were fragile innocents who might be damaged by too much educational rigor. The teachers and parents involved may have been totally unaware that they were perpetuating older values, for the specific behaviors were new; but the historical perspective was clear. Early in the twentieth century, for example, a number of parents rose up against extensive homework assignments—their goal being "to remove the obvious pressure which has been burdening the children. . . . These changes will leave more fully to parents the direction of the time of the child except during school hours." In 1901 the California legislature banned homework for any student younger than fifteen, and many other districts followed suit. The editor of the *Ladies' Home Journal* proclaimed that homework was "the most barbarous part of the whole system" because it left children too tired and jangled, incapable of sleep and removed from family cohesion. Only after World War II, and in many cases not until the 1960s, did this anti-homework crusade abate. But by this point a new attempt to allow for children's fragility entered the American scene. Grades began to inflate. With every evidence that actual school achievements were either stagnant or declining among American youth, flunking began virtually to disappear while a majority of students began to earn honor grades. The reason? Teachers and parents worried that bad grades would discourage children and unsettle their emotions. They wanted positive encouragement to "self-esteem"—a new buzz word in educational circles. It was better to be mild. From California high schools to prestigious universities like Princeton, the average student began to look like a winner, if grades were the measure. Again, this was a distinctive American pattern invested in dramatic new forms. Neither France nor Japan participated significantly in these kinds of changes, just as they had never bought into the fragility rhetoric in the nineteenth century. Continuity and modified continuity were not the whole story. There were new trends, or at least trends that displayed genuine novelty. Some were quite general in the industrialized nations. All three countries experienced massive pressure for additional educational opportunities. More people pressed into secondary schools and universities. The redefinition of childhood and youth toward seeking educational success had begun in the nineteenth century, but now it escalated, producing a growing thirst for higher degrees and additional diplomas. National patterns persisted to the extent that a far larger percentage of people went to college or university in the United States than in France or Japan, reflecting earlier differences in how educational opportunity was defined and the special role that American colleges played in sorting students out after a relatively democratic high school experience. But the expansion itself was universal, reflecting similar new needs and aspirations and everywhere pressing the industrial societies to spend more on schools, everywhere creating new patterns of mobility and crowding.

A second and related trend involved redefinition of educational adequacy. Higher levels of scientific and technical training were required of many schools in all three nations, as the industrial economy became more sophisticated. Demand for engineers, for example, though not a constant, clearly increased. The requirements of literacy became more rigorous. People who could merely read a bit and sign a name were no longer regarded as literate, given the reading requirements of advertising, instructions at work, and governmental red tape. Primary school instruction in reading and arithmetic had to escalate. The result left some people, particularly in the United States, worried that basic skills were not keeping up with need, as a larger minority now failed to meet the requirements. Or the need for greater educational skills simply demanded more concentrated instruction and more careful teacher training in the primary grades—the dominant pattern in France and Japan and in many American districts. With this intensification, an older issue was also redefined: To the extent that moral instruction and academic emphasis competed for school time, would the moral segment now more clearly take a backseat?

General trends were not the only change, however. Specific national responses to older issues reflected new departures as well. The United

States in the 1950s began directly to challenge older patterns of racial segregation in the schools—an unthinkable innovation by the standards of 1900. The old dispute between Catholics and republicans in France, though not entirely gone, ceased significantly to define educational issues. Any lingering vestige of the samurai in Japan's advanced education disappeared, with the abolition of the higher schools and the general demilitarization. Even the old conflict about how much to Westernize receded somewhat, as Japan became more confident about its own path to modernization.

Subjected to some common general trends—more rigorous academic goals, expansion of educational aspirations including new opportunities for women—and modifying some older national peculiarities, did the educational systems of France, the United States, and Japan begin to converge? Their modern systems had always shared a number of key features. In some respects, clearly, they now became more similar still. In the wake of Russia's space success, for example—in the post-*Sputnik* atmosphere of the early 1960s—the United States began to shore up its research universities and its graduate training, particularly in technology and science. The result was that major American universities began to look more like their counterparts in Japan or like some of the *grandes écoles* in France. Here was a clear case of convergence around a common need to have the educational system produce a world-class technical elite. Was convergence a more general pattern still? Or did comparative differences not only survive, but in some cases intensify in the complex late-twentieth-century dance of educational change and continuity?

FRANCE: RECONCILING ELITISM AND DEMOCRACY

While the tenor of the debate about education shifted considerably in France from 1918 to the present, and a huge growth in enrollment occurred, the system itself changed less than the rest of French society during the decades after 1950, when the nation experienced extraordinary economic growth. Despite many criticisms, the basic structure established by the early twentieth century remained serviceable, with one major modification. Long-standing discussions about the role of the church largely ended, though conservative politicians after World War II introduced modest state support to struggling Catholic schools in a gesture of reconciliation. The big issue was the relationship between the primary and the secondary school systems or, put in other terms, the democratization of the whole apparatus. Reformers, gathering speed even before World War I, objected to the elitism of the separate secondary schools, often arguing for what they called a "single system" that would flow smoothly from the initial grades, open to all, to the more advanced levels. Many also sought a further updating of the *lycée* curriculum—reducing, for example, the role of Latin—to improve its accessibility and its relevance for contemporary jobs and needs. Few attacked the idea of testing to determine advancement on the basis of merit; almost all the reformers accepted the need to modify pure educational democracy by sorting out talents. As one group put it in 1919: "Everyone must be taught," but also "the best must be drawn from the crowd and put in their real place which is the first." This difficult combination of access and division helps explain why the nineteenth-century system survived as well as it did, for it could be modified to answer these dual demands.

Despite elaborate discussion and many legislative proposals, little actually happened between the wars. This was partly because France was so polarized politically. Socialists wanted more access, but though their political power was growing they tended to be blocked by resurgent conservatives. Teachers themselves divided, with secondary school practitioners defending their turf. One set of reforms sought to make the elementary courses offered by the secondary schools more like those in the primary schools, to move toward a single system at this level. These feeder programs allowed wealthier parents to keep their children out of the standard primary schools. But while some modifications did occur, the secondary schools continued to charge fees for their elementary courses until after World War II, and thus they were largely reserved for the middle and upper classes. The only major change, passed in 1930, abolished fees for the secondary schools themselves. This made it easier for middle-class parents to send their children to the *lycées*, and enrollment expanded very rapidly during the 1930s as families sought to ensure opportunity for their children, amid the depression, by improving their educational levels. Worker and peasant children largely continued to attend the separate primary schools, with the most talented advancing to the lower technical or normal school level. As late as 1953, a farm laborer's child had only a 10 percent chance of getting into the secondary system, while a middle-class child had better than an 80 percent chance. Educational opportunity was expanding, but largely along existing class lines.

There was, however, a genuine upgrading of the technical school system, which helped prepare the patterns more fully installed after 1945. It was clear that both the national economy and educational demand from various social groups called for an expanded, practical, and more prestigious secondary school apparatus. Under the fascist-influenced regime of World War II, curricula were made more conservative but there was no durable change.

More vigorous governments after World War II effected more substantial reforms, including raising the legal school-leaving age past the primary level, to the mid-teens (the age was finally set at sixteen in 1963). Even at this point, the most sweeping efforts to create a unified system fell short, largely because middle-class parents and secondary school teachers insisted on preserving their advantages. But a series of ad hoc measures did in fact open the system up. In 1959 a system of observation for students age eleven to thirteen was established, to make it easier to place them accurately while preserving, in principle, some opportunity to reassign them to different tracks if their performance changed. By monitoring student performance, school officials no longer had to rely on one set of test results alone. In another adjustment an apprenticeship program, sketched earlier, was more fully realized, so that students who ended school early would still have sponsored training plus some regular classes for three additional years. By 1958, about 40 percent of all students ended their schooling a year past primary school; 25 percent took three additional years of technical training; and 35 percent aimed toward the *baccalauréat* by continuing on an academic track. Not surprisingly, various reformers worried that these overall levels were too low to ensure a qualified labor force and that they reflected and produced too much social inequality.

To address these problems, the *collèges d'enseignement secondaire* were set up in 1963 to provide a unified (though heavily tracked) system of early secondary training, from which students could in principle prepare for various upper secondary options later. Thus the base of French education was noticeably broadened, with a major bridge between primary and upper secondary schools. At the same time, the principle of separation by talent was preserved through the establishment of a complex system of tracks within the new colleges. Even before this, the *lycée* system was expanded through the addition of a serious technical program along with the prestigious classical option and the modern option. This measure greatly increased the number of students attending upper secondary school, taking the *baccalauréat*, and attending university, and the university system itself expanded rapidly, though it often lagged behind growing demand.

The percentage of the relevant age group attending secondary school rose from 7 in 1936, to 17 in 1951, to 47 in 1961, by which time 11 percent of the group were passing the *baccalauréat* and so were eligible for some sort of university entrance—up from just 4 percent in the 1930s. The *baccalauréat* itself was modified to allow students to choose more technical subjects, though the majority long continued to opt for science, mathematics, or philosophy. At the other end, after some complex adjustments in which middle-class parents for a time moved back toward private primary schools, increasing numbers of French students attended state-supported primary schools in common; the special *lycée* feeder programs were phased out.

In sum, reforms in France meant less separation among different types of students at the elementary level; more technical options for students of all sorts from secondary school onward; more ample access to secondary school and university, despite test-based tracking; and substantial increases in enrollment at all levels. Changes of this sort, while they did not create a perfect educational democracy, inevitably improved opportunities for mobility within the system, while also reducing the differentiation between males and females. Thus the percentage of children from worker and artisan families in the academic tracks of the upper secondary system rose from 7 percent of the total in 1936 to 15 percent in 1956, and increased further thereafter. An even larger percentage of youths of worker origins made it into the advanced technical schools. By this point, France was offering one of the more mobile educational systems in Western Europe. To be sure, the strict cutoffs between primary school and subsequent options continued to privilege those from middle-class backgrounds; and very few people of worker origins actually made it to university. But there was change, and a significant minority of working-class children—up to a quarter, by some estimates—was making it into advanced schooling (mostly but not exclusively technical) by the 1960s.

The French system remained vulnerable to criticism—indeed, one of the obvious characteristics of modern education, given the difficult goals the system tries to juggle and the personal and social importance of the educational experience, is that criticisms are virtually endemic. Many people continued to deplore the ways that massive social inequality seemed to be reproduced by the educational tracks. Continued preference in the middle classes for classical or liberal arts subjects created other problems, for not all graduates could always be placed. The sheer growth in demand for higher education was a strain; by the late 1960s, universities were frequently massively overcrowded, and new facilities were often of poor quality. Several of these factors—the social injustice, the crowding, the worries about jobs after graduation—fed into France's astonishing student revolt of 1968, when university students, headed by those in Paris, briefly seemed to threaten outright revolution. Subsequent reforms gave student groups greater voice in university affairs, and construction of additional university centers accelerated. Parent/student groups also formed to provide new participation in the secondary schools, and a mood of experimentation developed in French education overall.

A few more general changes evolved. Various governments tried to encourage private schools—attended, by the 1990s, by about one-third of all upper secondary school students—though basic state control continued since only the government was authorized to organize the *baccalauréat* examinations and so attest to successful graduation. The *baccalauréat* itself, though much discussed, continued its important guardianship role, with 30–35 percent of all students who attempted the exam failing and receiving a consolation certificate as a result. Policymakers tried again to work on the vexing problem of democracy at the secondary level. In 1975 a conservative government passed the Haby Reform (named for the minister of education, a former teacher). The first four years of secondary school were again reorganized, the *collèges d'enseignement secondaire* were replaced by new *collèges uniques*. During the first two years of this four-year program, students took essentially the same classes, while teachers monitored their work to advise them on subsequent tracking. At the end of the second year most students were urged to decide between a vocational and an academic track for their final two years (this decision was required by the third year, through consultations among teachers, parents, and students with appeal procedures available). Some students also took the fourth year as a preapprenticeship, essentially planning to end school as soon as they reached sixteen. The purpose of these reforms was to delay definitive choices and provide more opportunities to shift tracks, but in fact many of the old divisions persisted. A number of worker and peasant children dropped out after the apprenticeship year, while mostly middle-class children flocked to the academic track that still led to the *lycées*. Only 21 percent of all students by the early 1990s were completing the full, academic secondary school, while a larger number did three years of technical study. But by the mid-1990s almost 50 percent of French students were trying for the *baccalauréat* and almost 35 percent were obtaining it, through either academic or technical tracks, reflecting the twin themes of expansion and partial democratization.

For all the limitations on reforms and ongoing claims of undue elitism in France's educational choices, the nation continued to experience what was dubbed the *"explosion scolaire."* All levels expanded, which meant that considerable mobility continued, as children exceeded the school attainments of their parents. Between 1960 and 1988, for example, the number of university students rose from 270,000 to 1.2 million, 51 percent of them female—with twenty new universities and technology institutes founded in the process. Other schools grew as well, from the *grandes écoles* at the top to new provincial business schools alongside the university level. School expenditure per inhabitant more than quadrupled between 1974 and 1988, aimed particularly at secondary school growth. Both the government, bent on pushing a full half of the population through secondary schools by the year 2000, and ordinary families, seeking greater achievement or fulfillment through education, agreed that change must continue, whether the system itself shifted or not.

THE UNITED STATES: ANOTHER CASE OF EDUCATION EXPLOSION

As in France, the period between the wars saw few fundamental changes in American education. Enrollments expanded, as more students went on to high schools and a growing minority to university. By the 1920s the presence of women in universities was commonplace, a major factor in gender relationships throughout the nation. A number of earlier educational themes were powerfully restated. The philosopher John Dewey asserted in the 1920s a particular American educational tradition of pragmatism, with schooling at once vital to personal development and useful in terms of social needs. Some traditional subjects, like Latin, continued to decline. A social studies movement arose to apply history and kindred social science disciplines to the duties of citizenship; the movement held that rather than study the disciplines academically, they should be applied to produce good Americans, aware of national institutions and ready to participate in democracy.

Given the importance of American education, it was not surprising that some of the most significant developments between the wars extended the impact of schools into other facets of life. High schools, with their abundant extracurricular activities, helped center a new culture of youth, with special fashions and dance and music styles. Dating began to represent a common means of social contact between the sexes, based in the coeducational classes of high schools and many colleges. Instead of home-based courtships, students of the opposite sex, who met each other in school, shared entertainment outside the home and experimented with sexuality (usually, before 1960, stopping short of outright intercourse).

From a more strictly academic standpoint, key developments beyond the sheer growth of the existing systems occurred in the 1950s and 1960s. Cold war threats helped trigger new attention to the nation's scientific and technical training. Russian priority in the space race—punctuated by the *Sputnik* launch in 1957—prompted a surge of support for science education in the schools and for graduate training generally, often with federal funding. Medical advances called for new levels of training for specialist doctors. Expanded college enrollments meant new needs for professors. Additionally, more and more people sought to advance their own careers by seeking training beyond the college level. Graduate and professional schools grew rapidly, despite some fluctuations and unevenness. Corporations increasingly recruited people with master's degrees in business; engineering schools expanded. A significant minority of young adults now continued their education well into their twenties. New career aspirations among middle-class women, from the 1960s onward, increased female representation, though only a minority went on for advanced training in science or technology.

A second basic shift was more dramatic, addressing one of the long-standing anomalies in the national educational picture. On May 17, 1954, the Supreme Court rejected the legitimacy of educational segregation in its historical *Brown v. Board of Education of Topeka* decision. Arguing that separate schools were inherently unequal, the Court ruled racial segregation in education unconstitutional. "We conclude that in the field of education the doctrine of 'separate but equal' has no place," the Court declared. Subsequently the Court ordered school districts to desegregate "with all deliberate speed." The South largely resisted, and federal pressure was essential; in 1957, for example, authorities in Little Rock, Arkansas, agreed to desegregate the high school only after troops were sent in. In 1963, federal marshals enforced the entry of the first African American students to the University of Alabama. For virtually two decades, local courts issued decisions condemning segregation, requiring bussing to achieve greater racial balance, and in a few instances even insisting on redistricting among suburban school systems. Certainly the historical American position that schooling could be deliberately different for African Americans had changed.

The results of this shift were mixed. With new rights and a new attention to educational opportunity, the number of black students entering universities soared—there was a 350 percent increase in a single decade after the Civil Rights Acts of the 1960s. School integration did increase, though the result was sometimes heightened racial tensions within the schools. American localism, however, made full integration difficult. Many suburban school systems remained largely white, because they were based on residence and because many whites worked hard to keep their suburbs exclusive. African American school performance, including rates of high school graduation, continued to lag behind national averages. With a conservative resurgence in the 1980s and again in the mid-1990s, the federal government relaxed its pressure for school integration, without officially changing policies.

Racial issues triggered important curricular battles as well, again with indecisive though interesting results. A variety of groups began demanding changes in standardized, nationalist presentations of history and literature in the schools, seeking more representation of minority and women authors and experiences. Changes in research, such as the rise of social history, supported many of these shifts. Slavery and emancipation, long neglected in American history texts, gained new attention, and by the 1990s the Underground Railroad leader Harriet Tubman was one of the best-known names in national history (second only to George Washington, according to some surveys). These shifts, however, brought a conservative reaction and contributed to widespread claims that American students were falling behind in basic achievements. Various moves to tighten school standards, to impose more tests on learning outcomes, and to track students according to ability in the high schools dotted the final decades of the twentieth century. After a period in the 1970s when educational performance may indeed have declined (despite an increase in high grades awarded), test results began to suggest modest improvements by the early 1990s.

More than the French, Americans worried that students were not learning as much as their predecessors had, or as much as a modern economy demanded. There was a widespread tendency to blame education for problems in national competitiveness—part of a long-standing American attitude that assumed that education ought to be the key to social as well as personal success. More than the French also, Americans worried that education was not promoting appropriate national values. In the 1990s a host of conservatives began urging that schools return to a policy of teaching the superiority of American institutions, as part of creating a uniform and positive national culture during a period of uncertainty and stress.

Expansion of education continued. While the biggest growth in secondary education occurred in the decades after 1910, the percentage of high school graduates continued to expand, reaching 74 percent of the relevant age group by the late 1980s. But the biggest change was the explosion in university education. A major increase in enrollment after World War II was matched by another surge in the years 1975–1985, thanks among other things to the entry of new numbers of women. By 1970, the percentage of adults with four or more years of university education was 11 percent (up from 5 percent in 1940), and by 1987 the percentage had doubled again; 52 percent of the university population was female. These figures were complicated by the fact that the nature and rigor of various universities continued to differ widely—what a university education "meant" was much less clear than in France. The expansion of two-year or community colleges added to the complexity. Minority groups continued to lag behind whites in college enrollment rates. University training did lead to higher earnings; the relationship between education and economic achievement may actually have increased in the United States. Certainly, faith in education—despite measurable loss of confidence in schools and teachers—persisted, leading to the unique commitment of over half the population to at least two years of postsecondary training.

JAPAN: MORALS AND MERITOCRACY

Japan's educational system changed less than its counterparts in the West during the decades after 1950. This was hardly surprising, given that major shifts had occurred as recently as the 1930s and under American occupation in the late 1940s. Japan's great economic success in the period also limited the desire to change, though there was vigorous discussion. Finally, the general public, enjoying massive new educational opportunities (greater than those available in France, newer than those in the United States), displayed relatively little overall concern about the system itself. Japan's commitment to widespread education, graded on the basis of merit, seemed clearly established. By some measures, the Japanese were the best-educated people in the world.

The structural shifts introduced under United States sponsorship, before Japan resumed its sovereignty in 1952, had two prompt consequences. The first was the substantial expansion in enrollments, boosting Japan over many European levels in rates of attendance at secondary school and university. The reduction in social class barriers, particularly to secondary school, had a real impact, along with the general trend among the population in industrial societies—which Japan shared along with France and the United States—to push for higher levels of training in hopes of brighter prospects. In 1955, 51 percent of all Japanese of the relevant age group were already in upper secondary schools; by 1975, the figure had risen to 92 percent. In 1955, 8 percent of the relevant age group was attending university, and by 1975, the percentage had soared to 27 percent. Growth of this sort led to severe crowding of facilities and many other pressures, along with a substantial increase in competition for the most desirable slots (at the higher education level, beginning with the cherished admission to the University of Tokyo). But there is little question that improved access was widely welcomed by students and their supportive parents alike.

The expansion of education was accompanied by the establishment of new institutions, particularly to promote more advanced training in science and technology. A 1958 reform created two-year technical colleges, to allow students to extend training after the secondary school level. The number of technical graduates and engineers expanded rapidly. Women's education gained ground as well, and a variety of groups formed to promote it, though enrollment levels still lagged behind those of men.

The second reaction was a conservative effort to roll back some of the American reforms, in the interests of maintaining older traditions. The effort was only partially successful, but it did open an ongoing debate that in some ways continues to this day. Teachers, for the most part, supported the reform structure, which gave them greater autonomy, including rights of unionization. But the dominant political party leadership, vigorously conservative, thought otherwise. At first there was even talk of cutting back university admissions, to reserve slots for a more privileged group, but this move failed; conservatives did not, in the end, attack the egalitarian access to the system, by which students advanced according to merit. Conservatives were more successful in purging a number of teachers, including union leaders whom they regarded as radical. The teachers' political rights were limited. And the conservatives moved to recentralize the system, against teachers' objections. In 1958, national government control was established over curriculum and textbook choice, which effectively gave the state the power to decide what students learned and how, further reducing teacher initiatives. These changes were followed, in 1961, by standardized achievement tests. The public seemed to accept these changes, abandoning local controls so long as democratic access was maintained.

Conservatives also pressed for renewed attention to moral education, in place of the looser kind of citizenship training Americans had encouraged under the heading of social studies. In 1966 the Ministry of Education put out a paper called "The Image of the Ideal Japanese." The report praised the nation's economic advance but condemned "egotistic and epicurean attitudes" in the public at large; "there is still a feeling of spiritual hollowness and unrest left over from defeat in the war," the report claimed. A moral resurgence, launched through the schools, was essential to counter materialism. The report called for "the cultivation of ethical consciousness," which seemed to critics like a plea for some prewar version of nationalism. Liberal commentators urged more attention to human rights, rather than a traditionalist stress on group obligations. Reactions in the Japanese public were muted. Moral education gained support at a few points when acts of student violence occurred—such as the 1983 case in which a teacher stabbed a student in self-defense. Japanese opinion still sought an orderly, disciplined student body. But when student news was less dramatic, public interest in moral education seemed modest.

The reality of Japanese education had less to do with recurrent liberal-conservative debate than the compelling pressure of the system itself. School days were long, and the schools operated five and a half days per week with scarcely more than a month's worth of summer holidays. Homework began in the first year of primary school. Students and parents alike kept a firm eye on the importance of examinations for entry into the high secondary schools and then into university. In Japan's closely organized society, education determined status, and examinations determined how prestigious one's education could be. To prepare for the "exam hell," the majority of students in the lower secondary schools were sent to cram schools—*juku*—at some time or received private tutoring. The Japanese system continued to place heavy emphasis on rote learning and memorization, and parents, particularly mothers, spent a great deal of time monitoring the time children spent on their studies. Primary schools assumed that students could perform at a reasonably high level—there was little competition at this stage, but rather a supportive environment, which did seem to push achievement levels up in the basic skills. But competitiveness and stress mounted at the secondary level. There were many reports of bullying of weaker or eccentric classmates as a means of expressing a discontent that could not be explicitly stated and of extending the conformist tone of the schools. At the academic level, the government's insistence on approving all textbooks created a uniform presentation, often slanted toward nationalist ideals (for example, in avoiding significant discussion of Japan's role in launching World War II).

Liberals attacked elements of this system, claiming that it put too much pressure on children and too much emphasis on routine learning as opposed to creative thinking. They pointed out that even the advanced faculties at the major universities depended still on scientific and technical achievements in the West and that students at lower levels were pushed into constraining, uniform molds. Even language learning, the critics contended, suffered from its mechanistic quality. Students memorized long passages in English rather than being encouraged to use the language actively. Conservatives, in response, tended to argue that the deficiencies lay in inadequate moral training.

Debate resurfaced in 1967 and again in the 1980s. By this latter point, many observers felt that Japan's education was too narrow and insufficiently international to keep pace with the nation's global economic stature. Prime Minister Nakasone launched a major reform movement. Liberals began to talk about major strides toward greater individuality, often using stirring rhetoric. A First Report, in 1985, indeed identified individuality, creativity, and thinking ability as key principles in any reform, along with awareness of the information age and Japan's place in the international community. A Second Report used phrases like moving "from uniformity and homogeneity to more diversity and the expansion of freedom of choice" and a need "to identify and develop the personality, abilities, and aptitudes of individuals." A number of sweeping measures were discussed, including more local autonomy, more varied examinations, a wider range of criteria for university admissions, and a more flexible curriculum, but all these efforts failed, against widespread public apathy, liberal-conservative disputes, and rifts even within conservative ranks. Instead, minor adjustments surfaced. The Japanese encouraged more study abroad and admitted more foreign students into their own system. Government-sponsored internationalization of Japanese schools had real impact. Private universities received some tangible encouragement. At the same time, however, moral education gained some new emphasis, under headings like "proper national awareness" and "unique culture and traditions of Japan." As one conservative put it, "you have to teach tradition [to the children] whether they like it or not."

At most, the Ministry of Education remained aware of limitations and dissatisfactions, as discussion continued into the early 1990s. Ideas about greater diversity in the secondary system and new, more flexible methods of training for teachers remained current, as the once-complacent Ministry of Education admitted, "We should constantly strive to reform our educational system, envisaging what our society should be in the coming years." On paper, this admission included a commitment to an "emphasis . . . on individuality" and a desire "to make our education system cope with such changes of the times as internationalization and computerization." Educational budgets, one talisman of concern, began to rise again in the late 1980s, designed not only to address computerization but to facilitate smaller class size. Japan's educational success might still preclude massive redirection, but it had never guaranteed agreement on goals and now it seemed to inspire a more generalized dissatisfaction as well.

COMPARATIVE SIGNPOSTS: A FINAL LOOK

For almost a century and a half, the educational systems of Japan, France, and the United States have combined a set of common trends, outright imitations, and sharp contrasts. The same mix persists as the twentieth century draws to a close.

The convergences were striking after World War II. Societies like Japan, France, and the United States, sharing a rapid expansion of secondary and university education, also share a distinction from the much more limited school facilities in many other parts of the world. Other common features intensified among these educational leaders. While none of the three countries managed a fundamental overhaul of its educational system after World War II, specific modifications did reduce some of the special national features. Japan's unusual higher schools were replaced by more open secondary institutions. France ended its odd disjuncture between the primary and the secondary system. The United States, though still persuaded of the value of aptitude tests, also introduced more achievement tests—educational outcome tests. Changes of this sort softened national differences, though without eliminating them. All three countries shared an ongoing liberal-conservative debate about what education should be like. Specifics differed, but on the whole liberals pressed for more public control (as opposed to more centralized bureaucracies), greater opportunity and access, less nationalism, and, sometimes, less explicit attention to moral education. Finally, all three countries demonstrated heightened public commitment to education, visible in expanding school budgets and also in growing individual efforts to enter higher educational levels. Firmly converted to the role of formal education in shaping a major stage of life—despite the newness of the experience, in historical terms—French, Japanese, and American people all sought to obtain more than previous generations had achieved. Widespread faith that education mattered combined with growing needs for academic skills in advanced economies with large service and information sectors; national differences counted for little against this larger trend.

At the same time, however, serious contrasts persist among the three systems; comparisons remain complex. Further, educational practitioners often delight in pointing out the weaknesses of rival national patterns, sometimes exaggerating the differences. Japanese commentators, for example, worried about moral education at home, delight in pointing out American school discipline problems that seem worse. Americans, concerned about the quality of student learning, slam what they perceive as the dullness of the Japanese school experience.

Even without this hyperbole, distinctions are quite real. Drop in on a kindergarten art class. In the United States, teachers are at pains to praise the originality and creativity of each student's work—the goal is to create a sense of individual self-esteem. In Japan, teachers readily tell students that their drawings are or are not "right"—the goal is to create a sense of conformity to group standards.

Visit the buildings of a college. In France or Japan, college buildings tend to be somewhat shabby and mainly consist of classrooms and offices; eating facilities exist, but are utilitarian at best. The American college campus is opulent by contrast—in a society that is no longer richer, overall, than Japan or France. American colleges must have massive sports facilities, student activities buildings, and dormitories. They reflect a distinctive sense of what higher education consists of and, probably, a different degree of confidence in student abilities to fend for themselves.

Listen to national education debates in the late 1990s. In 1995 a new storm broke over the French *grandes écoles*. The French president, himself a graduate, blasted the schools for their elitism, arguing that most students were the children of upper bureaucrats; a further criticism focused on the general training, the lack of specialization, of some of the leading schools. A defender of the schools expressed horror at any idea of quotas for underrepresented social classes: "We believe we are already open to the best students regardless of background." American debate in the same period centered not on exclusivism but on the inadequacy of educational standards and, possibly, the excessive openness of many schools to students who did not really qualify. And there was concern, largely absent in France, about the lack of moral training as well. These different agendas reflected distinctive political climates, of course, though conservative politicians were dominant in both countries at the time. But they also reflected a longer history. The French, thanks to their educational tradition, normally worried less about quality, more about access; the Americans, though sometimes eager to talk about democratic access, were more prone to worry about rigor, in academic subjects and school discipline alike.

Comparisons of this sort require care and knowledge as well as a grasp of the role of history in shaping ongoing patterns. Japan continued to spend a much higher percentage of its public education budget on the primary system than did either France or the United States. The difference goes back to Japanese interests as early as the 1870s plus a special concern for providing a solid set of basic skills and a universally shared moral code. Higher education was less important and of course was partly covered by private tuition payments in any event.

The United States and Japan shared a greater interest in schools as moralizers, though they defined moral standards somewhat differently. France—though probably neither more nor less moral as a nation—saw education in more strictly academic terms. The old church-state battle had limited the ability to define school morality, while the considerable focus on generating a talented elite reflected a different agenda as well.

Japan, for all its educational zeal, featured much larger classes than did the Western countries; more than forty students per primary school class was normal. This reflected confidence in the authority of teachers and also in the discipline provided by group loyalty, along with the special role mothers played in supporting their children's early education and in inculcating orderly classroom habits. Americans counted on schools for more socialization of children as family stability declined, though they were often dissatisfied with the results as they confronted the real or imagined unruliness of youth. And of course they were more ambivalent about how much discipline they wanted, as against cherished student individualism. Here again, historical precedents combined with recent social changes to produce measurable differences in approach.

Why did so many more Americans attend university than French or even Japanese? Well over half the relevant age group went to college or university in the United States, less than a third in Japan and about a third in France, by the 1990s. Obviously, these differences reflected distinctions in the number of students completing upper secondary school, but there was more involved. The United States, lacking a national school system and reluctant to track students too firmly or too early, used a massive but differentiated higher education system to accomplish some of the sorting that, in France or Japan, occurred earlier. American democratic expectations insisted on more access to higher education, even at great social and personal cost, while at the same time the more rigorous universities helped compensate for more relaxed standards (compared with those of France or Japan) at the secondary level. At the same time, the huge diversities among universities allowed for sorting students by ability and preparing graduates for very different social class rankings — elitist features that were rarely explicitly acknowledged. Overall, the American higher education system was a massive national peculiarity that showed every sign of persisting, though its causes were complex. By the same token, owing in part to the huge array of institutions available, the American educational experience overall was notably less competitive, less examination-driven, than the experience in Japan or France. This was unquestionably a striking feature in a society that praised competition so widely; it derived from older beliefs about democratic access and also the need to avoid too much stress for children. It marked yet another way in which national traits, even somewhat unexpected ones, fed into the ongoing educational comparison.

Finally, of course, many key comparisons continued to require careful statement. Americans often criticized the French for failing to teach schoolchildren the lessons of national collapse and complicity during World War II, and even more roundly lamented the Japanese failure to offer much instruction at all about the same war. Yet efforts to focus American classes on issues of racial injustice or mistreatment of Native Americans might easily encounter conservative resistance in the name of inculcating an upbeat message ultimately devoted to the superiority of the nation's history. There were some exceptions here — individual American instructors certainly did teach about the national warts — but they were not as great as was sometimes assumed. On a related point: American critics often noted that Japanese textbooks were not freely produced; they were issued only when the government invited them and were rigorously scrutinized for conformity. Citizen input was limited, and respect for the textbook remained very high, possibly reflecting remnants of Confucian reverence. In the United States, texts were issued by commercial companies whenever they wished to venture. There were far more texts available, as a result, with a greater variety of specific features and information. Yet most commercial companies were hesitant to innovate; most texts resembled the others, partly because state boards of adoption played a great role in the success or failure of a book. Real diversity was quite limited. And most students, in many classes even at the college level, learned little that was not in a text. How much difference did two undeniably distinct systems of textbook production actually make?

The need for sophisticated comparison and adequate knowledge could strike quite close to home. By the 1980s, American leaders, bemoaning student inadequacy, often compared the knowledge of high school graduates to that of their counterparts in Japan or Western Europe. The comparison might be useful, and it certainly was interesting in suggesting that new patterns of imitation might somehow develop, with the United States availing itself of outside example. But it was also flawed by a failure to note clearly that a higher percentage of students graduated from secondary school in the United States than elsewhere and that this difference would inevitably color other results. Comparison might be valid nevertheless, in urging the need for greater rigor in a more competitive world, but it frequently misled as well.

Finally, comparisons must remain flexible. Deep-seated differences among national education systems persisted, sometimes replicating factors dating back a century or even more. Yet change continued, even in systems as advanced and seemingly successful as those of France, Japan, and the United States. As higher education became more costly in the United States, would relatively democratic access continue, or would the nation fall back to more formal screening and limitation? With Japan ever more involved in international contacts, would the ongoing attempt to define a distinctive moral code for the schools continue? Educational systems move from past to future. Recent experience suggests that initial characteristics may prove surprisingly persistent, even amid significant change. Change does occur, however, and with it the need to compare systems and their results quite carefully. In a demanding world economy, will national peculiarities be as visible fifty years from now as they remain today?

Chronology

1860s   Victor Duruy sponsors teacher upgrades, education reforms.

1879–1886   Ferry laws make education free, replace Catholic personnel with secular teachers.

1882   Primary education law makes school obligatory and mandates secular schools.

1902   Coordination of secondary schools and generalization of *baccalauréat* exam.

1906   Final separation of church and state.

1963   School-leaving age raised to sixteen.

1968   Huge university student protests.

1970sff   Vast university expansion.

1975   Haby Reform reorganizes secondary schools.

UNITED STATES

1780–1830s   Spread of private academies.

1789   Massachusetts laws require educational access for women.

1820s   Beginnings of industrialization.

1833   Oberlin College, first institution of higher education open to women.

1837   Horace Mann reforms Massachusetts Board of Education.

1852   Massachusetts requires school attendance.

1850s–1860s   Spread of public high schools.

1860s–1870s   Spread of education requirements in North and Midwest.

1862   Morrill Act provides land grant support for public universities.

1865–1870s   Spread of African American education during Reconstruction.

1870s–1890s   Development of research universities.

1890s   Spread of high school sports.

1899   College Entrance Examination Board formed (first SAT exams, 1925).

1900–1920   Spread of high schools for majority of students; growth of aptitude testing (IQ exams in San Francisco, 1912).

1901–1960s   Anti-homework movement.

1920s   Spread of coeducation, rise of dating.

1950s   Great growth in university enrollments.

1954   *Brown v. Board of Education of Topeka* orders desegregation in schools.

1968–1973   Student protest movements.

1980s   Women surpass men in university attendance.

JAPAN

1853   Perry mission opens Japanese markets to the West.

1860s–1870s   Visits to Western schools; Westerners hired to teach languages.

1865   First European hired to teach science.

1868ff   Meiji era.

1869   Non-samurai admitted to elite schools.

1871   Foundation of Ministry of Education.

1872   Education Code establishes national system for mass education, expands teacher training.

1879   Imperial rescript limits Westernization.

1881   Memorandum for Elementary School Teachers stresses Japanese loyalty, morality.

1886   Middle School Ordinance provides two-tiered secondary schooling (five-year school followed by three-year school).

1894   Vocational Education Law and Higher School Ordinance establish lower secondary schools and technical schools.

1899   Higher Girls' School Law aims at providing one secondary school for females in each district.

1900   School fees abolished.

1901   Japanese Women's University founded.

1937   Bureau of Educational Reform established for national control of education.

1945–1949   Reforms under U.S. occupation.

1958   Two-year technical colleges established; government resumes control over curriculum, textbooks.

1961   Standardized achievement tests administered by government.

1985   First Report (reform) on limits of Japanese education tradition.

Selected Bibliography

For general overview, see Fritz Ringer, *Education and Society in Modern Europe* (Bloomington: University of Indiana Press, 1979); Andy Green, *The Education and State Formation: The Rise of the Modern Educational System* (New York: St. Martin's, 1990); Ronald Dore, *The Diploma Disease: Education, Qualification and Development* (Berkeley: University of California Press, 1975); Robert A. Levine and Merry White, *Human Conditions: The Cultural Basis of Educational Development* (New York: Routledge and Kegan Paul, 1986); and Mary Jo Maynes, *Schooling in Western Europe* (Albany: State University of New York Press, 1985). Studies of literacy provide extensive sweeps. See Harvey J. Graff, ed., *Literacy and Social Development in the West: A Reader* (Cambridge: Harvard University Press, 1982), and Daniel P. Resnick, ed., *Literacy in Historical Perspective* (Washington, D.C.: Library of Congress, 1983). On France, see F. Furet and J. Ozouf, *Reading and Writing: Literacy in France from Calvin to Jules Ferry* (Cambridge: Cambridge University Press, 1982).

On premodern schooling, see Robert Muchembled, *Popular Culture and Elite Culture in France, 1400–1750* (Baton Rouge: University of Louisiana Press, 1985); Mary Jo Maynes, *Schooling for the People: Comparative Local Studies of School History in France and Germany, 1750–1850* (New York: Holmes and Meier, 1985); Lawrence Cremin, *The American Common School* (New York: Harper and Row, 1951) (see also the first volume of Cremin's masterful survey *American Education,* cited below); Conrad Totman, *Early Modern Japan* (Berkeley: University of California Press, 1993); R. P. Dore, *Education in Tokugawa Japan* (Berkeley: University of California Press, 1968); R. Rubinger, *Private Academies of Tokugawa Japan* (Princeton: Princeton University Press, 1982); Harvey Chisick, *The Limits of Reform in the Enlightenment: Attitudes toward the Education of the Lower Classes in Eighteenth-Century France* (Princeton: Princeton University Press, 1981).

On developments in nineteenth-century France: Donald Baker and Patrick Harrigan, *The Making of France: Current Directions in the History of Education in France, 1679–1979* (Waterloo, Ont.: University of Waterloo Press, 1980); Robert J. Smith, *The École Normale Supérieure and the Third Republic* (Albany: State University of New York Press, 1982); C. R. Day, *Education for the Industrial World: The École d'Arts et Métiers and the Rise of French Industrial Engineering* (Cambridge: MIT Press, 1987); Phyllis Stock-Morton, *Moral Education for a Secular Society: The Development of Morale Laique in Nineteenth-Century France* (Albany: State University of New York Press, 1988); John Weiss, *The Making of Technological Man: The Social Origins of French Engineering* (Cambridge: Harvard University Press, 1982); Georgs Weisz, *The Emergence of Modern Universities in France, 1863–1914* (Princeton: Princeton University Press, 1983); Joseph Moody, *French Education since Napoleon* (Syracuse: Syracuse University Press, 1978); R. D. Anderson, *Education in France, 1848–1870* (London: Clarendon Press, 1875); Anne T. Quartaro, *Women Teachers and Popular Education in Nineteenth-Century France* (Newark: University of Delaware Press, 1995); Linda Clark, *Schooling the Daughters of Marianne: Textbooks and the Socialization of Girls in Modern French Primary Schools* (Albany: State University of New York Press, 1984); Sharif Gemie, *Women and Schooling in France, 1815–1914: Identity, Authority, Gender* (Keele, Eng.: Keele University Press, 1995). See also two excellent surveys in French: Felix Ponteil, *Historie de l'enseignement en France: les grandes étapes, 1789–1964* (Paris: Presses Universitaires de France, 1966), and Antoine Prost, *Histoire de l'enseignement en France, 1800–1967* (Paris: Armand Colin, 1977). Another study on student life is fascinating: Paul Gerbod, *La Vie quotidienne dans les lycées et collèges au XIXe siècle* (Paris: Presses Universitaires de France, 1968).

On the United States, the best overview is Lawrence Cremin, *American Education,* vol. 1, *The Colonial Experience* (New York: Columbia University Press, 1970); vol. 2, *The National Experience* (New York: Columbia University Press, 1980); vol. 3, *The Metropolitan Experience* (New York: Columbia University Press, 1988). See also Lawrence Cremin, *The Genius of American Education* (New York: Random House, 1965). Other key studies include Carl Kaestle, *The Evolution of an Urban School* (Cambridge: Harvard University Press, 1973); Harvey Kantor and David B. Tyack, eds., *Work, Youth, and Schooling* (Stanford: Stanford University Press, 1982); Michael Katz, *The Irony of Early School Reform: Education*

Innovations in Mid-Nineteenth Century Massachusetts (Cambridge: Harvard University Press, 1968); Carl Kaestle and Maris A. Vinovskis, *Education and Social Change in Nineteenth-Century Massachusetts* (New York: Cambridge University Press, 1980); Maris Vinovskis, *Education, Society, and Economic Opportunity: A Historical Perspective on Persistent Issues* (New Haven: Yale University Press, 1995); William Reese, *The Origins of the American High School* (New Haven: Yale University Press, 1995); David Tyacks, Thomas James, and Aaron Benarot, *Law and the Shaping of Public Education, 1785–1954* (Madison: University of Wisconsin Press, 1987); David Tyack and Elisabeth Hansot, *Learning Together: A History of Coeducation in American Schools* (New Haven: Yale University Press, 1990), and *Managers of Virtue: Public School Leadership in America, 1820–1980* (New York: Basic Books, 1982); Joel Perlmann, *Ethnic Differences: Schooling and Social Structure among the Irish, Italians, Jews, and Blacks in an American City, 1880–1935* (New York: Cambridge University Press, 1988); B. Edward McClellan and W. J. Reese, eds., *The Social History of American Education* (Urbana: University of Illinois Press, 1988); and Carl Kaestle et al., *Literacy in the United States: Readers and Reading since 1880* (New Haven: Yale University Press, 1991). Among several source collections, the most comprehensive is Sol Cohen, *Education in the United States: A Documentary History,* 5 vols. (New York: Random House, 1978).

On Japan, see Michael Stephens, *Japan and Education* (New York: Macmillan, 1991), for a useful overview. Other important studies are Donald Roden, *Schooldays in Imperial Japan: A Study of the Culture of a Student Elite* (Berkeley: University of California Press, 1980); D. Eleanor Westney, *Imitation and Innovation: The Transfer of Western Organizational Patterns to Meiji Japan* (Cambridge: Harvard University Press, 1987); Gail Bernstein, ed., *Recreating Japanese Women, 1600–1945* (Berkeley: University of California Press, 1990); Carol Gluck, *Japan's Modern Myths: Ideology in the Late Meiji Period* (Princeton: Princeton University Press, 1987); David Dilworth and Hirano Umeyo, *Fukuzawa Yukichi's "An Encouragement of Learning"* (Tokyo: Sophia University Press, 1969); Henry Dewitt Smith, *Japan's First Student Radicals* (Cambridge: Harvard University Press, 1972); W. G. Beasley, *Japan Encounters the Barbarians: Japanese Travellers in America and Europe* (New Haven: Yale University Press, 1995); Akira Kubota, *Higher Civil Servants in Postwar Japan: Their Social Origins, Educational Backgrounds and*

Career Patterns (Princeton: Princeton University Press, 1969); Tetsuya Kobayashi, *Society, Schools, and Progress in Japan* (Oxford: Oxford University Press, 1976); and International Society for Educational Information, *The Modernization of Japanese Education,* 2 vols. (Tokyo, 1986). For more general context, see Ronald P. Dore, ed., *Aspects of Social Change in Modern Japan* (Princeton: Princeton University Press, 1970).

On twentieth-century developments, see the surveys cited in the national sections as well as John Talbott, *The Politics of Educational Reform in France, 1918–1940* (Princeton: Princeton University Press, 1969); Leonard Schoppa, *Education Reform in Japan: A Case of Immobilist Politics* (London: Routledge, 1991); David Tyack, Robert Lowe, and Elisabeth Hansot, *Public Schools in Hard Times* (Cambridge: Harvard University Press, 1984); John Modell, *Into One's Own: From Adolescence to Adulthood in America, 1920–1975* (Berkeley: University of California Press, 1989); Michael D. Stephens, *Education and the Future of Japan* (London: Sandgate, Folkestone, Kent, 1991); Edward R. Beauchamp, ed., *Japanese Education since 1945: A Documentary Study* (New York: M. E. Sharpe, 1994); Robert Leestra and H. J. Walberg, eds., *Japanese Educational Productivity* (Ann Arbor: Center for Japanese Studies, University of Michigan, 1983); N. J. Haiducek, *Japanese Education: Made in the USA* (New York: Praeger, 1991); Harold Stevenson, Hiroshi Huma, and Kenji Hakuta, eds., *Child Development and Education in Japan* (New York: Freeman, 1986); Ken Schoolland, *Shogun's Ghost: The Dark Side of Japanese Education* (New York: Bergin and Garvey, 1990); Merry White, *The Japanese Educational Challenge: A Commitment to Children* (New York: Free Press, 1987).

Index